Praise for Patrick Cockburn's

MUQTADA AL-SADR AND THE BATTLE FOR THE FUTURE OF IRAQ

"Fascinating . . . essential reading for anyone seeking to understand Iraq today."

—Rajiv Chandrasekaran, *The Sunday Times* (London)

"Mr. Cockburn has a reporter's eye for detail and for the absurdities of power."

—*The Economist*

"Well researched and highly readable."

—Con Coughlin, *The Sunday Telegraph* (London)

"Poignant . . . truly impressive."

—Charles Tripp, *London Review of Books*

"Deftly written, superbly researched."

—Michael J. Bonafield, *Minneapolis-St. Paul Star Tribune*

"Compelling."

—*Library Journal*

"In his latest book, *Muqtada,* Iraq's best reporter has now told the most important story in Iraq . . . few among today's Iraq reporters have the sophistication to tell such a tale. Cockburn has erudition, long-standing experience of Mesopotamia, and elegance of mind and pen to complement a high level of physical bravery. . . . Cockburn's book is by far the most useful that has been written about post-Saddam Iraq."

—Bartle Bull, *Prospect* magazine

"No subject could be more important and, of course, Patrick Cockburn knows Iraq as few foreigners do. The right writer and the right book."

—David Rieff

"Patrick Cockburn is one of the few journalists who has covered the Iraq crisis almost from its beginning. His peerless reporting has been instrumental in uncovering the true dimensions of the tragedy in Iraq. His new book on Muqtada al-Sadr and the radical Shia of Iraq is probing and perceptive."

—Ali Allawi

"No serious student of Iraq has failed to incur a debt to the intrepid and intelligent Patrick Cockburn."

—Christopher Hitchens

ALSO BY PATRICK COCKBURN

The Occupation: War and Resistance in Iraq

The Broken Boy

Out of the Ashes: The Resurrection of Saddam Hussein
(with Andrew Cockburn)

MUQTADA AL-SADR

AND THE BATTLE FOR THE FUTURE OF IRAQ

PATRICK COCKBURN

SCRIBNER

New York London Toronto Sydney

SCRIBNER
A Division of Simon & Schuster, Inc.
1230 Avenue of the Americas
New York, NY 10020

Copyright © 2008 by Patrick Cockburn

All rights reserved, including the right to reproduce this book or portions thereof in any form whatsoever. For information, address Scribner Subsidiary Rights Department, 1230 Avenue of the Americas, New York, NY 10020.

First Scribner trade paperback edition October 2008

SCRIBNER and design are registered trademarks of The Gale Group, Inc., used under license by Simon & Schuster, Inc., the publisher of this work.

For information about special discounts for bulk purchases, please contact Simon & Schuster Special Sales at 1-800-456-6798 or business@simonandschuster.com.

Designed by Kyoko Watanabe
Text set in Minion

Manufactured in the United States of America

3 5 7 9 10 8 6 4 2

Library of Congress Control Number: 2008273129

ISBN-13: 978-1-4165-5147-8
ISBN-10: 1-4165-5147-6
ISBN-13: 978-1-4165-5148-5 (pbk)
ISBN-10: 1-4165-5148-4 (pbk)

Originally published in hardcover in 2008 as *Muqtada* by Scribner.

To Janet, Henry, and Alexander

Contents

1. The Road to Kufa   1
2. The Shia of Iraq   16
3. The First Martyr   27
4. An Eight-Year Whirlwind   44
5. The Shia Rise Up   55
6. Saddam's Revenge   70
7. The White Lion   78
8. A Second Assassination   95
9. Muqtada Survives   110
10. Murder in the Shrine   119
11. Seizing the Moment   127
12. The Siege of Najaf   138
13. The Fall of Najaf   150
14. A Turn to Politics   163
15. The Battle of Baghdad   175
16. The Surge   187
17. The Disintegration of Iraq   199

Afterword   205

Acknowledgments   215

Notes   217

Index   227

250 km

TURKEY

Tigris

SYRIA

Tel Afar ○   ○ Mosul
        ○ Erbil
            Sulaimaniyah ○
        Kirkuk ○

Euphrates

IRAN

Tikrit ○

Haditha ○   Baquba ○   *DIYALA*
    Ramadi ○
Fallujah ○   □ Baghdad

ANBAR

Kerbala ○ ○ Hilla   ○ Kut
    Kufa ○   Ad
Najaf ○   Diwaniyah ○   Amara ○

Euphrates   *Tigris*

SAUDI
ARABIA   Nassariya ○

            Basra ○
            Umm Qasr

KUWAIT

Iraqi territories:

Kurdish   Sunni Arab   Shia Arab

Mixed Kurdish/   Mixed Sunni/   Sparsely
Sunni Arab   Shia Arab   populated

Source: CIA

Iraq and Its Ethnic and Religious Groups

75% Shia

51% Shia/ 25% Sunni

75% Sunni

51% Sunni 25% Shia

Mixed Sunni, Shia, and Christian

Abu
● Ghraib   ⑩
Jordan St.

Baghdad
International
Airport

Airport Rd.

Rabia St.

14th July St.

Tigris

Abi Talib St.

Sadr
City

Army Canal

Green
Zone

Jamia St.

□ Baghdad
University

Hilla Rd.

Dora Expw.

Tigris

Diyala R.

0   2   4
⊢──┴──┴──┤
Miles

⑧

Religious Divisions in Baghdad, November 2007

MUQTADA AL-SADR

AND THE BATTLE FOR THE FUTURE OF IRAQ

CHAPTER ONE

The Road to Kufa

"He's an American spy!" shouted the Mehdi Army militiaman as he leaned in the window of my car and grabbed the red-and-white kaffiyeh, the Arab headdress, I was wearing as a disguise. It was April 19, 2004, and I was trying to get to the holy city of Najaf, where Muqtada al-Sadr, the mysterious Shia cleric whose men had seized much of southern Iraq earlier in the month, was under siege by American and Spanish troops. A U.S. general had said he would be killed or captured. I was wearing the kaffiyeh because the sixty-three-mile-long road from Baghdad to Najaf passes through a string of very militant and very dangerous Sunni towns where foreigners had been attacked. I have fair skin and light brown hair, but I had hoped that the headdress might convince anybody glancing at the car that I was an Iraqi. It was not intended for close inspection.

I should have been more wary. I was traveling in a white Mercedes-Benz of a type not very familiar in Iraq that might easily have attracted attention. I sat in the back to be less conspicuous. In the front passenger seat was Haider al-Safi, a highly intelligent and coolheaded man in his early thirties who was my translator and guide. An electrical engineer by training, he had run a small company fixing photocopying machines in the years before the fall of Saddam Hussein. He lived in the ancient Shia district of Khadamiyah in Baghdad, site of one of the five great Shia shrines in Iraq. He neither drank nor smoked but was otherwise secular in outlook. My driver was Bassim Abdul-Rahman, a slightly older man with close-cropped hair. A Sunni from west Baghdad, he had shown he had good nerves ten days earlier, when we were caught in the ambush of an American fuel convoy near Abu Ghraib on the road to Fallujah. All three of us had got out of the car and lain on the ground until there was a break in the firing, when Bassim had driven us slowly and deliberately past bands of heavily armed villagers running to join the fight. I crouched down in the back of the car hoping they did not recognize me as a foreigner.

We had come across the Mehdi Army militiamen in their black shirts and trousers as we approached the city of Kufa on the west bank of the Euphrates River, a few miles from Najaf. They were standing or sitting cross-legged in the dust beside the road where it turned off to Kufa before crossing the bridge over the river. They were well-armed young men, carrying Kalashnikov assault rifles, with rocket-propelled grenade launchers slung across their backs and pistols stuck in their belts. Many had ammunition belts filled with cartridges crisscrossed over their chests. There were too many of them for a normal checkpoint. They were edgy because they expected U.S. troops to attack them at any minute. In the distance, to the north, I could hear the distant pop-pop of gunfire along the Euphrates.

Checkpoints in Iraq did not at this time have the reputation they later gained of being places of terror, often run by death squads in or out of uniform, looking for somebody to torture and kill. Probably we were too relaxed, because the worst danger seemed to be behind us in the grim towns of Mahmudiyah, Iskandariyah, and Latafiyah, where permanent traffic jams gave passersby plenty of time to look us over. There was also a truce. It was the Prophet's birthday and Muqtada's spokesman in Najaf, Sheikh Qais al-Ghazali, had declared that there would be no fighting with the Americans for two days in honor of the event and to protect the pilgrims flooding into the city to celebrate it. I had lived long enough in Lebanon during the civil war to have a deep suspicion of truces. When they were declared, as happened frequently, I used to jokingly tell friends: "It's all over bar the shooting, so keep your head down." True to form, we could already hear the menacing crackle of machine-gun fire coming from somewhere in the date palm groves around Kufa. But the sound was still intermittent and far away, and was not discouraging the thousands of enthusiastic Shia pilgrims I could see marching on both sides of the road, banging their drums and waving green and black flags as they walked to the shrine of Imam Ali in Najaf. One of the most surprising and attractive aspects of the new Iraq was the popularity among the Shia of pilgrimages, which had been banned or limited in number by Saddam Hussein.

Haider told Bassim to stop so we could ask the militiamen if we were on the right road to Kufa—they would know if the Americans were firing on the road—and if they had heard anything about a press conference being given by Qais al-Ghazali. They were immediately suspicious. Some ran to the car and started staring at me. It was then that one of them started to yell: "This is an American! This is a spy!" Things then got worse very fast. They dragged me out of the car and started handing around the kaffiyeh to one another as evidence of guilt. Haider was trying to say I was Irish and a journalist. It did no good. Other militiamen took up the shout: "He is an American! He is an American!" Two of the militiamen turned on Haider and said: "How dare you bring him to the shrine of Imam Ali." Haider protested he came from a family of sayyids, descendants of the Prophet Mohammed, and furthermore his family originally came from Najaf.

The Mehdi Army men started to go through my brown shoulder bag. I had bought it in Peru three years earlier because it was exactly the right size for carrying the small number of items necessary for a journalist. They found the contents very incriminating as they took out a notebook; a Thuraya satellite phone, which looked like a large black cell phone; and a camera. For some reason cameras have always been regarded with deep suspicion by Iraqis as evidence of espionage. The militiamen waved it around saying that I wanted to photograph them and send the photos to the Americans who would then arrest them. They started to push me around and one of them kicked me. I thought they were working themselves up to kill us. Bassim thought so, too. "I believe that if Patrick had an American or English passport they would have killed us all immediately," he said later.

One of the militiamen was peering at me suspiciously and suddenly sniffed. He pointed at me and said: "He is drunk; he drank alcohol before coming here." A second Mehdi Army man turned on Haider and accused him of drinking alcohol with foreigners. Bridling at this, Haider, who was losing no chance to stress his Shia credentials, shot back: "How dare you accuse me of coming to the Holy City drunk when I don't drink and come from a sayyid's family? If I was drunk you would smell the alcohol."

While this curious argument was going on—the militiamen probably had no idea what alcohol smelled like—two of the angriest men were trying to hustle me into a separate car. I thought if they did succeed in driving me away they would in all likelihood shoot me. I put my hand flat on the chest of one of them and pushed him back firmly, but I was also very eager to avoid a fight. Nobody seemed to be in charge of this Mehdi Army detachment, and there was no reason why one of them should not decide to end the argument there and then with his pistol or Kalashnikov. They looked like men who killed very easily.

They asked, reasonably enough, why I was wearing a kaffiyeh. Haider explained that it was "to avoid kidnappers in Latafiyah."

"Are you scared for your money?" asked one of the Mehdi Army.

"It is for our life, not just our money," Haider replied. He kept repeating that we had come to meet Qais al-Ghazali, the one aide to Muqtada of whom we hoped they might have heard. Finally, to my intense relief, one of the militiamen said that they would take us to the main mosque in Kufa, where "the sheikh [a sheikh is a cleric not descended from the prophet who wears a white turban; a sayyid wears a black turban] will decide what to do with you." There was a casualness about our reprieve, just as there had been a chilling casualness about the way they had come close to killing us a few moments earlier. Bassim asked if he could drive our Mercedes to wherever they wanted us to go, but the man said: "No, you are hostages." Three gunmen clutching their weapons and festooned with ammunition pouches crammed into our car. We followed a second car, also filled with fighters, which made for the green-domed mosque of Imam Ali in the center of Kufa. Haider was crushed against the door of our car, so he could hardly speak. Nevertheless he kept talking, he told me later, in order to make us appear less strange to our captors. There was no doubt about their commitment to Muqtada's cause. They were poor men. Most came, not from Kufa or Najaf, but the great Shia shantytown in east Baghdad that had once been called al-Thawra, then Saddam City, and within the last year had been renamed Sadr City after Muqtada's revered father Mohammed Sadiq al-Sadr, assassinated with two of his sons in Najaf on the orders of Saddam Hussein in 1999. It was less a district than a twin city to Baghdad, and its two million impoverished people were the core of Muqtada's movement.

One man in the car explained fervently that joining the battle was the most important thing in his life. "I left my wife, who has just given birth to our daughter, so I could come here and fight for Muqtada," he said. "I took up a collection from my friends so I could get transport here." Turning to Haider, he asked: "If you are from a sayyid's family you are a cousin of Muqtada's, so why don't you fight for him, too? If either of us dies we will be martyrs."

"Everybody must play his role in life," replied Haider. "You are fighting while I'm writing about your fight and telling the facts about American defeats and crimes." Bassim, meanwhile, was berating them for threatening to kill a disabled man—myself—since they could see I walked with a severe limp (the result of catching polio as a child in 1956).

Our car stopped on a patch of open ground outside the Imam Ali mosque, named after the son-in-law and cousin of the Prophet. It was here that Muqtada, wearing a white shroud to show he was ready to die, had delivered a sermon two days earlier, defying the gathering U.S. forces and saying: "I am ready to face martyrdom." The gunmen ordered Haider and Bassim out of the car and took them through a door into the mosque. I did not like us being split up, but I was reassured by the fact that the militiamen were becoming less aggressive. One of them offered me a cigarette, and though I had given up smoking, this did not seem a good moment to reject a friendly gesture. I chain-smoked five cigarettes, one after another. Another gunman discovered a copy of *The New Yorker* I had been reading lying on the backseat and leafed through it. At the sight of a cartoon of a woman in a low-cut blouse he muttered "*haram*" [forbidden] and peered at it for a long time. Inside the mosque, Haider was being politely interrogated by a well-educated man who called himself Sayyid Abbas. "I don't know anything about a truce," he told Haider, confirming my skepticism about the cease-fire we had heard about in Baghdad. "You shouldn't have taken the risk of coming because there's fighting here and this is a battlefield." Getting up, he gave Haider some tea and brought me a glass of orange juice to drink in the car. Suddenly we were being smothered in politeness. "We Iraqis don't want war," Abbas told me, "but the Americans want our oil and the Israelis want to rule the Middle East. As for you, we want just to be sure you are who say you are. Don't worry. We'll take you to Najaf." My belongings were all returned except for my satellite phone, which I saw a gunman in black Arab robes tucking into his belt. I thought of demanding it back but was so relieved that we had got away with our lives that I did not want to start a fresh dispute.

Sayyid Abbas got into his own car to drive ahead of us so we would not be stopped by other Mehdi Army militiamen. He was immediately proved wrong in saying our worries were over. We had only gone a few hundred yards and were driving past the high white wall of another mosque, the Muslim bin Qaleel on the outskirts of Kufa, when there was a staccato burst of gunfire. It seemed to come from a heavy machine gun on the far bank of the Euphrates. I could see the bullets smashing into the masonry of the wall above our heads, sending little chips of plaster flying into the air. At the sound of the first shots the marching pilgrims began to run down the road in panic, clutching their flags and drums as they looked desperately for cover. We had the same idea and swerved off the road so we could shelter behind the far side of the mosque. Above us, black-clad gunmen raced along the top of the walls to take up firing positions. A commander, waving his pistol, was shouting orders to them. In the face of this common threat to all of us, the gunmen, who earlier in the day had debated whether or not to kill us, appeared keen to win us over to their point of view. There was one point they kept on repeating, as if it mattered a lot to them. "It is wrong," they asserted, "for people to call us a militia: we are an army." The distinction in their eyes was that they were not just a Shia defense force but a real army in the service of Islam and the most revered leader of the faithful on earth, Muqtada al-Sadr.

Shielded by the mosque, we waited for the firefight to end. I thought about Muqtada and why he was able to inspire young men to borrow small sums of money to go to fight and, if necessary, die for him. The Iraqi police and the army that the United States was trying to rebuild were notorious for taking their pay while making it very clear that they did so only to support their families and without the intention of being killed for anybody. President George W. Bush and Prime Minister Tony Blair repeatedly stated that American and British troops would leave when Iraqis were ready to take over. They never seemed to understand that the problem was not training or equipment, but legitimacy and loyalty. Few Iraqis outside Kurdistan felt that the U.S.-led occupation was legitimate, and they therefore did not give their loyalty to it or the Iraqi governments it sponsored. Sayyid Abbas might be leading an undisciplined and dangerous rabble, but they believed their cause was not only right but sanctioned by God, and they were willing to die for it.

The firing on the other side of the Muslim bin Qaleel mosque finally died away. We peered gingerly around the corner but could not see much because of the broad green leaves of the date palms growing on the banks of the Euphrates. The pilgrims began to return to the road to resume their journey. Nobody had been killed or wounded, and many were laughing with relief. Sayyid Abbas got back in his car and led us toward Najaf. He drove very fast. It was obvious that we would not have got through without his help. There were many other Mehdi Army checkpoints blocking the road, and several times gunmen ran forward to stop us, but they waved us through as soon as Sayyid Abbas leaned out the window of his car and they saw his face.

Najaf was not far away. In AD 661, Imam Ali, the son-in-law and first cousin of the Prophet Mohammed, whose followers became the first Shia, had been assassinated by a dissident Muslim named Ibn Muljam. Wielding a poisoned sword, Ibn Muljam struck Imam Ali on the head as he entered a mosque in Kufa to perform the morning prayer. The blade was partly deflected by the wooden door frame, so Ali was only badly wounded. It took two days for him to die,[1] giving him time to instruct his followers that, after he died, they should strap his body to the back of a white camel, which was to be allowed to wander freely. Wherever it finally stopped they were to dig his grave. The camel did not roam far. Six miles south of Kufa, on the edge of the desert, it stood still, and Ali was buried on the spot. Over the centuries his tomb became a shrine and Najaf grew up around it, the true center of Shia Islam, the home of its most revered leaders, and the longed-for destination of millions of pilgrims.

I always found Najaf an entrancing city, one of the strangest in the world. It is a dusty place on the edge of the desert, always short of water in the past, unlike Kufa, which is on the cool-looking banks of the Euphrates. The road linking the two small cities runs between tawdry modern villas and looks no better than the depressing ribbon development in the rest of Iraq. But suddenly, in the distance, the visitor sees the golden dome and minarets of the great shrine where Ali lies buried. It springs into view like a burst of sunlight in the sky as it rises above the low buildings of brown brick that surround it. People, groping to explain the significance of Najaf, would sometimes describe it as "the Vatican of the Shia," but this is true only in the loosest of senses. Unlike the Vatican in Rome, the shrine of Ali is surrounded not by architectural marvels but by a souk, or bazaar, its small shops and battered corrugated iron roofs shabby even by Iraqi provincial standards. The outside walls of the shrine are of brick and are pierced by gates adorned with mosaics portraying birds and flowers. These gates lead to the wide, stone-paved courtyard that surrounds the shrine. The courtyard is often filled with pilgrims, most very poor, the women all dressed in black, sitting on the ground eating from packages of food they have brought with them. They line up quietly to enter the shrine itself, bright with neon lights reflecting from mirrors and mosaics.

I first visited Najaf in 1977, guided by an amiable young man from the Ministry of Information in Baghdad named Adnan Sabri. A Christian and a committed, if naïve, Baathist, he spoke sincerely of Saddam Hussein as the great secular modernizer, and showed me around Najaf as if we were visiting Stonehenge or the Pyramids, picturesque survivals from earlier times but irrelevant to the development of the Iraq of tomorrow. Even so, his confidence faltered at the doors of the shrine, and he said that, since both of us were non-Muslims, it would perhaps be best not to enter. Adnan turned out to be wrong about the place of both Saddam and Najaf in Iraqi history. Within three years the great leader, by now president of Iraq, had started a long and bloody war with Iran that left little money for developing anything else in the country. When Saddam was hanged in Baghdad at the end of December 2006, it was the Shia religious leaders in their modest houses in Najaf who held the future of the country in their hands. Some of the witnesses to Saddam's execution chanted "Muqtada! Muqtada!" as he went to his death.[2]

I had other memories of the shrine. During the bombing of the Iraqi army in Kuwait by the U.S.-led coalition in 1991, I would go there to look at sad processions carrying the cheap wooden coffins draped with the Iraqi flag containing the bodies of dead soldiers. Desperate to conceal its military losses, the regime insisted that mourning be kept to a minimum, but it did not dare prevent families from carrying their dead sons into the shrine before they were buried in Wadi al-Salaam, Najaf's vast cemetery, which stretches over twelve square miles. The largely Sunni regime in Baghdad always distrusted the Shia masses and their religious leaders, but was wary of provoking them. Its suspicion of their loyalty was correct. A few months later, I was back in Najaf, permitted to go there by an Iraqi government eager to tell the world it had crushed the Shia uprising, which, in March 1991, had followed Saddam's shattering defeat in Kuwait. The pale stone flags of the courtyard were pitted where mortar rounds or rocket-propelled grenades had landed, the blasts tearing off tiles around the shrine. The only people there were tough-looking soldiers in their camouflage uniforms. At this time, the Iraqi army was showing how far it had advanced by putting up pictures of Saddam. On a chair on a pile of rubble at the entrance to the shrine, soldiers had placed a ludicrously inappropriate picture of the leader. It showed him in tweeds climbing a mountain slope in what looked like Austria, the whole thing reminiscent of a scene from *The Sound of Music* with Saddam about to burst into song.

* * *

Najaf's buildings are not the sole reason it is such an extraordinary place. The great shrine does not have the splendor of the Taj Mahal or the Dome of the Rock in Jerusalem. Kufa, Najaf, and Kerbala, another shrine city fifty miles to the north, make such a strong impression because it was here, in a small area west of the Euphrates, that so many of the dramas and tragedies of early Islam were played out fourteen hundred years ago. It is not just that Ali was murdered and buried here. In Kerbala are the tombs of his sons Imam Hussein and Abbas, who died, betrayed by their friends and hopelessly trapped by their enemies, in their last battle in AD 680. The great festivals and rituals of the Shia revolve around commemorating the tragedy of their deaths much as Christians commemorate the crucifixion of Christ.

What makes Najaf so different from Jerusalem and Rome is that here martyrdoms have not ended. The Shia religious leaders who congregated in the city lived on the edge of torture and death under Saddam. Many of them were killed with hideous cruelty in his prisons. Others disappeared, taken out into the desert to be shot or enduring a living death in one of his dungeons. Ayatollah Mohammed Baqir al-Sadr, a leading thinker of Shia Islam and a resolute opponent of the Baath party, had been tortured and executed by Saddam along with his sister in 1980. He became known as the First Martyr, or Sadr I. Muqtada, a cousin of the Ayatollah, went on to marry his daughter in 1994. The father of Muqtada, Mohammed Sadiq al-Sadr, had received Sadr I's and his sister's mutilated bodies and buried them in Najaf in 1980. Sadiq then built up the Sadrist movement in the 1990s, until he in turn was assassinated with two of his sons and became known as the Second Martyr, or Sadr II. The semidivine attributes of his father and father-in-law were crucial to the rise of Muqtada and to the awe with which he was regarded by his followers.

In the wake of the uprising in April 1991, I was brought by Ministry of Information officials to see the Grand Ayatollah Abu al Qasim al-Khoei, the leading figure in the Shia hierarchy, in his home beside the Euphrates in Kufa. A white-bearded man in his nineties, he had played little part in the rebellion but was under house arrest. Twelve years later, soon after the U.S. invasion, I was back in Najaf looking at the room pockmarked with bullet holes where the Grand Ayatollah's son, Sayyid Majid al-Khoei, whom I had come to know and esteem in London, had been trapped by an armed and angry mob reportedly led by followers of Muqtada. When he gave himself up he was hacked to death in a street outside the shrine.

The blood of the martyrs is famously the seed of the church. The Shia religious leaders had shed blood in torrents under Saddam and were to go on doing so. This helped give them an authority in their community that Shia politicians, exiled after fleeing Iraq and deemed by many Iraqis, sometimes unfairly, to have spent their years abroad cavorting in five-star hotels, could never match. In the summer of 2003, I had gone to a narrow alleyway in Najaf, halfway along which was the house of Grand Ayatollah Ali al-Sistani. There was a long line of people outside the door, waiting to submit petitions or seeking an interview. The leader of the Shia community since the death of al-Khoei, Sistani was the most influential figure in Iraq. American officials in Baghdad knew of his importance, though he refused to meet with them. At the same time, these arrogant men could never quite comprehend that this aging cleric—he was in his seventies—sitting on a frayed carpet, was going to play a far more important role than they in determining the future of Iraq.

On the day in April 2004 when Haider, Bassim, and I entered Najaf after our nasty experience with the Mehdi Army, the mood was a peculiar mixture of religious celebration and warlike preparations. Thousands of pilgrims were happily sitting on the ground in front of the Imam Ali shrine watching ritual mourning dances in which troops of men strike their backs with symbolic metal flails to the beat of an enormous drum and chant prayers. But there were also fighters with their machine guns and bulging ammunition pouches wandering through the knots of pilgrims. At the end of one street we heard cheering. The skirmish near the Muslim bin Qaleel mosque in Kufa that had forced us to take cover earlier in the day turned out to have been with American and not Spanish troops, as we had supposed. The two-hundred-strong Spanish contingent was being withdrawn by the new Madrid government, which opposed involvement in Iraq. It was a newly arrived American unit that had been doing the shooting. Some of its men had advanced too far toward the Mehdi Army positions and had been forced to abandon an armored vehicle. Its burned-out remains were now being displayed as a trophy in the streets of Najaf to delighted applause from gunmen and pilgrims.

We finally located the press conference with Sheikh Qais al-Ghazali, Muqtada's spokesman, which was taking place in the open courtyard of a dilapidated building near the shrine, and could only be reached by clambering up broken brick steps. I spoke to al-Ghazali, a tall unsmiling man in gray robes, and asked if he expected the Americans to launch an offensive into the heart of Najaf. "I think the Americans understand about Iraq's holy places," he said. "I don't think they are so stupid as to attack us." Having seen Paul Bremer, the U.S. viceroy in Iraq, in action over the previous year, I was by no means as confident about relying on his wisdom or restraint. Most American military and political leaders in Baghdad underestimated the capacity of Iraqis, both Shia and Sunni, to cause them trouble. During his year in power as virtual dictator of Iraq, Bremer showed a peculiar inability to learn from his mistakes. On this occasion, however, with the Sunni insurrection escalating by the day, even he and his advisers hesitated to storm Najaf and provoke a wider rebellion by the Shia community.

I have given an account in some detail of what happened to us on the road to Najaf on a single day in April 2004, because it was an ominous foretaste of what was to come.[3] In the following years, thousands of Iraqis would die because they were stopped at checkpoints just like the one we had encountered. By the end of 2006, the UN, employing Iraqi government figures from the Health Ministry and the Baghdad morgue, reported that some three thousand civilians were being killed every month. Iraqis began to carry two sets of identity papers, one showing that they were Sunni and the other that they were Shia. Faked papers avoided identifiably Sunni names like Omar and Othman. Shia checkpoints started carrying out theological examinations to see if a person with Shia papers was truly familiar with Shia ritual and history and was not a Sunni in disguise. Many of the dangerous young men manning these checkpoints came from Sadr City and belonged, or claimed to belong, to the Mehdi Army, just like the detachment we had met. If Haider had been less persuasive or I had been carrying an American or British passport, instead of an Irish one, they would certainly have killed us.

There is a final reason for dwelling on our brief abduction by the Mehdi Army. Complicated though Iraq is, both as a country and a society, it is possible to set out the main themes of its politics before and after the invasion in a way that is comprehensible to those who have not experienced Iraq firsthand during this time. It is far more difficult to convey the atmosphere of permanent fear in which Iraqis lived. "Can a man who is warm understand a man who is freezing?" asks Aleksandr Solzhenitsyn in *One Day in the Life of Ivan Denisovitch*. A similarly deep emotional chasm separates those who are afraid from those who are not. The divide is not simply between different individuals. Even a few seconds after the handful of occasions I thought my life was truly in danger in Iraq, I found it impossible to recapture the terror I had felt at the time. Nor did I try very hard to do so—I wanted to forget such grim moments as quickly as possible. But it is worth remembering that Iraq was full of people who had every reason to be terrified both before and after Saddam Hussein was overthrown. The Mehdi Army militiamen we met outside Kufa were trigger-happy and suspicious because they knew they would soon have to fight better-armed and better-trained American and Spanish troops. They feared, rightly, that many of them would be killed.

In Baghdad I would see parents become frantic with fear if they could not immediately find their children at the school near my hotel; they instantly suspected they had been kidnapped. Once I watched police commandos, terribly wounded by a suicide bomb, being carried on stretchers into Yarmouk Hospital in west Baghdad. Their faces were hidden by black masks and they were more worried that these would be removed while they were under anesthetic, revealing their identity, than they were by the thought that their mangled legs or arms might be amputated. Over the coming years the number of Iraqis killed and wounded each month came to be seen as a barometer of the gravity of the war in Iraq, but these raw casualty figures did not begin to convey the sense of misery and fear that was engulfing the country. By June 2007 the UN High Commission for Refugees was announcing bleakly: "The situation in Iraq continues to worsen with more than two million Iraqis believed to be displaced inside Iraq and another 2.2 million sheltering in neighboring states."[4] By then the Mongol invasion of 1258 was the only cataclysm in the last one thousand years of Iraq's history comparable to the disasters that have followed the invasion of 2003.

I hoped, but did not really expect, to see Muqtada in Najaf. I had heard he was moving from house to house. This was scarcely surprising since U.S. generals had spoken glibly of killing him and evidently believed that, if he disappeared, so would many of their problems in dealing with the Iraqi Shia. It was already evident that Paul Bremer, the U.S. army, and the Iraqi politicians in Baghdad had grossly underestimated the strength of Muqtada and the Sadrist movement that he led.

Muqtada was a figure of mystery in April 2004, and has largely remained so to the present day. The foreign media had commonly called him a "maverick," though his main policies, such as his hostility to the U.S. occupation, have been unwavering. Another journalistic cliché frequently used to describe him is "firebrand cleric," but in practice he has proved a cautious and skillful politician, knowing when to advance and when to retreat. U.S. media and government commentary on Muqtada has come to admit his importance, though it usually demonizes or belittles him, shifting between presenting him as a clerical gangster or as a successful demagogue of limited intelligence and ability who somehow leads the only mass movement in Iraqi politics.

Part of the mystery concerning Muqtada has its origin in simple ignorance. Few non-Iraqis have much idea of the rich and complex history of Shi'ism in Iraq. "The Americans seem to think," a Shia friend once snapped at me, "that the history of Iraq started when they invaded in 2003." This is not quite fair, but it is true that very few people outside the Iraqi Shia community understood the religious, political, and social forces that produced the Sadrist movement. The sudden emergence of Muqtada as a powerful figure at the time of the fall of Saddam is only surprising if one does not know this background and, above all, the bloody and dramatic story of resistance to Saddam Hussein by Iraqi Shia as a whole and the al-Sadr family in particular. Readers of this book may be surprised that in a biography of Muqtada al-Sadr the chief protagonist only takes center stage in chapter nine. But his delayed appearance in the course of this narrative is wholly necessary. Muqtada and his followers are intensely religious and see themselves as following in the tradition of martyrdom in opposition to the tyranny established when Hussein and Abbas were killed by the Umayyads on the plains of Kerbala fourteen hundred years ago. Little about the Sadrists or modern Iraq will be explicable without an understanding of the Shia faith. Moreover, the heroic resistance of the Shia to Saddam is little known because so many of the protagonists were killed or, if they survived, never related what had happened to them. I was in Iraq just before and just after the great Shia Intifada, or uprising, of 1991 and wrote what I could about it. I thought that in the coming years others would gather more information about the rebellion, in which some 150,000 Shia Iraqis were killed. To my surprise, few detailed accounts of the fighting, so important to the more recent history of Iraq, have been published, which is why I have described the uprising in detail.

Biographies of individuals normally include an account of their family background and some reflections on how far this influenced their character. There is no doubt that Muqtada strongly identifies with his father, Sadr II, and father-in-law, Sadr I, to the point that his own personality and beliefs become shadowy. Muqtada and his advisers are acutely aware of the reasons behind their political appeal. Posters pasted on every wall in Kufa and Najaf on the day we were there in 2004 illustrated the sources of Muqtada's popularity. The red, white, and black Iraqi flag formed the background, in front of which stood the figures of three men in dark clerical robes: Muqtada himself, his father, and his father-in-law. The power of this blend of religion and patriotism among the Iraqi Shia was to be demonstrated many times in the years to come, but it first displayed its strength in April 2004.

The mystery surrounding Muqtada's personality has another source. Shia sages and leaders have traditionally been old men. Born on August 12, 1973, and only thirty years old when he first confronted the U.S. Army in Najaf, Muqtada needed to cultivate the gravitas of a man who stood close to God. His father would tell jokes to his followers, but there are no accounts of Muqtada doing the same. His opponents later claimed that his father ignored him, but in fact he played a central role in his father's political and religious organization during the 1990s. Few people in Iraq had more on-the-ground experience of organizing the Shia masses. After the assassination of his father and two brothers in 1999, he survived by persuading Saddam Hussein that he was too simple-minded to be a threat. Stories of his incapacity may well have been spread, and certainly not denied, by his own family in order to keep him alive. Few people have lived so long knowing that each day could end with their death. The picture that emerges is of a man who is highly intelligent but moody and suspicious. It is notable that no rivals have emerged within his inner circle. And there was another aspect to his character that was not obvious during his first armed clashes with the Americans in April 2004: he learned from his mistakes. He might wear the white martyr's shroud, but after the battles for Najaf, he always sought to avoid struggles he did not control and could not win.

The energy with which U.S. officials and their Iraqi allies demonized Muqtada was perhaps because he personified the broader dilemma facing the U.S. occupation from the moment it began. The stated U.S. objective in the war was to overthrow Saddam Hussein. But if he was to be replaced by a democratically elected government then this was inevitably going to be dominated by the Shia, since they make up sixty percent of the population. They believed their day had come. And not only was the government going to be Shia, but it would be led by religious parties with links to Iran. Muqtada represented the ultimate American nightmare. They had not got rid of Saddam only to see him replaced by a black-turbaned, virulently anti-American, Shia cleric. Whatever reason the United States gave for invading Iraq, it was not for this.

CHAPTER TWO

The Shia of Iraq

In April 2003, the U.S. troops that had just captured Baghdad and overthrown Saddam Hussein saw a sight they did not understand. All over central and southern Iraq more than a million Iraqis had taken to the roads and started walking toward the holy city of Kerbala. The journey took them between three and five days and they often slept in the fields at night. Many of the pilgrims carried green flags, the symbol of Imam Ali, or black flags, a sign of mourning. Others bore once-green palm fronds that were turning yellow as they dried in the intense heat of the Iraqi plain. Young men poured out of the great Shia stronghold, now called Sadr City (a fortnight earlier it had been Saddam City), in Baghdad and headed for Kerbala, sixty miles away. Straggling along the roads from other parts of Iraq were knots of people representing every Shia city, town, and village in the country. Often the pilgrims were accompanied by an elderly vehicle, usually a battered white pickup van, carrying their food and a few people too old or sick to walk. The mood was buoyant and confident, but they were not celebrating the fall of the Baathist regime, though if it had still been in power the giant assembly could scarcely have taken place. The pilgrimage was in fact the first demonstration of the ability of Muqtada al-Sadr to mobilize great masses of pious Shia. In his first Friday sermon in his martyred father's mosque in Kufa, on April 11, Muqtada, liberally quoting his father's words, had called for people to walk on foot to Kerbala as a sign of their faith.[1]

The American troops who sped past the walkers in their trucks would have been surprised to learn that the people were commemorating a battle. It was not one that had just been fought as the American army advanced north, but rather a battle that had taken place fourteen hundred years earlier at Kerbala. In military terms, it was no more than a skirmish that ended in a massacre. But it was here, not far from the Euphrates, that the great Shia martyr, Imam Hussein, and his warrior half brother Abbas had been killed in AD 680. The grandson of the Prophet Mohammed and the son of Ali, assassinated in Kufa nineteen years earlier, Hussein with his small caravan of soldiers and family members was overwhelmed by the greatly superior forces sent against them by their archenemy Yazid, the devilish ruler of Damascus and Hussein's rival to be ruler of the Muslim world. It is this battle at Kerbala that is at the center of the Shia faith. The story of what happened so long ago on the banks of the Euphrates has become a symbol, like the crucifixion in Jerusalem for Christians, of the eternal conflict between good and evil. The legend of the death of Hussein, Abbas, and their followers tells of courage, martyrdom, and redemption through sacrifice on one side; and betrayal, cruelty, and violence on the other. It is the tale, too, of a righteous minority against a powerful but evil government authority.

The pilgrimage I saw on the roads around Baghdad in the days following its capture was the Arba'in, which marks the fortieth day of mourning after Imam Hussein's martyrdom. In any country of the world, at any time, so many pilgrims on the roads at one time would have been a striking event. The processions and marches dwarfed in size the Roman Catholic religious processions in Mexico. They were hundreds of times larger than those that I had seen as a child in Ireland, where the columns of carefully ordered marchers belonging to religious organizations blocked the main street of Youghal, the small town where I was born in County Cork. But what made this pilgrimage unique was not only its size but its timing: it was taking place within days of the end of a war. The roads were not safe. Burned-out Iraqi tanks had only just stopped smoldering beside the road. Well-armed looters were still active, their trucks piled high with stolen property. Edgy American soldiers were beginning to earn a grim reputation among Iraqis for opening a torrent of fire at anything that made them feel nervous.

Astonishing though the Arba'in may have been, it passed almost unnoticed in the United States and Western Europe. This was a pity because what we were seeing was of great significance for the future of Iraq. The throngs of people answering Muqtada's call and making their way to Kerbala was the first open display of the strength of the Shia of Iraq, who made up sixteen million out of the country's total population of twenty-seven million. The giant pilgrimage showed their religious commitment, their solidarity as a community, and their ability to mobilize vast numbers. The United States, supremely confident after its easy initial victory, was about to try to fill the power vacuum left by the fall of the old regime itself. Prewar plans for an Iraqi provisional government were cast aside. "Occupiers always call themselves liberators," said my friend the Kurdish leader Sami Abdul-Rahman disgustedly when told just before the war that America's plans for democracy in Iraq had been put on hold. Nobody in Washington paid any attention to the pilgrims, numerous though they were, or foresaw that they were serious competitors to the United States for control of Iraq.

Perplexity among American soldiers over the religious rituals of Iraqis did not diminish over the coming years. The next Arba'in came in April 2004. A year into the occupation, the mood was angrier in the Shia community. On March 2, Sunni insurgents had planted five bombs in Kerbala and Khadamiyah that killed 270 worshippers and injured 570. The confrontation between the Mehdi Army and the U.S. military was escalating by the day. The American forces were having great difficulty distinguishing between the Mehdi Army and the pilgrims marching across Iraq waving green flags to commemorate Arba'in. One day in early April, I was driving on the main road on the northern outskirts of Baghdad when I saw that a heavily armed U.S. patrol had herded about a hundred Iraqis into a field and forced them to sit down. The American soldiers were eyeing their captives with suspicion and demanding to know why they were carrying green banners. It turned out the pilgrims came from the town of Dujail, one of the few Shia centers north of Baghdad. It was famous as the place where Shia fighters had tried to assassinate Saddam Hussein in 1982, and 147 townspeople had subsequently been executed or tortured to death in retaliation. It was for this crime that Saddam Hussein was hanged on December 31, 2006.

We came across a group of six men carrying a green flag walking beside a date palm grove near a main road. They had come from Sadr City and were very willing to talk. A slightly built man wearing black clothes, who seemed to be their leader, said his name was Hamid al-Ugily, and he and his friends were spending two or three days walking to Kerbala. Surprisingly, he said he had made the pilgrimage under Saddam but had had to do it secretly, walking mainly at night. He showed no gratitude to the Americans for overthrowing the old dictator. "The Americans are just as bad as Saddam Hussein," he said. "We think they will attack Muqtada in Najaf. We will defend our religious leaders." These opinions were not unexpected. The occupation was becoming ever more unpopular among the Shia. I asked the pilgrims what jobs they held, and the answers they gave underlined the fragility of the Americans' hold on Iraq. All six men said they were soldiers in the Iraqi Civil Defense Corps (ICDC). This paramilitary body, created by the Coalition Provisional Authority (CPA), was supposed to take over duties currently being carried out by American soldiers. Abbas, one of the marchers, said: "I have been in the ICDC one year, and the Americans didn't do anything for Iraq." The ICDC was just the first in a series of Iraqi military and paramilitary organizations created by the United States on whose loyalty it found it could not rely.

I had visited Kerbala, the site of the golden-domed shrines to Hussein and Abbas, a few weeks after it was recaptured by the Iraqi army in March 1991, after the Shia had risen up in the wake of Saddam Hussein's defeat in Kuwait. The desperation of the Shia rebels besieged by Saddam Hussein's Republican Guard cannot have been so different from that of the outnumbered followers of Hussein and Abbas trapped in the same place in AD 680. The original martyrs of the Shia faith likewise knew that they could expect no mercy from their murderous enemy. In both cases defeat was inevitable. Iraq is full of the ghosts of terrible tragedies, both recent and buried in the distant past, but nowhere do they jostle one so closely as in Kerbala, Najaf, and Kufa. Here, just to the west of the Euphrates, the death by assassination or in battle of the progenitors of the Shia faith was mirrored by the persecution and massacre of their followers during the thirty-five-year rule of Saddam Hussein.

The Mesopotamian plain is the birthplace of civilization, where writing was discovered, but few Iraqis identify with Ur of the Chaldees, the Babylonians, or Nebuchadnezzar and the Assyrian empire. (An exception was Saddam Hussein, who portrayed himself as being in the tradition of Iraq's ancient rulers, and had ugly yellow bricks inscribed with his name used to rebuild parts of Babylon.) It is what is believed to have happened after the first Islamic army burst out of the desert into the lush Euphrates Valley in AD 633 that Iraqis, and above all the Shia, see as belonging to a past they feel is truly theirs. Saddam attempted to create a nationalist anti-

Iranian countermyth surrounding the battle of al-Qadassiya, when the Islamic Arab army decisively defeated the Persians (Iranians) in AD 637. As a propaganda ploy it never quite took wing. Saddam's dismal lack of success on the battlefield also belied his attempts to present himself as being a successor to the great Arab conquerors. The only positive outcome of this self-regarding myth was to give employment to Iraqi artists adept at painting battle scenes showing the triumph of the Arabs. The lobby of the al-Hamra Hotel, where I stay in Baghdad, is to this day dominated by an enormous picture of the battle of Qadassiya in which Arabs and Iranians swirl around one another as they wield their swords and spears, while in the center of the picture towers a stricken Persian war elephant with an arrow stuck in its eye.

The central drama of the Shia faith begins with the departure of a small expedition from Medina fourteen hundred years ago. Earlier, in AD 680, the seventy-seven-year-old caliph Muawiya, whose rule over the newly conquered Islamic world had been secured by the assassination of Ali, had died in Damascus. An astute and determined empire builder, he was the founder of the Umayyad dynasty. The claim of Ali to the caliphate had been based on being the first cousin of Mohammed, the husband of the Prophet's favorite daughter Fatima (Mohammed left no sons), as well as the father of Mohammed's best-loved grandsons, Hussein and Hasan. When Ali was killed in AD 661, his followers—the Shi'at Ali—were simply those who had supported his right to the caliphate. But this became transmuted over the centuries into a more revolutionary belief that Ali's piety and virtue, as well as his claim as a member of the Prophet's family, should have counted for more than the wealth and power of the Umayyads, the new dynasty based in Damascus, in selecting the leader of the Islamic world. Shi'ism was starting on its way to being the faith of the dispossessed and opponents of the powers-that-be.

Upon his death, Muawiya was succeeded as caliph in Damascus by his son Yazid, deemed by Shia to be a licentious drunk and the epitome of evil. Messengers hurried from leaders in Kufa to Medina pleading with Hussein to cross the desert to their city, where they would join him in raising his banner as the true leader of Islam. Hussein and his brother Abbas, urged on by their supporters in Medina, responded to the call. In the event, like so many exiles and would-be revolutionaries, Hussein found his friends more prudent and his enemies more proactive than he had hoped. His cousin Muslim, who had ridden ahead to Kufa to scout out the ground, found his presence in a safe house betrayed, and he was captured and killed. The ruthless governor of Kufa and Basra, Ubaydullah, had secured both cities for Yazid long before Hussein began to approach. Hussein, who had left Medina with only thirty cavalry and forty foot soldiers, expected to recruit an army from enthusiastic supporters when he reached the Euphrates Valley. Bedouin tribes along his route, however, kept their distance from what they saw as a doomed venture. A poet named Farazdaq rode out from Kufa bearing the news of betrayal: "for though the heart of the City is with thee, its sword is against thee."[2]

Unable to advance or retreat, Hussein pitched his tents to the north of Kufa on the edge of the desert, close to the west bank of the Euphrates. At first the little band was shadowed by a small cavalry detachment sent by Ubaydullah, and then by a larger force of four thousand cavalry and archers from Kufa. At the campsite where the city of Kerbala now stands, Hussein dug a ditch behind his men, filled it with brush wood, and prepared to set it afire to make sure he was not attacked from the rear and to show that he would not retreat. His followers, already cut off from the river, were very thirsty. Abbas, seeing the women and children in the camp crying out for water, stole to the riverbank and filled his waterskin. On his way back to the camp, he was detected and fought a lonely battle with enemy soldiers until first his right arm and then his left were cut off. Propping his body against the trunk of a date palm, he tried to resist until Ubaydullah's men bludgeoned him to death with sticks and clubs. On the day before the final battle, Hussein told his close family to give themselves up to the enemy, but they refused.

In the face of hopeless odds, Hussein's followers made a valiant charge, but they fell one by one, pierced by a rain of arrows. Hussein, standing at their head with Koran in one hand and sword in the other, died with thirty-three lance and sword wounds. The survivors were ridden down and their heads chopped off by the triumphant Umayyad horsemen. By evening, the heads were being rolled out of leather sacks to show Ubaydullah in Kufa the completeness of the victory and, days later, to the caliph Yazid in his palace in Damascus. It is the anniversary of this great defeat, on the tenth day—Ashura—of Moharram, that is commemorated by Shia across the world as a day of penitence and mourning equivalent to the Christian celebration of Good Friday. Hussein's last battle and death is presented not as a failed bid for power, but as an intentional martyrdom, deliberately sought to expose the sinfulness of the worldly Umayyads as persecutors of the pious and the good.[3]

Shia religious leaders today are highly conscious of parallels between what happened in the seventh century and what is happening today. When Muqtada al-Sadr was trapped in Kufa in April 2004, he denounced President Bush as a modern Yazid. The significance of the reference no doubt eluded political operatives in the White House. I was perplexed to notice on the website of Grand Ayatollah Ali al-Sistani, where the most detailed questions from the faithful are answered, that the game of chess is strictly forbidden. One questioner who asked if he could play chess on his computer was firmly told: "Playing chess is *haraam mutlaqan* [prohibited absolutely or under any circumstances] even though betting is not used."[4] I asked an Iraqi friend why Sistani objected so strongly to chess. He explained impatiently, as if it was something everyone should know, that "the reason Sistani condemns the game is that Yazid was playing chess in his palace in Damascus when the head of Imam Hussein was brought to him."

The legacy of the grim circumstances in which Shi'ism was born has had a profound effect on the beliefs and actions of its followers. It is a faith conceived in defeat and subjection and contrasts with Sunni Islam, which is a doctrine of victory and power. The details of the bloody skirmish at Kerbala provided the building blocks out of which was created a religious faith of high sophistication as well as a folk religion of great intensity and appeal. Shi'ism, with its emphasis on the endurance of suffering under an oppressive state, was peculiarly well-suited to the psychological needs of a community living under the rule of a leader as cruel as Saddam Hussein.

The Shia believed that the descendants of the Prophet should exercise leadership over the Islamic community. The imams, starting with Ali, were the true heirs of Mohammed, who, when the time was right, would overthrow tyrannous governments and establish justice in the world. Predictably, the time was never quite right for the establishment of this new order. Those Shia sects that did succeed soon abandoned their Messianic pretensions once they were in power, while those that did not were extirpated as perpetual rebels. The branch that triumphed in Iran and Iraq—the great majority of Shia today—was known as the "Twelvers" because its followers believe there have been twelve imams in succession. The Twelfth Imam, al-Mehdi, disappeared in Samarra north of Baghdad in the ninth century, but did not die and will one day return to purify the world of evil.

The imams—most lived and died obscurely after the death of Hussein—did not bid for political power, but the Shia developed a distinction between spiritual and temporal leadership that is similar to the Christian distinction between church and state. In contrast to Sunni Muslims, Shia obedience to the government of the day is qualified and conditional. The Shia were never Islamic Bolsheviki, underground dissidents permanently plotting the destruction of the status quo, but the doctrines and institutions of their faith provided a fertile breeding ground for dissent.

Popular Shia religious culture in Iraq remained vibrant despite persecution by Saddam's regime. State-sponsored secular nationalism was discredited by the disastrous Iran-Iraq war, in which half a million Iraqis were killed, wounded, or taken prisoner; the defeat in Kuwait; the uprising of 1991; and the economic disaster of sanctions. The government tried, at different times, guardedly, to tolerate or covertly restrain prayer meetings and processions. They were always suspicious that these meetings might be used by opponents of the regime. When these gatherings did take place, they were carefully monitored and video was taken so participants could be identified.[5] Despite this constant persecution, secular Baathism failed to erode the popularity of such expressions of Shia identity. It was an important failure. The Shia clergy focused on sacred texts and canonical traditions, and the Shia middle class in the cities was partly secularized. But the political punching power of the Shia community came from the religious solidarity of millions of people that, at times, made even Saddam Hussein hesitate to confront them directly.

Shia religious culture is expressed in many forms. In contrast to the Sunni, it is highly pictorial. Folk art, using highly colored paintings or elaborate embroidery, recalls dramatic incidents in the battle of Kerbala, such as Hussein's riderless but noble white horse returning to camp with blood dripping from the saddle. An oft-repeated motif is the severed arm of Abbas, whose fierce bravery has always had a strong appeal to Iraqi tribesmen. The Shia tribes in the marshes north of Basra consider swearing by the name of Abbas a far stronger oath than swearing by the name of Hussein.[6]

The elaborate ten-day-long rituals of Ashura and the Arba'in pilgrimage that follows it are central to the Shia sense of identity and solidarity, though the form the celebration takes varies markedly in different parts of Iraq. In the market town of Twaireej, on the Euphrates, fifteen miles from Kerbala, the birthplace of Iraqi prime minister Nouri al-Maliki, the Ashura ritual is spread over ten days, starting with green, black, and red flags being raised over the roofs of houses. The green represents the sayyids, members of a familial succession leading back to the Prophet; the black symbolizes sorrow and grief over the battle of Kerbala; and the red is the blood of the murdered Imam Hussein. Men of the town wear long black shirts to show grief. In another, more exotic symbol, water pots and water tanks are displayed covered with black cloth from which drinking water is offered for free in memory of the searing thirst of Imam Hussein's besieged followers. In the burning heat of the plains of Mesopotamia, every Iraqi can visualize the suffering of those trapped without water to drink. It is a symbol of life itself.

Over ten days, the faithful in Twaireej gather for two or three hours every evening for recitations, the chanting of hymns, young men beating their chests and whipping themselves or slightly cutting their scalps with a sword so as to draw blood. Passion plays and recitations retell stories from the days leading up to the last hopeless fight. "The stories are known to every individual taking part in the ritual, whether as performer or spectator," writes Faleh Jabar, the great expert on the Shia of Iraq. "It is the journey of Hussein to Kerbala to regain his deserved caliphate. He is betrayed by supporters; outflanked and outnumbered by a brutal enemy; cut off from water; left almost alone with a few loyal supporters, a stranger in a foreign land with his children and his sister." Stories are woven out of the individual fates of the martyrs, touching not only violence and death but also love and marriage. The sacred and the mundane are combined in a way that is closer to the luxuriant displays of medieval Christianity than to more puritanical strains of Islam.[7]

It is important, however, not to read history backward: the successful political activism of the Shia in the Middle East only developed over the last half century. Few paid much attention to the radical potential of Shi'ism before the Iranian revolution of 1978–79; the rise of Hezbollah in Lebanon following the Israeli invasion of 1982; and the Shia uprising in Iraq in 1991, followed by their gradual takeover of power after the U.S. invasion of 2003. Shi'ism may have had its birth in schism and dissent, but for most of its history it was an apolitical faith. It might be the religion of the underdog, but it primarily taught resignation and endurance in the face of oppression, not revolt. The Abbasid dynasty replaced the Umayyads in 750 and established Baghdad as the center of the Muslim world. It was during the

Abbasid period that Shi'ism took its present form, and its doctrinal differences from the Sunni took root. But the Shia believers were still a minority community. The last Shia dynasty to hold power in the Arab world was the Fatimids in Cairo, who were overthrown by Saladin—a Sunni Kurd from Tikrit in northern Iraq—in 1171. When Ibrahim al-Jaafari became prime minister, leading a Shia-dominated government in Baghdad in 2005, a Shia official proudly remarked to me: "It is the first time we Shia have held power in the Arab world since the Fatimids."

The position of the Shia in Iraq was changed by three events that have a fundamental impact to this day: the enforced conversion of Iran to Shi'ism by the Safavid dynasty in the sixteenth century; the rise of a powerful Shia clergy; and the conversion of the southern Iraqi tribes to Shi'ism in the eighteenth and nineteenth centuries. The first Safavid shah, Isma'il, a Turkish-speaking warrior who established his capital in Tabriz, seized power in Iran in 1501. He used Twelver Shi'ism as the ideological glue to bind his disparate new realm to his dynasty through forced conversion. Shi'ite clergy were imported from Lebanon and Bahrain to indoctrinate Iranians. The first three caliphs—Abu Bakr, Omar, and Othman—who had displaced Ali were formally cursed during Friday sermons. The Safavid shahs claimed to be descended from Ali through the seventh imam. The Shia identity of Safavid Iran was further enhanced because it was continually at war with the Ottoman Empire as the supreme Sunni power. Baghdad changed hands a number of times, but the Ottomans were able to maintain their grip, and with a Sunni in power locally, the Iraqi Shia became permanently subordinate. Sharing a common religion with Iran, they were suspected as possible traitors. "Safawi"—Safavid—became a derogatory term used by Sunni to imply that Iraqi Shia are Iranian pawns. Saddam Hussein spat out the words at his tormentors just before he went to the gallows.

A second development significant for the Shia was the rise of the power of their clergy, or *ulema*. More specifically, it was the *mujtahids,* the qualified interpreters of the Sharia law, who became central to the organization of the Shia religion. The clerical hierarchy was chosen because of its scholastic learning, but they were willing to advise on all aspects of life. The most learned and highly regarded of the *mujtahids* were the Marji'iyyah, and the supreme religious figure was the paramount Marji' al-Taqlid. Pious Shia chose one of the senior clergy to emulate as a source of inspiration. All this took time to evolve, but it introduced a further difference between the Shia and the Sunni that was pregnant with consequences for the future

of Iran and Iraq. Unlike the Sunni community, the Shia now possessed a
clergy and a religious organization that was separate from the state. Potentially, it could provide an alternative leadership for the Shia.

This was an important development because, for the first time, the
majority of Iraqis belonged to the Shia faith because of the conversion to
Shi'ism of the Sunni tribes in southern Iraq. The clergy in Najaf and Kerbala needed the loyalty of the newly converted tribes. The shrine cities were
wide open to attacks from across the desert to the west. Najaf was twice
besieged by anti-Shia Wahhabi from the Arabian peninsula and Kerbala was
sacked in 1801. The Shia leaders of the shrine cities had every reason to con-
vert the Sunni tribes surrounding them in order to gain protection. The
tribes may also have converted to Shi'ism because they needed a new focus
for their identity, as they abandoned nomadic herding and adopted settled agriculture. This in turn bound them more closely to Najaf, Kerbala,
and other urban centers.[8] This conversion of the tribes had a political consequence that was to dominate the country's politics in the twentieth century: Iraq became a country with a Shia majority but was ruled by the
Sunni. The rough British census of 1919 showed that the Shia were 53 percent of the population;[9] a fuller census in 1947 showed Shia Arabs as making up 51.4 percent of Iraqis, Sunni Arabs 19.7 percent, and Sunni Kurds
18 percent.[10]

Iraq differed from most other Middle Eastern states in another significant way. The first urban civilizations grew up along the fertile banks of the
Tigris and Euphrates five thousand years ago. But Iraq has an equally long
history as a frontier zone squeezed between civilizations centered on the
Iranian plateau: Anatolia, Arabia, and the eastern Mediterranean. It was not
only a frontier but a battlefield: Alexander the Great died in Babylon; the
Romans were never able to hold the Mesopotamian plain; and Ottoman
control was tenuous for much of their long rule. From the destruction of
Baghdad by Hulagu the Mongol in 1258 until the monarchy was established
under British auspices in 1921, central government control was always limited and often nonexistent. This helps explain the continuing strength of
nonstate agencies such as tribe, clan, and extended family in Iraqi life, and
also, perhaps, the extreme ferocity of its politics. There is a violent anarchic strain in Iraqi life. Commenting on this just after the fall of Baghdad,
an Iraqi neurosurgeon, who had only narrowly dissuaded looters from ran-
sacking his hospital, warned me: "Remember, even Saddam had difficulty
ruling this country."

CHAPTER THREE

The First Martyr

"If my little finger was Baathist, I would cut it off" was the defiant retort of Mohammed Baqir al-Sadr, the Shia revolutionary thinker and leader, when he was asked to submit to the Baathist government in Baghdad.[1] His uncompromising words became a catchphrase for the Shia resistance to Saddam Hussein. Baqir was the progenitor of the politically activist Shia religious movement whose followers became known as the Sadrists. He was executed by Saddam in 1980. In death, Baqir's reputation was enough to make his cousin and student Mohammed Sadiq al-Sadr the Iraqi regime's most dangerous opponent, until its gunmen in turn assassinated him with two of his sons in 1999. After the U.S. invasion in 2003, it was the al-Sadr family name, by now twice sanctified by martyrdom, that promoted with astonishing speed Sadiq's little-known son Muqtada al-Sadr into one of the most powerful men in Iraq, to the horror of the United States and its Iraqi allies.

Baqir became known as the First Martyr, or Sadr I, and Sadiq, the Second Martyr, or Sadr II. Baqir was the only grand ayatollah to be executed in modern history. His followers hoped, and the government in Baghdad feared, he would be the "Khomeini of Iraq." (He openly supported the Iranian revolution in 1978–79.) Saddam Hussein was determined not to share the fate of the Shah, forced to flee Iran as the Shia revolution triumphed in the streets of Tehran. Repression of Shia militants in Iraq was savage and carefully planned. On April 4, 1980, Baqir was arrested in Najaf, and four days later he was executed, along with his sister Amina

Sadr Bint al-Huda, in a prison in Baghdad. Stories were whispered, and widely believed in Iraq, that his torturers had hammered an iron nail into his head and raped his sister before they were both killed. The cruelty of their deaths explains why hatred for the Baathists persisted for so long after the overthrow of Saddam Hussein. "Many Shia believe that they raped Huda in front of her brother before they executed them," a Shia journalist in Baghdad told me in 2007. "That is why the thirst among the Shia for revenge against the Baathists is so strong, and why they get so angry when the Americans want to reverse de-Baathification."[2]

Baqir suffered the same dire fate as many revolutionary leaders in history who hoped to emulate successful revolutions elsewhere. Throughout the twentieth century, Islamic parties sought to overthrow secular states. All had failed. Now in Iran, to the amazement and bewilderment of the world, Ayatollah Khomeini had succeeded in overthrowing what had appeared to be a powerful government, flush with oil money, protected by ferocious security services, and supported by the West. Euphoria gripped Islamic parties in the region. If it could be done in Iran, why not in Iraq, where the Shia were also a majority?

Baqir was not entirely swept away by religious enthusiasm. He and many of his followers knew all too well that they faced a strong and ruthless security apparatus. Their own resources were limited. The Shia religious hierarchy was not united behind them and rightly feared a confrontation with the Baath. In Tehran, the Iranian leaders were making the same mistake as successful socialist revolutionaries in Moscow, Beijing, and Havana had made in the course of the twentieth century. They thought their own recipe for revolution could be successfully exported to other countries. From Bolivia to Indonesia, socialist supporters paid a price in blood for their overconfidence. A revolution needs an element of surprise if it is to win. The powers-that-be must be caught napping. In Iraq the reverse was true. The government was prepared and the revolutionaries were not. In the summer of 1979, Shia militants hopefully chanted: "In the name of Khomeini and al-Sadr, Islam will always be victorious." Baqir himself sensed that such open defiance of the regime would lead to his death.[3]

Baqir was a member of one of the great religious families of the Middle East. Born in 1935 in the Khadamiyah district of Baghdad, he was one of the al-Sadrs, part of the clerical aristocracy. "The family lineage," says his son Jafar al-Sadr, "goes back to the Prophet Mohammed through the seventh Shia imam, Musa al-Khazim. Our forefathers were living in the Jabal Amel [in Lebanon] from the 12th century to the 18th century when the family's grandfather Sayyid Saleh bin Ibrahim Sharaf al-Dun emigrated to Iraq in 1785."[4] Established in Khadamiyah, they were prominent in the affairs of their community. During the last years of Ottoman rule, Sayyid Hussein al-Sadr was a revered *mujtahid*. His son Sayyid Mohammed al-Sadr had a leading role in the 1920 uprising against the British, preaching jihad against the occupation of Iraq; later, he became a long-term president of the senate, briefly prime minister in 1948, and was known as the "Rasputin of Iraq" because of his influence in court circles.[5]

Baqir's father, Haydar, died young, and his elder brother, Ismail, who was to be a religious leader in Khadamiyah, played an important role in his upbringing. His mother came from the al-Yassin family that was also well connected to the Shia clerical leaders. Her brother Sheikh Murtada al-Yassin was a highly regarded religious activist in Khadamiyah. It was an advantage, from the point of view of Baqir's future clerical career, that he came from Khadamiyah, one of the four shrine cities of Iraq, the other three being Najaf, Kerbala, and Samarra. It had originally been a separate township in a loop of the Tigris River, just north of Baghdad, until the capital grew around it. Baqir, as a child, would have seen the shrine's golden dome and four slender minarets outlined against the sky whenever he looked across the city. Devout pilgrims, many from Iran, poured into its spacious courtyard; they bought golden necklaces for weddings in the jewelers' shops that lined the ancient streets around the shrine. Originally built in AD 799, it houses the double tomb of the seventh and ninth imams; Musa, the ancestor of the al-Sadrs, who died in AD 799, and his grandson Mohammed Jawad, who died in AD 835. Destroyed by the Mongols in the thirteenth century, it was rebuilt by the Turkish Ottomans and the Persian Safavids when each in turn occupied Baghdad in the sixteenth and seventeenth centuries. Both vied for Shia support by rebuilding and adorning the shrine.

At the age of eleven, Baqir moved to Najaf with his family to study at the religious schools, where he was, by all accounts, a highly talented student. His subsequent martyrdom makes it difficult to discover the real character of the young religious student whose personality now lies hidden beneath layers of hagiography. "In his eleventh year he studied the science of logic and genealogy, of which he showed himself a uniquely brilliant student," says Hussein al-Shami, who was one of his students.[6] He joined a hawza (a Shia seminary similar to an academic college; the term is also used to describe the Shia clerical community as a whole) of such leading *mujtahids* as Ayatollah Mohammed Rouhani and later the Grand Ayatollah Abu al Qasim al-Khoei, who was to be his political and ideological competitor in future years. Al-Khoei is said to have altered several of his judgments after discussion with his young student.

Baqir was joining a very hierarchical and introverted, but also comatose and beleaguered, world. The Marji'iyyah, the most senior members of the Shia clergy, were somewhat akin in status to cardinals in the Roman Catholic church, though they are less numerous (there are, at present, nine) and there is no equivalent to the pope. They are traditionally not only venerated but emulated by the Shia, who will choose one of them as his model, though go to a lower-ranking cleric for rulings and advice. The Marji'iyyah themselves were not very approachable, and sat in their houses with their students. "They all thought they were superior to each other in learning and wisdom, so they would seldom deign to visit another member of the hierarchy," comments Ghanim Jawad, a well-informed observer of Shia clerical politics.[7] "So sometimes they didn't see each other for years, but would communicate by sending messengers carrying pieces of paper." Authority was fragmented. There were divisions between Arab and Iranian ayatollahs. The grand Marji' al-Taqlid (the highest Shia religious authority) when Baqir was in his twenties, Muhsin al-Hakim, whose family was to play a critical role in opposition to Saddam Hussein, had been selected with the support of the Shah of Iran. The Shah wanted the position to go to an Arab rather than an Iranian cleric, because the Arab had fewer followers in Iran and thus would be less of a menace to the Shah's regime. One of the strengths of the Shia hierarchy was that those clerics critical of the Iraqi regime could live in Qom, and those hostile to the Iranian government could live in Najaf.

The strange world of the Shia clerical class was under ever-growing threat in the 1950s. Secularism was undermining Islam, both Shia and Sunni, across the Middle East. Religion seemed to limp behind socialism and nationalism in devising an effective response to the political, cultural, and economic impact of the West. The Shia clergy saw their grip on education weakening. Their income from *khums*—donations—was inadequate. The

Shia community was split: there were the very wealthy Shia business elite in Baghdad; disaffected peasants on the great estates of southern Iraq; the workers in the cities increasingly under the influence of the Iraqi Communist Party; and a secular, highly educated professional middle class. Many of the problems facing Iraqis were common to all Islamic countries seeking to throw off imperial control, direct or indirect, and to modernize. Iraq was different because its problems were more acute. Neither socialists nor nationalists turned out to have workable solutions to them. With the overthrow of the monarchy in the bloody coup by General Abdel Karim Qassim in July 1958, the country entered a period of turmoil that has lasted fifty years and shows no sign of stabilizing to this day.

At first sight, the Shia clergy looked peculiarly ill-equipped to cope with the coming challenges. The fall of the Hashemite monarchy opened the door to mass politics, and religious rituals suffered. In 1959, the numbers taking part in the pilgrimages to Najaf and Kerbala fell to an all-time low. "The Communists and the nationalists were powerful in the government and on the streets," recalls one Najaf cleric. "They got a tremendous boost from the support they were getting from Egyptian president Gamal Abdel Nasser."[8] In the face of these menacing developments, the way was open for Baqir and some of the younger clergy to try to make reforms aimed at protecting the hawza and the collective of senior clerics. They took the obvious course of setting up a political party, called al-Dawa (the Call), the first meeting of which took place in Najaf in 1957. Its aim was to defend Islam and its institutions. The traditionalists in the clerical leadership were briefly frightened enough to accept change even if the foundation of a party potentially challenged their authority. They could see the need to emulate the Iraqi Communist Party with a cell structure, discipline, and chain of command. Alarmed by the swift growth of communism among the Shia masses, Grand Ayatollah Muhsin al-Hakim assented to its creation.

A safeguard against the new party competing against the clerical hierarchy was that its founding members were almost all young men from families in the inner circle of Iraqi Shi'ism. There were representatives from many of the noble clerical families, including Baqir himself. Almost all were young, ninety percent of them under thirty-five. Baqir al-Hakim, later the founder of the Supreme Council for Islamic Revolution in Iraq, was only fourteen when he joined. Many of the founding members were to be executed, assassinated, or tortured to death, but half a century later, the Iraqi government was dominated by the relatives and descendants of the men who had established al-Dawa.

Baqir himself was only twenty-three years old in 1958, which, in normal times, would have been too young to play a prominent role in a clerical elite where authority came only with age and prolonged training. He had the advantage of his family background, but he also needed the patronage of a senior and well-established religious figure. The way this was done—Iraqi clerical politics have some similarities, notably in the venom with which they are conducted, with university politics in the West with Najaf playing the role of Oxbridge or Harvard—was to write a laudatory book on the work of a senior cleric, the recently selected Grand Ayatollah Muhsin al-Hakim. Khomeini had a similar sort of book. Modernizer he might be, but Baqir could not hope to accomplish anything without the support of well-established elders. Despite his intelligence, ability, energy, popularity, family connections, and powerful patrons, he still had a long way to go before he could join the Marji'iyyah. General Qassim's coup gave Baqir and his new party their chance. Iraq was entering revolutionary times. Aging and conservative Shia clerics might be uncomfortable with the innovations Baqir proposed, but they could scarcely do without him.

The extent to which Iraq had always been divided between Shia and Sunni became a matter of furious dispute in the years after the U.S.-led invasion of 2003. The arguments were bitter because several of the protagonists were in search of an alibi. If it could be shown that Iraq was always a mosaic of competing communities that hated one another, then the United States and its allies could not be blamed for provoking a sectarian and ethnic civil war. The Sunni, for their part, were reluctant to admit that, as a minority, they had wielded power over the Shia who were three times more numerous than themselves.

It is true that there was no apartheid between Sunni and Shia. They occasionally intermarried. Some Shia rose high in the Baath party and the government. And religion was not the only means through which Shia Iraqis established their identity. But in the exercise of power, Iraq was a Sunni-dominated state and became more so during Saddam Hussein's long rule.

At first the 1958 coup opened doors to the Shia. The leaders of the powerful Iraqi Communist Party were Shia and swiftly radicalized the urban and rural poor. President Qassim was himself partly Shia. In east Baghdad he started building basic housing for impoverished Shia immigrants from the countryside. Fifty years later, the area had become a political and military bastion of Muqtada al-Sadr, having gone through three changes of name from al-Thawra (the Revolution), to Saddam City, and finally to Sadr City. Containing one-third of the capital's population, it was less of a district than a densely populated twin city to the rest of Baghdad.

The military coup in February 1963, in which the Baath party took a leading role, was seen as an "anti-Shia" action because the Iraqi army and security services were Sunni-dominated. The slaughter of communists was also a massacre of the Shia, and the sectarian balance began shifting decisively against them. The Baath party was ousted from power later in 1963 by its former allies, but most of the security police still came from Dulaim (later Anbar) province, which, then as now, was almost entirely Sunni. Shia members of the Baath party found they were far more ruthlessly treated by the security police than its Sunni members. Saddam Hussein, beginning to emerge as an important Baathist leader, recorded how in 1966 he escaped from imprisonment. His account, given to a sympathetic biographer, shows how well-connected Sunni from the provinces were treated with kid gloves. He was appearing before the Higher Security Court charged with plotting to storm the presidential palace and machine-gun members of the government attending a meeting. Despite the seriousness of the offense, on his way back to jail Saddam persuaded his guards to stop and let him eat a meal at a restaurant in Abu Nawas Street beside the Tigris. During the meal, he and six companions simply walked out the back of the restaurant.[9]

Arab nationalism could be a mask for sectarianism in a way not immediately obvious to non-Iraqis. In 1964, for instance, many banks and commercial and industrial companies were nationalized. The ostensible reason for this was to bring the Iraqi economy in line with state socialist Egypt, with which Iraq was supposedly to combine in the name of Arab unity. But the reality was that the majority of Iraqi businessmen were Shia and the state officials who took over the nationalized companies were mostly Sunni. Sectarian divisions between Sunni and Shia in Iraq in the 1960s were not as deep as those dividing Arab from Kurd, but if they were not always dominant, they were also never absent.

The divisions were also about to get worse. The Baath party returned to power in a military coup in 1968 and did not intend to share power with anybody. It soon disposed of most of its military allies and showed an exceptional capacity for using violence against its opponents. Authority was concentrated in the hands of President Hassan al-Bakr and his cousin Saddam Hussein, vice chairman of the Revolution Command Council. Saddam wielded power primarily through different agencies of the security police and the intelligence services. The most important posts went to his half brothers and cousins, members of the Bejat clan of the Albu Nasir tribe from Tikrit. "If you want to know how we rule Iraq," reflected one of Saddam's relatives in later years, "we do it just the same way as we used to run Tikrit."[10] Military, police, tribal, and party allegiances were adeptly combined to make the regime coup-proof. Most important, the jump in oil prices after 1973 provided the Baathists with vast funds, sufficient to raise the living standards of all Iraqis and quell popular discontent. Should the Shi'ite clerics or the politically active Shi'ites in al-Dawa choose to confront such a powerful and violent state machine, their chances of success looked remote.

While these dramatic events were happening in Baghdad, Baqir was living a modest but energetic life in Najaf. "He did not own a house but rented one and he did not drive a car," says one of his students from those days, Hussein al-Shami. "He used to say that 'while I am in this position, the leader of a Shia congregation, I must live at the same level as my students.'" He was ascetic but did not see asceticism as being at the heart of religion. On the contrary, he was eager to attract the younger Iraqi intelligentsia into the hawza by finding well-qualified teachers, and he believed the students should be properly rewarded. "He guaranteed them the same socioeconomic status that they might have gained from government jobs." He sought to get the Marji'iyyah to pay for religious instructors to be sent to poorer areas. Previously, these had been paid for by people in the districts into which they were sent, which inevitably meant that the richer parts of Iraq were oversupplied with religious teachers and poorer parts like al-Thawra (now Sadr City) were poorly provided for.[11]

It was in the three years after the fall of the monarchy that Baqir sought to lay the ideological basis for an Islamic counterattack on Western capitalism and communism. He wrote two books—*Falsafatuna* (Our Philosophy) and *Iqtisaduna* (Our Economics). His first ideas about how to save the Islamic *umma* (community), though couched in abstract language, appeared in a periodical he had helped set up called *Adhwa.* At this stage, it was still surprising that the Shia clergy, living in an essentially medieval world, should even have contemplated allowing a magazine to function. Baqir's contributions almost immediately caused him trouble. In 1960 he was forced to stop writing for the magazine and to sever his open connection with the Dawa party. For the next twenty years of his life, up to his execution, his political activism had to be masked or, at least, diluted in public, though in times of crisis the mask would slip.

During this whole period, Baqir felt squeezed between the Baath and its brutal security agencies, on the one hand, and, on the other hand, those in the Marji'iyyah who saw him as a dangerous radical. Hussein al-Shami recalls that this lack of understanding and continual criticism by Baqir's clerical colleagues "made him feel so lonely that he wished for death sometimes, though he tried to be patient and carefully conceal this." Clerical jealousies ran deep. "He was so harshly criticized when he established the Islamic Dawa party that he used to say: 'It is very strange that some religious people allow their sons to join the al-Baath party but they attack me for establishing the al-Dawa party.'" He felt his promotion within the ranks of the clergy was being blocked by unfair allegations from critics who thought he was too emotional as a personality and a divisive figure. Some of his opponents within the hawza allegedly made use of his bad relations with the Baath party to further isolate him. "They used to terrify anybody going to see him by saying that, if they did so, they were likely to be arrested by state security."[12]

The Baath party's merciless security organizations always had the strength to crush the traditional Shia leadership. Saddam Hussein's real skill, though he enjoyed playing the role of military commander, was as a secret policeman. He and his lieutenants had seized power through a military putsch. They were determined that nobody should do the same to them. For all their revolutionary rhetoric they thought of politics in terms of plots devised by a small number of people probably backed by a foreign power. For this reason they wholly failed to foresee the success of the Iranian revolution, based on mass street protests, until the last moment. Saddam prided himself at his skill in smelling out his enemies. "We used to be able to sense a conspiracy with our hearts before we even gathered the evidence," he had once boasted to Baath party leaders.[13] The Dawa party had little chance against such well-organized ferocity. The Marji'iyyah could also be intimidated. The real vulnerability of the regime, however, became evident when political dissent combined with popular piety as the

Shia masses carried out the age-old rituals of Ashura and Arba'in. These self-organized demonstrations and pilgrimages, which had no real leaders, were to pose the greatest threat to the Baath in the 1970s.

Skirmishes between the Shia leaders and the Baath party started early. A decision came in 1969 to deport all Iranian nationals in Iraq. The regime claimed they totaled half a million, though this was an exaggeration. Whole groups, such as the Faili Kurds (Shia Kurds), were to be targeted in coming years. There was a drumbeat of propaganda, similar to that emanating from Washington during the U.S.-led occupation after 2003, insisting that Shia militants were pawns manipulated by Iran. At times, there was enough substance to give this claim some credibility. In January 1970, the government alleged that it had discovered a plot to overthrow it that included Shia figures close to Dawa, such as the Grand Ayatollah's son Mahdi al-Hakim, who was forced to flee abroad. When the grand *marja* Muhsin al-Hakim himself died in June 1970, the enormous numbers attending his funeral chanted verses against the Baath (there are in fact several grand ayatollahs who collectively form the Marji'iyyah, but one is usually identified as the leading figure). His successor, Grand Ayatollah Abu al Qasim al-Khoei, took a more pacifist and apolitical line than his predecessor, which led the politicized Shia laity to turn to Baqir. He had a further advantage: his family, though it might have had links with Iran in the distant past, was identifiably Arab, while al-Khoei had been born in Iran.

Repression increased. The General Directorate of Security Services was still circumspect in dealing with senior clergy, but not with the laity. In 1972, Baqir was arrested but was detained in a Kufa hospital because he was ill. In 1974, five of the most important Dawa party leaders from Najaf, Kerbala, and Basra were executed. The party leader for Baghdad, Sahib al-Dakhil, disappeared in 1971 and was never seen again.[14] The executions and heavy sentences for other militants led to a mass flight of party supporters. Baqir issued an edict in the same year, severing any connection between the hawza and political work. This was partly a defensive measure. He feared that if the hawza and Dawa were too closely linked then "the demolition of the political organization by the Baath government would have a devastating effect on the hawza."[15] A second motive, according to a former student of Baqir, was recognition that the hawza was meant to be linked to the Shia community as a whole and not a single group. Too close an association with the Dawa would alienate some of the faithful.

Distancing himself publicly from a party opposed to the Baath was a matter of common sense, but Baqir maintained covert links. He appointed one of his students to liaise with Dawa and channeled money to it whenever possible.[16] He may have had deep differences with the Grand Ayatollah al-Khoei over the extent to which the Shia clergy should become involved in active politics, but he was highly conscious of the vulnerability of the Shia institutions to state action. The Baath government could, for instance, simply deny residency to the many Iranian students studying in Najaf, or it could call up Iraqi Arab students for military service. It could also target funds controlled by the clergy. Baqir may have advocated political activism, but he was not without caution. Asked by the head of the Directorate for General Security, Fadhil al-Barak, to omit a passage criticizing socialism from one of his books—because the Baath party was itself socialist—he complied on the grounds that government agents would probably change the passage anyway.

The government in Baghdad made intermittent attempts to cultivate him. Remarkably, he was asked to ghost a book on religion that would appear under the name of President Hassan al-Bakr. He refused without hesitation. On another occasion, al-Barak said he was prepared to ignore all the critical reports about Baqir made by the security directorate in Najaf. Unfortunately, he added spitefully, he could "do nothing about reports that had been delivered direct to the leadership by members of the hawza." In other words, some of Baqir's clerical colleagues would not have been sorry to see him disappear. Over the coming years it was to be a constant and angry complaint of what was to become the Sadrist movement that their rivals for leadership of the Shia community betrayed them in their hour of need.

The greatest challenge to the Baath came by surprise and came from below. It happened spontaneously in 1977 during the Arba'in pilgrimage. This was a year before the beginning of the revolution in Iran, indicating that many Iraqi Shia were in a militant mood even before the emergence of Ayatollah Khomeini. There were many reasons for their discontent. Anti-Baath feeling among the Shia peasantry was exacerbated by a drought caused by low water in the Euphrates, the result of a new dam built upriver in Syria. Some fifteen thousand soldiers, mostly Shia, had been killed in the war with the Kurds in 1974–75 and many of their coffins had been brought to the great Wadi al-Salaam (Valley of Peace) cemetery in Najaf. The government banned the pilgrimage in 1977 claiming it had discovered a Syrian plot to plant a bomb in the shrine in Kerbala.

The march went ahead anyway, organized by villages and city quarters. Marchers from Najaf to Kerbala were in a militant mood and chanted "Noble Najafis, hoist aloft your banners." On the second day of the march, a crowd of some thirty thousand neared a place called Khan al-Nus, halfway between Najaf and Kerbala. The police and security forces opened fire. In retaliation, the pilgrims, many of them farmers who themselves carried guns, stormed and sacked the local police station. Meanwhile in Najaf, Baqir, who had played no role in organizing the march, was worried enough to send an emissary, Mohammed Baqir al-Hakim, to warn the marchers not to shout slogans against President Ahmad Hassan al-Bakr and Saddam Hussein. The pilgrims ignored the advice and chanted:

> *Saddam take your hands off.*
> *Neither our army nor our people want you.*

The outcome of such defiance was inevitable. Attack helicopters and armored units commanded by Saddam Hussein's cousin Khairallah Tulfah were rushed to the spot and opened fire. Some sixteen demonstrators were killed and two thousand arrested. Eight members of a spontaneously formed organizing committee were executed and two died under torture. Mohammed Baqir al-Hakim and fourteen others were given life sentences. True to his character, Saddam Hussein regarded the sentences passed by the special court as far too lenient and had two of the judges expelled from the Baath party.[17]

The critical moment in the twentieth century for the Iraqi Shia was the Iranian revolution of 1978–79. Baqir became its advocate and an open supporter of Ayatollah Khomeini. But Shi'ism in Iran and Iraq have very different histories. In the former, it has been the state religion since 1501 and is followed by ninety percent of the population; in the latter, it was the religion of only sixty percent and they were without political power. The revolution would not necessarily have spread to Iraq, but Saddam Hussein was taking no chances. In 1979 he seized absolute power, massively repressed the Dawa, and, in the following year, launched a military attack on Iran. He thought he would win a quick and easy victory, but in reality he had started a series of hot and cold wars that ultimately

destroyed not only the Baath party rule but the centuries-old Sunni predominance in Iraq.

Baqir knew Khomeini during the latter's long exile in Najaf between
1964 and 1978, though there are differing accounts of the degree of inti-
macy. He encouraged his students to attend Khomeini's seminars on
genealogy and other topics even though these were conducted in Farsi. In
an extraordinary miscalculation the Shah asked Saddam Hussein to expel
Khomeini from Najaf, where he had been forced to take refuge in 1964
and was largely isolated from the outside world. He left in October 1978
for Paris, where he had instant access to the international media. His every
word was recorded and relayed to his millions of supporters in Iran. Vast
crowds defied riot police, martial law, and curfews to demonstrate in the
streets of Tehran and other Iranian cities. Clerics united with liberals and
the Marxist left in opposition to the regime. In February 1979 the Shah's
nerve broke and he fled Iran to be replaced by Ayatollah Khomeini. Both
the Baath party and the Iraqi opposition were astonished and uncertain
how to respond.

Khomeini and Baqir were at one in their advocacy of political activism
by the Shia clergy. They both opposed the tradition of quietism as represented by Grand Ayatollah al-Khoei. This concentrated on the morality and
behavior of the individual. Its supporters decried direct political involvement by the clergy as corrupting. Sadrists later quoted with approval
Khomeini's jibe at Shia religious dignitaries: "You busy yourself with
Islamic laws concerning menstruation and giving birth; I am leading a revolution."[18] For Khomeini, Islam is, and had always been, political. During
the lectures in Najaf that Baqir had advised his students to attend, Khomeini spelled out his belief in "the guardianship of the jurist" under which
the supreme leader is a jurist, an expert on Islamic law. Baqir agreed with
Khomeini about the leading role of the *mujtahids,* but he gave the belief a
critically democratic and less authoritarian twist. He proposed a division
of powers between the nation and clerical class, retaining "executive and
legislative powers for the nation, while reserving judicial powers for the
mujtahids—both accountable before the law and the constitution." Baqir,
unlike Khomeini, saw the traditional clerical leadership as fallible. He
argued that the prophets and the imams may be chosen by God, but the
selection of the Marji'iyyah is "determined by the nation."[19] Elections were
at the center of his vision of an Islamic state.

Two months before the Shah fell, lay leaders of the Dawa party visited

Baqir in Najaf. They looked to him because he was a founder of their party, was of Arab lineage, and, unlike al-Khoei, was a proponent of political activism. His response was cautious. He said he needed two or three years to enhance his religious standing. He did not get them. Events were beginning to build up their own momentum. When Khomeini flew into Tehran to be greeted by millions, Baqir abandoned his earlier caution and began to force the pace. He declared a three-day holiday at the Najaf hawza on February 11, 1979, to celebrate Khomeini coming to power—demonstrators carried pictures of the Iranian leader. Baqir also sent his own disciple Sayyid Mahmoud al-Hashimi to Tehran. In messages he exchanged with Khomeini, Baqir was addressed as a subordinate. In street demonstrations Shia militants sought to repeat the tactics that had brought down the Shah. Iraqi security held its hand but collected detailed intelligence about Islamic militants. At five a.m. on June 12, 1979, some two hundred security and policemen arrested Baqir and took him to the General Security Directorate run by Fadhil al-Barak in Baghdad. There were demonstrations and protests on an unprecedented scale in the Shia quarters of Baghdad and in Shia cities and towns across the country, as well as in Lebanon, United Arab Emirates, Britain, and France.[20]

The government backed down and Baqir was released from prison. The threat was serious enough, and differences within the Baath leadership over the degree of violence to be used in combating it were enough to provoke a crisis within the ruling Revolution Command Council. This was the moment when Saddam Hussein seized total control of Iraq. The government changed its tactics. This time Baqir was held under house arrest, but his disciples and members of the Dawa party were targeted. Some four thousand to five thousand were arrested and more than two hundred were executed. Baqir's position in his house in Najaf was not comfortable. A supporter recalls that Iraqi security "cut off electric power, the water supply and the telephone line . . . and even made it difficult for him to buy food." This went on for months. "Baqir's younger daughter suffered from a severe toothache, but he could not get medicine for her." Baqir himself became physically weak and spent much of his time praying. His hopes for an Islamic revolution in Iraq were ebbing and his followers were being arrested, tortured, and executed. He could see that other members of the Marji'iyyah were distancing themselves from him. Even so, the government in Baghdad preferred to neutralize him rather than kill him. A presidential envoy came to his house to ask him to make a conciliatory gesture by publicly criticizing the Islamic revolution in Iran or showing support for the Baathist government in Baghdad. The envoy said that this could be done by public praise for some important government measure, such as the nationalization of oil, Kurdish self-government, or the campaign against illiteracy. Baqir rejected the offer. "Sayyid Mohammed Baqir chose death," recalls his son Jafar al-Sadr, "after he had seen that his friends abandoned him and Iran let him down despite his support for it."[21]

As Islamic militants were eliminated, survivors began to turn in desperation to the idea of individual attacks to kill Baathist leaders. The Dawa party was shattered by arrests and executions even before the Baath Revolution Command Council issued a decree in March 1980 that made membership in the party punishable by death. It was no longer able to mobilize the Shia masses. Its efforts to do so had, as Baqir feared, made its activists too visible to the ever-watchful Iraqi intelligence services. If the Iranian recipe of ever-escalating street demonstrations was not feasible, what other means could be used to overthrow the government?

According to a student of Baqir in Najaf at the time, the Shi'ite leader covertly fell back on other means of confronting Saddam, who, from the summer of 1979, was the sole ruler of Iraq. He looked to recruit anti-Baathist soldiers, hitherto the traditional means of staging a coup in Iraq. "He worked on contacting critically placed officers in the armed forces. He knew of the crucial role the Iranian armed forces played in the victory of the Iranian Islamic Revolution." By some accounts Baqir went further. A cleric close to the members of Baqir's entourage, who were with him in the last days of his life, says: "He started building commando cells, connected indirectly with himself, whose primary goal was the assassination of Saddam Hussein. He put in charge al-Sheikh Abdul Ameer Muhsin al-Saidi and Jalil Mal Allah." Their job was to find somebody who had enough access to Saddam to kill him and was willing to die doing so. A suitable candidate was found—a doctor who had joined the presidential medical staff—but he was found out and executed before he could carry out his mission.[22]

Baqir was not alone in thinking that single acts of terror were now the only way left to attack the regime. The Islamic Action Organization, a smaller Shia militant group founded in Kerbala in the 1970s, had been forced into exile in Beirut. It had been radicalized by contact with militant Palestinians in Yasser Arafat's Fatah movement and the Lebanese Shia Amal militia. It trained a number of cadres who, on their return to Iraq, remained undetected by Iraqi intelligence. On April 1, one of them, Samir Nuri Ali, threw a hand grenade at the Iraqi foreign minister Tariq Aziz as he was visiting Mustansariya, the ancient university in the heart of Baghdad. As the grenade exploded, Ali drew a gun. He was killed, along with several students, in the shooting that followed. The next day, standing in the pouring rain, Saddam told a meeting of students: "The Iraqi people is now a large and powerful mountain they cannot shake with all their bombs. By God, the innocent blood that was shed at Mustansariya will not go unavenged."[23] A few days later a second bomb was thrown at the funeral of those killed at Mustansariya.

The riposte by the regime was immediate, savage, and presumably long prepared. Baqir was arrested. His sister Bint al-Huda, who had long worked with him and led a women's religious study group, was detained with him. By one account she tied her dress to her wrists to try to avoid it being torn off when she was tortured. Both Baqir and Bint al-Huda were taken secretly to Baghdad. Did Saddam offer Baqir one last chance? Hussein al-Shahristani, the nuclear scientist and prison escapee, says that at the last moment the Baathists offered Baqir a deal. "They said they would release him in return for a promise of silence. Sadr says, 'No, I have closed all doors, there is no escape for you now. Now you have to kill me so the people can rise up.'"[24]

Baqir and his sister were hanged on April 8. By one account, Baqir's body, but not that of his sister, was returned to Najaf in a coffin on April 9 for burial in Wadi al-Salaam. Another, more detailed, account says that at about nine or ten p.m. on April 9, the electricity suddenly went off in Najaf (presumably to get people off the streets). Security men went to the house of one of Sadr's relatives, Mohammed Sadiq al-Sadr, the father of the man who was to rebuild the Sadrist movement in the 1990s, and took him to a government building. There they handed over two coffins, one containing the body of Baqir and the other of Bint al-Huda. Marks on the faces of both showed that they had been tortured. Iraqi security ordered Mohammed Sadiq to take the coffins but not to tell anybody that Bint al-Huda had also been executed. If he told anyone of her death he would be killed himself. It was only on his deathbed that Mohammed Sadiq spoke of what he had seen.

The government at first blacked out all information about the executions. But news leaked out through Baath party members in Najaf and was confirmed by Khomeini and in an announcement on the Arabic service of Iranian radio. As news spread there were sporadic demonstrations in Shia areas. They were bloodily repressed. Many were silent because the government was arresting and killing anyone who showed the slightest sign of dissent. Those who did demonstrate must have known they were going to their deaths. Even so, there was an attempted protest march from Najaf to Kerbala led by the Abu al-Kalal family. It was dispersed in the al-Khan al-Nus area by the security forces, who killed or arrested participants.[25] In al-Thawra in Baghdad, two hundred people took part in a demonstration. Surviving members of the Dawa party attended. The demonstration was led by Sayyid Qassim al-Mubarqaa, who wore a white shroud to show that he knew he would be killed.[26] He was shot down along with other marchers. In the days after the execution of Baqir, even distant relatives of members of Dawa were arrested and tortured. Women who were rounded up at this time had difficulty getting married later, because it was assumed they had been raped. Terrible stories were told of prisoners being fed into wood chipping machines or of acid being dripped into their open wounds. A wave of terror engulfed Shia districts. By executing Baqir and crushing his movement, Saddam appeared to have won a total victory over the Shia radicals in Iraq, but he had also infuriated much of the Shia community. If his repression ever faltered they would confront him.

CHAPTER FOUR

An Eight-Year Whirlwind

On April 8, 1980, the very day Mohammed Baqir al-Sadr was executed, an agent of the Defense Intelligence Agency (DIA), the intelligence arm of the Pentagon, sent a tantalizing message from Baghdad warning that Saddam Hussein might invade Iran. The agent was evidently well-informed and in contact with the Iraqi elite, though his name is blacked out in the declassified note. "There is a 50 per cent chance that Iraq will attack Iran," he reported. "Iraq has moved large numbers of military personnel and equipment in anticipation of such an invasion." Skirmishes had already started. An Iraqi commando unit had carried out a rocket attack on an Iranian oil field two days earlier. The agent concluded by saying that Iraqi leaders were convinced that "the Iranian military is now weak and can be easily defeated."[1]

The likelihood of Iraq going to war with Iran increased with the passing days. The Iraqi security services understood that the attempt to assassinate Tariq Aziz at Mustansariya showed that the militant Shia opposition was desperate and "on its last legs."[2] But they systematically exaggerated the gravity of the threat posed by a few sporadic bombings and shootings. These were a convenient excuse to portray the execution of Mohammed Baqir and the slaughter of anybody connected with the Dawa party as a defensive act directed against Iranian-orchestrated terrorism (so convenient indeed that one Baathist ex-minister believed that the assassination attempt on Tariq Aziz was faked by Iraqi security).[3] Saddam Hussein made an angry speech on April 5 defining for the first time the conflict with Iran as one between "the Arabs and the Persians" and denouncing Khomeini as "a Shah in a turban." He demanded that Iran restore Iraqi territorial rights on the Shatt al-Arab waterway, ceded by Iraq to end Iranian support for the Kurds in 1975, and sought to give the coming conflict a pan-Arab dimension by asking Iran to leave three small but strategically important islands, the Lesser and Greater Tumbs and Abu Musa at the entrance to the Gulf, that had been seized by the Shah in 1971. On April 9, Saddam deported 9,700 Iraqi Shia of supposed Iranian origin and in the coming days expelled another 16,000. Some 400 businessmen were lured to the Ministry of Commerce in Baghdad for a meeting and were then stripped of their belongings, forced onto buses, driven to the Iranian border, and dumped in no-man's-land.[4] Houses, land, and businesses were confiscated. The definition of who was an Iranian was haphazard and the relatives of many deportees found themselves conscripted into the Iraqi army as full-blooded Iraqis. In retaliation, Iran escalated its rhetoric. On April 22, Khomeini revealed that Baqir and his sister had been executed and called for the overthrow of the Iraqi government. He asked Iraqi soldiers to "leave your barracks and do not suffer this humiliating regime a minute longer: Overthrow Saddam Hussein as we did the Shah." [5]

On September 22, Saddam Hussein launched what he called the Whirlwind War, a classic misnomer since the bloody conflict that ensued was to last eight years. His main motive was that he believed, as the DIA agent had explained to him six months earlier, that he could win a swift and easy victory.

Saddam Hussein was at the peak of his power at home, having ruthlessly crushed all his opponents, destroying the Dawa party as an organization and intimidating the Shia clergy. The long-running Kurdish rebellion that had destabilized so many Iraqi governments had been defeated in 1975. For all Khomeini's bellicose calls to the Iraqi army to mutiny, Iran was in no position to launch a military attack on Iraq. The Iraqi government had plenty of money because oil prices had soared, thanks in part to the revolution in Iran. Iraq was ruled by an all-powerful leviathan state and it was under Saddam's sole control. He ended the rivalries between the government administration, the security services, the Baath party, and the armed forces and forced them to pursue common objectives. The loyalty of this formidable machine to Saddam was guaranteed by giving critical posts to members of his family. There were to be no more coups. The outlook for the anti-Baathist opposition looked very bleak.

Paradoxically, the weak point of the newly powerful Iraqi state was the very man who had created it. Adroit though Saddam had been in seizing and keeping power within Iraq, he consistently misjudged the balance of power in the Middle East as a whole. He was not a career military officer, though he liked to present himself as a warlord. And while often compared to Stalin as an authoritarian ruler, he had a tendency to stumble into self-inflicted disasters that were more characteristic of Inspector Clouseau. He gathered intelligent and well-informed men around him, but it was dangerous for them to counsel moderation. "The other leaders understood that the only safe way to deal with Saddam was to be ten percent tougher than the boss," reflected a senior Russian diplomat stationed in Baghdad for most of the Iran-Iraq war.[6] By starting a war with Iran, the Iraqi leader was taking a gamble that was likely to turn out badly. Powerful though the Iraqi state was in the summer of 1980, it was not strong enough to defeat Iran. Unless the rule of Ayatollah Khomeini collapsed in the face of the Iraqi army offensive, Saddam Hussein would find himself fighting a unified state with three times the population of Iraq. Khomeini had already proved during the Iranian revolution that he could mobilize millions of people for street demonstrations. He could certainly put the same number into uniform with guns in their hands.

True, Saddam Hussein had powerful allies. His war effort was backed by the United States, the Soviet Union, the West European states, and most of the Arab world with the important exception of Syria. But the Iraqi state was more fragile than it looked. The passivity of the Shia might be enough in peacetime, but not in war. They were estimated to make up twenty percent of the officer corps of the army but eighty percent of the rank and file. Furthermore, this predominantly Shia army would be fighting their coreligionists in Iran. The depth of soldiers' loyalties might not matter in a short, victorious war. But the conflict in which Iran and Iraq were about to engage proved to be very drawn out. The struggle along the Iran-Iraq border—neither side was able to penetrate far inside the other's territory—came to resemble the static but lethal trench warfare on the Western Front in the First World War. Even if Iraq had been a country united by strong religious and ethnic bonds, the loyalty of its soldiers would have been under strain.

The failure of the mainly Shia Iraqi army to mutiny en masse between 1980 and 1988 was later used as evidence that the soldiers were Iraqis before they were Shia. This argument was somewhat specious, though it may have sounded convincing to Americans in the run-up to the invasion of 2003, when the Shia opposition to Saddam Hussein was eager to convince Washington that by overthrowing Saddam the United States would not be doing Iran a favor. In reality, the attitude of Shia soldiers was more nuanced and it changed over time. "Early in the war I and other Shia soldiers used to shoot high in the air during battles," recalled Jafar Ali, a Shia sergeant from Basra who fought throughout the war. "We used to say it would be better for Saddam to fight the Israelis than kill Shia Muslims. But later on, when we had seen our friends killed or wounded in the fighting, we shot to kill at the Iranians. Soldiers who didn't believe in the war would still go on fighting because they knew they didn't have much choice." By Jafar Ali's account, Shia soldiers deserted at the beginning of the war because they did not approve of it, while eight years later they were deserting simply because they were weary of war.[7] Iraqi government propaganda about Iranian atrocities had enough substance to be effective. "Initially I was against the war," said Mohammed Yassin, a Shia army captain from Kerbala who also fought throughout the war, "but later on we heard about the terrible time our prisoners were having in Iranian prisons and the way they were ill-treated. After that we began hating the Iranians and we fought very hard. We started to feel a sense of Iraqi national unity, regardless of whether or not Saddam was president."[8]

It soon became clear to Iraqis that Saddam had made a disastrous blunder in invading Iran. It was October 5, 1980, before Iraqi soldiers captured Khorramshahr despite it being close to Basra, just on the other side of the Shatt al-Arab waterway, and even longer before they took the nearby Iranian oil terminal at Abadan. Iraq had a large superiority in tanks, but Iranian light infantry fought to the death. Foreign journalists invited by the Ministry of Information in Baghdad to witness the easy triumph of the Iraqi army found that shells from Iranian artillery were exploding around them long before they had left Iraqi territory and entered Iran. Local people in Basra had also noticed that Iranian shells were falling in their midst despite self-glorifying claims on Iraqi radio about the rapid advance of the Iraqi military. They nervously asked the journalists what was really happening at the front.

The war was fought in the predominantly Shia and Kurdish areas of Iraq. Shia civilians immediately felt its impact. In the first days of the war my colleague Robert Fisk visited the salt-marsh peninsula of Fao facing Iran across the Shatt al-Arab. "Fao was almost deserted," he discovered. "I watched many of its inhabitants—part of the constant flow of millions of refugees which are part of Middle East history—driving northwest to Basra in a convoy of old Chevrolet taxis, bedding piled on the roofs and chador-clad mothers and wives on the backseats, scarcely bothering to glance at the burning refineries of Abadan. They were Iraqi Shia Muslims, and now they were under fire from their fellow Shias in Iran, another gift from Saddam."[9] Much of the war was fought in the marshes where the Tigris and Euphrates meet and where a few years earlier I had watched graceful canoes gliding between villages of reed houses built on artificial islands on the shores of shallow lakes. Within fifteen years the impact of war and Iraqi government repression would end the five-thousand-year-long history of the marsh people. Ominously for a country as wholly dependent on oil revenue as Iraq, the Iranians began firing ground-to-ground missiles at the Iraqi oil terminals Al-Amaya and Al-Bakr, twenty miles offshore, the vital outlets through which much of Iraq's crude was exported. Idling at anchor in the Basra port were ninety freighters trapped by the war closing the Shatt al-Arab, which was their only exit to the sea. Over the next eight years the vessels slowly rotted as they waited in vain for the conflict to end.

The Iranians held the Iraqi advance and then counterattacked. In 1981 they won their first big victory at Dezful, capturing fifteen thousand prisoners. On several occasions whole battalions of Shia soldiers surrendered without firing a shot. In May 1982, Iranian forces recaptured Khorramshahr, and in June, Iraq offered a truce, declaring a voluntary withdrawal from the few pockets of Iranian territory it still held. Iran turned down the cease-fire and demanded the removal of Saddam Hussein as the price of peace. By the end of 1982, American intelligence estimated that Iraq had lost forty-five thousand prisoners and the same number were dead. By then Khomeini had taken the critical decision to carry the revolution west on the bayonets of the Iranian army. Iran now exaggerated its strength just as Iraq had done two years earlier. Mass surrenders by Iraqi Shia units ceased. In July 1982, nine Iranian infantry divisions hurled themselves at the Iraqi lines defending Basra, but failed to break through. This was to be the pattern for the next four years. Then, in 1986, the Iranian army suddenly captured the Fao peninsula in a surprise assault. Saddam Hussein mobilized more troops for a counterattack. "When Iran occupied Fao everybody began to fight back," said Jafar Ali. "This was the natural reaction to foreign invasion in all the Shia towns."[10]

Many Iraqis had divided loyalties. One commando officer from a Shia family had three of his brothers executed by Saddam Hussein, but still fought because he thought it was his duty as a professional soldier and an Iraqi.[11] Others took a wholly opposite point of view. Rasheed Abdul Gafoor, many of whose relatives had been executed by Saddam Hussein, secretly listened to Iranian radio broadcasts in Arabic because only there could he hear religious songs and lectures. He was loyal to Imam Khomeini, though it was too dangerous to talk about him with anybody except close family members. It was only after the fall of Saddam Hussein that he felt it safe to decorate the walls of his house with pictures of Khomeini, al-Khoei, and al-Hakim.[12]

A simple but compelling reason why Shia soldiers did not desert or fail to fight was that it was lethally dangerous to do so. "Anybody who failed to fight during a battle was executed instantly," says one former soldier. "His coffin was marked with the word *traitor* and his family was charged the price of the bullets used to execute him. Saddam's people were everywhere, and when they captured a deserter they cut off his nose and ears and made a special mark on his forehead. On top of this a deserter would be banned from work and his rights as a citizen revoked."[13] Armies have always used draconian means to keep soldiers from running away, and in this case mutilations and executions were largely successful in imposing discipline.

There were other reasons why Shia soldiers fought against their Iranian coreligionists. Iranian Shi'ism was intertwined with Iranian nationalism. Khomeini was able to overthrow the Shah in 1978–79 not only because he was a revered Shia religious leader, but because he was a more convincing advocate of Iranian nationalism than the Shah. Ever since the Safavid dynasty forcibly converted Iran to Shi'ism five hundred years earlier, Iranian identity has been substantially religious. Khomeini had been expelled from Iran in 1964 when he denounced an agreement to exempt U.S. soldiers in Iran from Iranian law.

The Shia of Iraq were also nationalist, though their definition of what this meant in terms of Iraqi national identity was different from that of the Sunni. The *mujtahids,* the Shia clerical leaders, had been the inspirers of the revolt against the British occupation of 1920. Unlike the Kurds, the Shia demand had never been for the destruction or weakening of the Iraqi state, but rather for a fairer share of power within it and an end to anti-Shia discrimination.[14] This helps explain the surprising popularity of Sadrism when it was relaunched by Mohammed Sadiq al-Sadr between 1992 and 1999 and, under the U.S. occupation, by his son Muqtada al-Sadr after

2003. The movement combined Iraqi nationalist and Shia religious identity in a potent blend. Both Saddam and the United States were at different moments astonished by the Sadrist success, but Iraq is not the only country where nationalism and religion march together. In Europe, Poland and Ireland are traditionally two of the most nationalist countries, and also two of the most religious, because of the bonding of Roman Catholicism and Polish and Irish national identity.

Saddam Hussein had crushed effective political opposition by the Shia by the summer of 1980. In the first months of the war he felt confident enough to give speeches in solidly Shia areas of Baghdad and Kerbala, where he called on the faithful "to fight with the spirit of Ali." He paid for gold leaf to decorate the shrine of Abbas. Visiting Najaf, he announced that he would "fight for justice with the swords of the Imams" and made the birthday of Imam Ali a Shia national holiday. For all this, there was one voice he wanted to hear supporting the war that remained stubbornly silent. Abu al Qasim al-Khoei, the paramount religious leader of the Shia, had remained quiescent during the 1970s as persecution intensified against Dawa. This angered the supporters of Baqir al-Sadr, who accused him of collaboration with the Baath, but al-Khoei's quietism was consistent. He did not approve of clerics becoming politicians or aspiring to become direct rulers of the state. He was vigorously opposed to Ayatollah Khomeini's doctrine Wilayat al-Faqih, under which the senior clergy would be the supreme authority in an Islamic government. In al-Khoei's view, the Marji' al-Taqlid must adhere to its traditional role of providing spiritual and moral guidance for the laity.

This apolitical role, and the quietism so frequently criticized by the Sadrists in the future, was never quite as otherworldly as it appeared. Al-Khoei genuinely believed—and this was also the belief of his successor, Grand Ayatollah Ali al-Sistani—that the main concern of the Shia clergy should be spiritual. Aside from his theological stance, there was also a simple but sensible calculation behind his apolitical position. He could see that in any confrontation between the clerical leadership and the all-powerful Iraqi state, the former was bound to lose. Avoiding such a conflict fitted in with the long Shia tradition of Taqqiyya (dissimulation and evasion by the faithful in order to avoid confrontation with more powerful authorities) in order to ensure survival. Allegations that the senior clergy stood idly by while members of Dawa were persecuted, arrested, tortured, and murdered during the 1970s underplays the fact that there was little the so-called quietists could have done to help their coreligionists. Al-Khoei did not openly support the revolution in Iran, but he did not oppose it, either. When Farah Diba, the wife of the Shah of Iran, visited Najaf in October 1978, and suddenly turned up at his house accompanied by Iraqi officials, he saw her, but during their conversation strongly criticized the Shah's treatment of protestors in Tehran.[15] The following year, when Baqir was executed, his followers were furious about the religious leadership's lack of response. "It was al-Khoei's duty to eulogize the martyr al-Sadr, but he did not," said one cleric in Najaf. "Nor did he say anything when seventy-nine scholars were executed on a single day."[16] In Tehran, Iranian clergy claimed that al-Khoei had secretly supported the Shah in his final days. At a press conference, one of the clergy brandished a letter from al-Khoei to the Shah, found after the Shah had fled, thanking him for an agate ring sent as a present. Tehran later concluded the letter was a fake.[17] The anger and desperation of the Dawa supporters was understandable, but at this moment the Baath party could have liquidated the surviving institutions of Iraqi Shi'ism very easily.

With the opening of the war with Iran, the regime in Baghdad had a greater need for al-Khoei's support for the Iraqi war effort. It was more difficult to move against him because of the possible impact on the Shia soldiery. Al-Khoei's failure to endorse the war effort spoke volumes. A tone of impatience, if not desperation, began to creep into the government's desire to demonstrate that he supported the war. In October 1980, Iraqi television managed to catch him at a mosque in Najaf, where prayers were said for the victory of Iraq's Arab army "over the Persian aggressors."[18] In May 1981 the state media proclaimed as a major scoop that al-Khoei had prayed for the health of Saddam Hussein.[19] More brutal but covert pressure was put on al-Khoei and his followers to support the war. When the regime organized the First Popular Islamic Conference in Baghdad in April 1983, the Grand Ayatollah and his family refused to attend. "The hawza was almost destroyed," says Ghanim Jawad, an important activist in the al-Khoei Foundation in London. "They arrested activist *ulema* [clergy] or active students and accused them of being supporters of Iran or al-Dawa." Foreign students were denied visas to stay in Iraq, and Iraqi students were conscripted into the army. Iraqi security chipped away at the circle of advisers, friends, and relatives around the Grand Ayatollah.[20] The UN Special Rapporteur on human rights in Iraq visited Najaf in January 1992. He said "the number of clergy at al-Najaf had been reduced from eight or nine thousand twenty years ago to two thousand ten years later, and eight hundred before the uprising of 1991."[21] Al-Khoei himself survived perhaps because his open differences with Khomeini over the clerical control of the state were useful to the government in Baghdad, as they denied the Iranian leader primacy over the Shia community worldwide. For those Shia militants who wanted to oppose Saddam more directly, the only alternative to al-Khoei's quietism was to flee the country.

The Iranians, meanwhile, pressed for a single credible Iraqi Shia Islamic umbrella group to be established under their auspices. This was all the more necessary from the Iranian point of view after Iraqi forces had been driven from Iranian soil in the summer of 1982. If Iran was to advance into Iraq and appeal to the Iraqi Shia to overthrow Saddam Hussein, then it needed an organization uniting its Iraqi Shia friends. On November 17, 1982, Mohammed Baqir al-Hakim announced the formation of the Supreme Council for Islamic Revolution in Iraq (SCIRI), which was to bring together his own following, Dawa, and the Organization for Islamic Action—the group whose members had carried out attacks in Baghdad in April 1982—under his leadership. Al-Hakim, the fifth son of Grand Ayatollah Muhsin al-Hakim, the preeminent Shia cleric before al-Khoei, was born in Najaf in 1939, and was a founding member of Dawa. He had been jailed and then amnestied after trying to mediate during the bloody Arba'in of 1977. He fled to Syria in 1980 and then to Tehran, the city that, along with Damascus, was to become a base for Islamic militant groups. Al-Hakim's family was to pay a fearful price for their opposition to Saddam and alliance with Iran. In 1983, alarmed by the formation of SCIRI, Saddam carried out mass arrests of al-Hakim family members still in Iraq. Sayyid Mohammed al-Musawi, a family friend from Najaf, estimates that sixty-three members of the family were executed by the Baathists during their years in power.[22] Eighteen were executed and only one—Sayyid Hussein al-Hakim—was released after being forced to witness the killing of his relatives. He was told to go to Tehran to tell Mohammed Baqir al-Hakim about their fate. The cycle of deaths did not end there. Sayyid Mahdi al-Hakim, the brother of Baqir, was attending an Islamic conference in Khartoum in 1988 when a gunman sent by the Iraqi embassy shot him dead in a hotel lobby.

The fortunes of SCIRI were wholly dependent on the success of the Iranian war effort. The Iranians wanted the organization set up quickly in case the regime in Baghdad collapsed, and they needed an Iraqi Islamic leadership to put in its place. SCIRI was in a position similar to that of communist parties that advanced with the tanks of the Red Army into Eastern Europe in 1945 and took over local administrations. The difference was that the Iranian army did not advance very far into Iraq. The armed wing of SCIRI, the Badr Organization, drew its recruits from Islamic militants, Iraqi prisoners of war, and the one million Iraqi refugees in Iran. Badr was commanded by an Iranian colonel at this time and was wholly under the control of Iran. It swiftly acquired a dubious reputation in Iraq for doing the Iranians' dirty work. "They tortured Iraqi prisoners during the war," says one professor at Najaf University. "They tortured the Sunni and the Shia twice as badly because they used to ask them: Why did you join Saddam's army if you are a Shia?"[23] In the coming years, SCIRI never quite shook the reputation, in the minds of many Iraqis, of being stooges of Iran who tortured their fellow countrymen.

The reign of terror against any sign of domestic discontent in Iraq intensified. Islamic militants arrested anywhere in Iraq knew what fate to expect. Punishment of family members of suspects, including children, became common. After one raid in Najaf in 1980, during which many families were arrested, a former prisoner found a one-month-old baby crying beside the road. The child had presumably been dropped or deliberately left behind by his mother as she was bundled into a security police vehicle. "Such was the atmosphere of terror in Najaf at the time that the man who found me did not dare ask people whose family I belonged to," recalls the foundling, now a well-educated twenty-seven-year-old man living in Amara in eastern Iraq. "The man decided to look after me, but this created a further problem because his neighbors would think the baby was a bastard or the child of prisoners, which would mean serious trouble with the government. He sent me to Amara to be brought up by an old couple. I have never found out who my real family is."[24]

It was never likely that Iraq would win a decisive victory in the war, though dissidents in Tehran and Damascus optimistically packed their suitcases each time there was an Iranian offensive. The Iraqi defeats of 1981–82, when Saddam Hussein's defeat seemed possible, frightened the United States and its allies. Donald Rumsfeld famously visited Baghdad in 1983 to deliver a carefully phrased letter from President Ronald Reagan to Saddam saying that Washington backed Iraq. Iraq started using poison gas on a mass scale for the first time since the First World War without the rest of the world protesting. The U.S. embassy reopened in Baghdad in 1984, and the CIA provided a flow of satellite photographs of Iranian positions. The United States, along with Western Europeans, granted loans and gave credit and the tide began to turn. Advancing behind a blizzard of chemical weapons, including mustard gas and sarin and tabun nerve gases, the Republican Guard recaptured Fao from Iran in April 1988. Iraqi planes attacked Iranian oil tankers with French Exocet missiles. When the Iranians retaliated against Kuwait, the United States agreed that the Kuwaiti oil tanker fleet should sail under the American flag. The United States was effectively joining the Iraqi side in the war. After a U.S. naval vessel shot down an Iranian passenger plane flying to Dubai in July 1988, the Iranians concluded that the odds against them were too great. Ayatollah Khomeini announced that he must "drain the bitter cup" and agreed to a cease-fire on August 8, 1988.

Saddam Hussein might have been able to unify many Iraqis behind patriotic slogans when an Iranian victory seemed possible, but the long and bloody conflict had served to discredit Iraqi nationalism. When Saddam invaded Kuwait in August 1990, he found the patriotic well had run dry. Iraqis did not want to fight again, particularly in a war they knew Iraq must lose. When officers who had spent their youth in the army were called up in the fall of 1990, many broke down in tears. The official braggadocio was the same: Saddam pledged to raise a million-strong army. When, on one occasion, Ministry of Information officials took me to see part of this great force being trained, I watched bewildered Sudanese waiters and sullen Egyptian construction workers drilling with elderly Kalashnikovs. In Najaf, the most influential Shia religious leader, al-Khoei, issued a fatwa saying that people should not buy goods looted by the Iraqi army in Kuwait. Another fatwa said that Shia soldiers were forbidden to pray on Kuwaiti territory; if they were already in Kuwait they should pray only in cars or trucks.[25] This, by Shia standards, was a surprisingly direct sign of al-Khoei's disapproval of the invasion. Government-sponsored rallies in Baghdad were ill-attended. The largest gathering I saw in the streets of the capital just before the war started on January 17, 1991, turned out to be a gathering of pigeon fanciers. Savage punishments no longer maintained discipline in the army. When the U.S.-led forces finally advanced, they found that as much as half the Iraqi army had already deserted. Few of the remainder did any fighting. Iraq lost 2,100 tanks in Kuwait, but American damage assessment teams were surprised to discover that only ten percent had been destroyed in battle. The rest had been abandoned. Iraqis would no longer fight for Saddam.

CHAPTER FIVE

The Shia Rise Up

Grand Ayatollah al-Khoei was lying on a couch beside a window in a house in Kufa. His straggly white beard covered his chest and he was looking all of his ninety-two years. He stared ahead with a detached gaze as if he did not notice the Iraqi security men who had suddenly filled his room. It was a few weeks after the Shia of Iraq had risen up, in March 1991, in the wake of the Iraqi army's devastating defeat in Kuwait. At the height of the rebellion, mutinous Shia soldiers held every city south of Baghdad and came close to overthrowing Saddam Hussein. Then, as the U.S.-led coalition refused to interfere, Iraqi army units loyal to the regime launched fierce counterattacks, crushed the uprising, and began to exact a terrible vengeance. Along with other reporters, I had been expelled from Iraq and was in Jordan when the news of the uprising first reached Baghdad at the beginning of March. Then, to my surprise, I was allowed back in. The Iraqi government must have wanted to show the media and the world that it was once more in control. Leaving early from the al-Rashid Hotel in Baghdad on April 15 in a convoy of cars with the Information Ministry "minders," we were told we were going to Kufa and Najaf, but not that we would be seeing al-Khoei. When we reached the nondescript house where he was staying, I saw it was surrounded by guards and there were plainclothesmen inside the gates. It was clear he was under house arrest. He seemed to be alone—I could not see any of the myriad relatives and retainers I would have expected to find around the Grand Ayatollah, who was, after all, the supreme spiritual leader of 150 million Shia around the world. I have always felt uneasy interviewing prisoners, because it is impossible to know what pressures or threats have been made against them. It seemed particularly unfair to badger an old man surrounded by Iraqi secret policemen. Nevertheless, I asked al-Khoei what he thought about the uprising. For some minutes he said nothing, and I was beginning to think he had not heard my question. Then, speaking very low in a gasping voice, he said: "What happened in Najaf and other cities is not allowed and is against God." His answer was carefully ambiguous, not making clear if he was condemning the actions of the insurgents or the government. He went on to say: "Nobody visits me, so I don't know what is happening. I have trouble with my breathing."[1]

I was right to think that al-Khoei was under intense pressure from the regime to condemn the uprising. It had all started in Basra on March 1, and by March 4 had spread to Najaf. Two days later, after the capture of the city by antigovernment forces, al-Khoei had issued the first of two fatwas urging Muslims to "to look after the holy places" and guard people's property and government institutions. He appealed for dead bodies lying in the streets to be buried, though without success. A second directive, issued as the insurgents consolidated their victory, set up a Supreme Committee under which the Shia would provide for security and public order. To somebody as suspicious as Saddam Hussein, this may have looked as if al-Khoei was authorizing an alternative administration. When Iraqi troops recaptured Najaf ten days later, they arrested al-Khoei. A Najaf resident who was later interviewed by a human rights organization said: "I watched from a nearby house as some soldiers captured the Imam [al-Khoei], four members of the leadership, and some of the rebels. They forced the Imam, who is over 90 years old, to walk without assistance and, since he cannot, he fell to the ground. Then his son helped him up and all were taken away."[2] Al-Khoei and his son Mohammed Taqi were taken to the military intelligence headquarters in Baghdad on the night of March 19; the next morning they were summoned to what would be a two-hour meeting with a furious Saddam Hussein. Mohammed Taqi, who sat silent throughout, later recalled that Saddam said to his father: "I didn't think you would do something like this." The Grand Ayatollah said he had only been trying to control the violence. "No, you wanted to overthrow me," the Iraqi leader replied. "Now you have lost everything. You did everything the Americans wanted you to do."[3]

Saddam compelled al-Khoei to appear with him on television and make a statement denouncing violence. The Grand Ayatollah had little choice but to comply. The security police had detained 105 of his associates in Najaf at the time he was arrested, including his son-in-law Mahmoud al-Melawi, the eighty-nine-year-old Ayatollah Murtaza Kazemi Khalkali, and scores of Shia scholars. The al-Hakim family was once again targeted, with two clerics and eight other family members detained. Despite a long campaign by human rights organizations to find out what had happened to the men arrested, only one, a Pakistani, was freed. The rest ended up in mass graves with tens of thousands of other Shia who were being murdered at this time. Only al-Khoei and his son Mohammed Taqi were allowed to return to the heavily guarded house in Najaf, where I saw him a few weeks later.

The rebellion, known in Iraq as the Sha'aban Intifada after the Muslim month of Sha'aban, broke out at the beginning of March and reshaped the political and religious landscape of Iraq. It was immediately and explosively successful in the Shia south and in Kurdistan, but not in Baghdad and the Sunni heartlands of central Iraq. Here, Saddam Hussein was able to hang on. Sunni terror of the Shia and Kurds probably consolidated support for him within the upper ranks of the regime. Sunni generals who had been planning a coup against him after the debacle in Kuwait thought again.[4] I had a friend, a sophisticated journalist, who in private always expressed to me his loathing for the regime and his hope that it would be overthrown. But he was also a Sunni, and during the uprising he confessed to me that he was so frightened for the safety of himself and his family if the Shia rebels seized Baghdad that he wanted the uprising crushed. He may have exaggerated the chances of an anti-Sunni pogrom, but he was right in suspecting that as soon as Saddam's iron grip was relaxed, a subterranean well of hatred against the regime would instantly burst forth in the Shia community. Sanaa Mohammed, a Shia woman who worked in local government in Kerbala, describes how, soon after the fall of the city to insurgents, she met two women in the street who were asking questions as to the whereabouts of certain men. The women were Shia and explained that they had traveled a hundred miles across war-torn Iraq because they were "searching for two of Saddam's security men who killed their brothers and wanted to take their revenge on them."[5]

The slaughter of Baathist officials during the uprising, and the even more savage retaliation by the government, made the gap between Shia and Sunni in Iraq almost unbridgeable. Each community had a wholly different vision of what had happened during the intifada. For instance, there is no evidence that the Iranian role in it was very significant. This angered many of the insurgents and their sympathizers. During the American bombing in early 1991, Hussein al-Shahristani, an Iraqi nuclear scientist who had been a member of Dawa, escaped to Iran from Abu Ghraib prison after twelve years' imprisonment. He had been arrested and savagely tortured in 1979 for refusing to help Saddam Hussein build a nuclear bomb. He was bitterly critical of the Iranian role. "They encouraged the uprising and then betrayed it," he said. "They only let a few people across the border to help, and they would not let them bring arms. They certainly did not put up posters [of Ayatollah Khomeini]—they were terrified of the American reaction."6 But the Sunni community was convinced that the uprising was fomented and sustained by Iran. This made them even more brutal in their treatment of any Shia unlucky enough to be detained during it or afterward. They saw them as pawns of Iran and traitors to their country. Colonel Othman, a former Sunni officer stationed in Kerbala at the time of the intifada, is wholly unrepentant about his role in suppressing the uprising, firmly believing to this day that "Iran was providing aid [to rebels] across the border in the form of food, weapons, and secret intelligence agents. Iran was arming the rabble and supporting them psychologically and financially."7

The cause of the uprising was the humiliating defeat of the Iraqi army in Kuwait. This discredited the regime and weakened its instruments of repression. In the six months following Saddam Hussein's invasion of Kuwait, many Iraqis thought he would make a deal with the United States at the last moment. They knew they could not fight the vast coalition President George H. W. Bush was assembling. "We didn't expect a war," said a general who later fled to England. "We thought it was all a political maneuver."8 When round-the-clock bombing of the Iraqi army in Kuwait started on January 19, the soldiers, mostly Shia and Kurdish conscripts, knew the war could have only one outcome. They deserted in droves. A few months later, in Kurdistan, I interviewed Captain Azad Shirwan, an intelligence officer of a tank brigade that had been stationed in Kuwait. He told me that by the time the U.S.-led ground offensive started on February 24, most of his men had disappeared: "In our brigade, positions were mostly defended by officers, because the private soldiers had deserted."9 Iraqis of all sorts are astute at sniffing the political winds. They were well-informed because they secretly listened to transistor radios; the soldiers in

Kuwait knew that the battle was lost before it began. When Saddam Hussein ordered a withdrawal from Kuwait a day into the allied ground offensive, the army simply broke up.

"We were anxious to withdraw, to end the mad adventure, when Saddam announced withdrawal within twenty-four hours—though without any formal agreement to ensure the safety of the retreating forces," one officer recalled bitterly. He and his men suspected that Saddam did not care if regular army units were wiped out so long as he could preserve his praetorian Republican Guard divisions. "We had to desert our tanks and vehicles to avoid aerial attacks. We walked 100 kilometers towards the Iraqi territories, hungry, thirsty and exhausted." They arrived at the town of Zubair south of Basra. "In Zubair we decided to put an end to Saddam and his regime. We shot at his posters. Hundreds of retreating soldiers came to the city and joined the revolt; by the afternoon, there were thousands of us. Civilians supported us and demonstrations started. We attacked the party building and the security service headquarters."[10]

The mutiny soon spread to Basra, where the streets were full of angry soldiers separated from their units. It became part of the mythology of the revolt that its opening shot was discharged in Sa'ad Square in Basra on March 1 by a tank gunner who fired into the smiling face of Saddam Hussein on one of the giant posters that decorated every street in Iraq. This was said to have ignited the uprising and was an iconic moment in the rebellion. Everybody recalls having heard the story, the first cathartic moment of defiance against the dictator, but the tank gunner himself has proved elusive. There is no doubt, however, about what happened during the rest of the day as anti-Baathist crowds rampaged through the streets. "The streets were full of people, many of them soldiers," recalled an exiled Iraqi businessman who had returned to Iraq from Iran just before the uprising. "They were shouting slogans and writing them on the wall, destroying Saddam's pictures and monuments, executing members of the Baath party."[11] Fighting was particularly intense because some six thousand loyalists from the Republican Guard held out against five thousand defectors from the regular army.

So many events were packed into the first euphoric but bloody hours of the uprising that participants had varying accounts of what had happened. A month later, after Saddam's tanks had recaptured the city, I asked Dr. Walid al-Rawi, the coolheaded administrator of Basra Teaching Hospital, about his memories of the revolt. He said it was a little slower to develop than others had related. The first he knew about it was when a policeman told him there were violent incidents in small towns and villages on the edge of the vast marshes between Basra, Amara, and Nassariya that had always been hiding places for antigovernment guerrillas. "Later that day, a band of fifty rebels came to the hospital and took away three patients who were security men, one of whom they shot in the hospital grounds." Walking around the city center, I could see burned-out Baath party offices, but otherwise the visible damage was limited. From the beginning the insurgents showed their puritanical Islamic beliefs. Mohammed Kassim, the manager of the Basra Tower Hotel, told me that on the first day of the uprising, armed men came to his hotel. "They asked if there were any Baathists staying or any alcohol. I told them no and they went away." Not every hotel was so lucky. Another band of rebels burst into the Sheraton, notorious for its Filipino hostesses during the Iran-Iraq war. The hotel was closed but we could see from below in the street the dark scorch marks where the rebels had set fire to its top story and burned out nineteen rooms.[12]

There were sporadic lynchings in other parts of the city. The military intelligence headquarters were stormed by a crowd on the second day of the uprising, and the soldiers inside killed. On the quayside of the Shatt al-Arab was the dead body of a Baathist official tied by the neck, with a spike driven through his chest. Somebody had stolen his shoes—his feet were bare.[13]

Dr. al-Rawi was right in thinking that the first incidents in the uprising had started in the villages outside Basra. In a hastily commandeered villa in Baghdad, General Wafiq al-Samarrai, the burly forty-four-year-old head of military intelligence, was monitoring developments for Saddam Hussein in the disastrous days after the defeat in Kuwait. He had hurriedly moved into his emergency headquarters before the war in the correct expectation that the grandiose official offices of Military Intelligence would be destroyed by missiles and smart bombs in the first hours of the war. His earliest intimation that pinprick guerrilla attacks were starting came in a worrying phone call from Basra. An army general, Hamid Shakar, had been driving to Baghdad with one bodyguard when insurgents ambushed his car near a paper mill thirty miles north of Basra. This was on the fringe of the marshes and their vast reed beds, one of the few areas suitable for guerrillas to hide in the whole of southern Iraq. Samarrai called Saddam Hussein, who rushed to his headquarters. Just as he arrived there was a second call, this time from General Nizar al-Khazraji, who commanded the whole of southwest Iraq and had his headquarters in Nassariya, a Shia city with a population of one million. Shouting his words over the phone line, a connection so poor that General Samarrai could barely hear him, Khazraji said: "The rebels are trying to attack us." Fearing that he would not be believed, he held up his phone and asked: "Don't you hear the bullets?" Because of the bad reception, al-Samarrai could hear nothing. Khazraji asked for a helicopter to extract him. "I told Saddam, who was sitting in my headquarters, what was happening in Nassariya and he ordered a helicopter to rescue Khazraji," General Samarrai recalled. But the Iraqi army was disintegrating fast. The officer commanding the helicopters said there was nothing he could do because "we don't have any helicopters in the area." Soon afterward Saddam and General Samarrai heard that it was too late: the building Khazraji was in had been stormed by rebels and the general had been seriously wounded and captured.[14]

Events during the uprising are usually recounted either by the government or their opponents, but seldom by both. In the case of the capture of Khazraji, however, there is a reliable witness, a Shia notable of Nassariya named Kadhum al-Raysan, who saw what happened. His story is significant because it confirms what Samarrai, who escaped to London several years later, told me, and shows how scattered bands of Shia guerrillas hiding in the marshes were able to take advantage of the collapse of government authority. Raysan saw fourteen young men with light arms coming from the marshes and heading for the center of Nassariya. The men were chanting *"Allahu Akbar! Allahu Akbar!* [God is great!]" as they advanced. Soon they were joined by hundreds of other young men. As government authority broke down, General Khazraji was caught up in the fighting and besieged in a building with sixty or seventy loyalists. It is at this point that he must have made his anguished but vain plea for help from Baghdad. Raysan says that the fighting went on for hours and everybody in the building was killed except Khazraji, who was severely wounded. Surprisingly, the insurgents did not kill him but instead took him to the local hospital. From there he was rescued by a helicopter assault team that Baghdad was finally able to assemble. Raysan, who later fled to Saudi Arabia, did not know why Khazraji was spared when so many minor Baathists were being hunted down and killed.[15]

The intifada spread with extraordinary speed from Basra and Nassariya northward to the Shia cities strung along the Euphrates and Tigris rivers. As the heart of the Shia faith and the home of Grand Ayatollah al-Khoei,

Najaf was regarded with suspicion by the regime and was always filled with Baathist security men. Even so, there had been signs of dissent earlier in February. On February 14, at the funeral of Yusuf al-Hakim, a well-known cleric, a member of the family famously hostile to the regime, the mourners had chanted anti-Saddam slogans. People knew that the war in Kuwait was going badly. I had stood in the courtyard of the Imam Ali shrine after the start of the bombing campaign, watching the simple wooden coffins of dead soldiers draped with the Iraqi flag being carried past. The U.S. air attacks, which killed thirty-five people in Najaf, had also shown that there was nothing the government could do to protect its own people. I visited the pulverized remains of a house, once the home of the al-Habubi family, thirteen of whom had been killed by a misdirected bomb apparently aimed at a nearby electricity substation.

By March 2, angry soldiers who had escaped from Kuwait began to arrive in Najaf. One of them was a professional soldier from the city, named Abdul Hassan al-Khafaji, who bitterly recalls how he and his men were "chased like rats" out of Kuwait during the lost battle. "The streets were full of deserters," he said. "All structure in the army was lost. Everybody was their own boss. News was spreading that somebody had shot at Saddam's portrait in Basra." The following day he went to a demonstration in Imam Ali square close to the shrine. "At first there were about a hundred people, many of them army officers from Najaf who had deserted. The security forces were well-informed and were there as well. The demonstrators were shouting: 'Saddam, keep your hands off. The people of Iraq don't want you.'" Security men opened fire on the crowd. Only a few of the demonstrators had pistols but they shot back. One important local Baathist was caught and hacked to death with knives. The sound of the shooting attracted more people, mostly young men in their twenties and teenagers. The security men chased them into the bazaar, a warren of small shops and booths in the center of Najaf, and there was confused fighting for twenty minutes or half an hour, at the end of which the security forces fled to their headquarters. Their retreat was decisive. The crowd took over the shrine of Imam Ali, which had a generator to power its loudspeakers that called the faithful to prayer. Now the jubilant demonstrators used the sound system to rally people against the Baathists, shouting slogans such as "Seek out the criminals."

A legacy of Saddam Hussein's wars was that every Iraqi male knew how to use a gun. These were available in surprising numbers in Najaf and other Iraqi cities, because the Iraqi leader had unwisely stockpiled arms in schools around the country to arm the people in case of an American land-ing from the air. By the evening of March 3, the increasingly well-armed insurgents stormed a girls' school used by the Amn al-Khass security police and killed eight or nine people inside. Predominantly Sunni army units that previously guarded Najaf on behalf of the regime had all been sent to Kuwait. The Quds division of the Republican Guard was based just outside Najaf, but its barracks were empty apart from administrative staff. These did not resist when the rebels commandeered 82-millimeter mortars and used them against the Baath party headquarters. "Abdel Amir Jaithoun, my old headmaster, was killed there," relates Colonel Khafaji. "So, too, was Najim Mizhir, who was the only Baath leader in the city who actually came from Najaf and was quite liked, though he shot a demonstrator." Through-out the city, Baathists were hunted down while others hid in the great Shia cemetery that surrounds Najaf.[16] Many, but not all, who were captured abjectly pleaded for their lives. Yunis al-Sammari, the head of the security police in Kufa, rejected an offer to spare his life if he gave information about arms caches. As he was led off to execution he shouted: "I have lived a Ba'athi all my life and I will die one."[17]

In Kerbala, to the north of Najaf, Sanaa Mohammed, a Shia government employee, was astonished at the speed with which the regime was disinte-grating around her. From listening to the radio she knew of the retreat from Kuwait, but could not believe that Kerbala and the mid-Euphrates region had fallen to insurgents because of "the terrifying picture of Saddam and his regime we had in our minds." Then she heard strange noises from the street outside her house. "Young men were shouting 'We have been liber-ated' and 'Saddam is finished.' They were cheering for the glory of Imam Hussein and the hawza." Almost immediately, revenge killings began. "Two members of the Baath party were killed in our street," says Sanaa. "My fam-ily and I were terrified because my brothers worked in government jobs, so they fled from Kerbala. In fact, the killings were of people working for security, and the killers knew who they were, so they did not need guides. I myself saw a middle-aged man, in the sort of suit that Baath party mem-bers used to wear, running down the street until he was out of breath, with two or three men chasing him firing their guns. He was dodging right and left trying to avoid the bullets, but eventually he was hit and died there. They threw his corpse onto a pile of bodies of people who had been killed earlier in the day." Retaliatory killings increased when Baath party and security buildings were sacked and confidential documents were discovered revealing who had worked as an informer for the regime.

Liberation was followed by an orgy of looting. Everything was considered fair game. "I saw how they robbed government institutions and schools," says Sanaa with deep disapproval. "They stole machinery from livestock farms that they could not possibly use, just for the sake of destruction. The same thing happened at the Kerbala canning plant: some of the foodstuffs were distributed among the people and the rest just vanished. This happened although there was a declaration by the Marji'iyyah forbidding the theft of government property, which nobody paid any attention to."[18] Looting was very much an Iraqi tradition among both Arabs and Kurds, and is probably explained by a history of nomadic raiding in the not so distant past, exacerbated by a hatred of all authority. During the intifada in Najaf even traffic lights were wrecked as symbols of the state.[19] The looters were often in the front ranks of those seizing government buildings (so much so that, during the war of 2003, I avoided entering barracks and other state facilities if I could not see looters, on the grounds that if they thought such places were too dangerous to steal from, they were probably right). The intifada also revealed that Iraq was full of people desperate for vengeance against the agents of the state. In the city of Kut on the Tigris south of Baghdad, scene of the siege and surrender of a small British army in 1916, the regime only lost control for a single day. But Ali Mohammed, a teacher in Kut, says that even so, "we had the same killing of Baathists, and the stealing of government property that happened in other provinces happened here. They stole fabric from the Kut fabric factory. It was only when the authorities regained control and announced by loudspeakers that there was going to be a house-to-house search, that people began leaving stolen goods in the streets."[20]

The success of the uprising depended on the attitude of the Americans. Clear-sighted Shia rebels saw this from the beginning. "The biggest reason for the intifada is that they [the rebels] thought the Americans would support them," Sayyid Majid al-Khoei, the intelligent and perceptive second son of the Grand Ayatollah, told me. "They knew they couldn't beat Saddam on their own. They thought they could get control of the cities and the Americans would stop Saddam's army from intervening." In the first euphoric days of the uprising, people in the streets believed the same thing. Sayyid Majid kept a diary. On the night of March 4, just after the insurgents had taken Najaf, he went to the shrine of Imam Ali and wrote down what he heard people saying. Leafing through a battered notebook years later, he read their remarks out to me. "Iraq is finished," said one man. "The Western armies are in Basra and Samawa." People believed rumors that Saddam had fled from Iraq. "Kerbala and Najaf are in our hands," said others gathered at the shrine. "Let us go on to Baghdad."[21]

For a few days a march on Baghdad seemed possible. The regime was beset by enemies on all sides. On March 5 the Kurds had started their own uprising, which was instantly victorious across Kurdistan. In the city of Hilla, only sixty-six miles south of Baghdad, a tank commander joined the rebels and proposed leading an advance on the capital with his six tanks. "The way to Baghdad is open," he said, but his unit disintegrated as his men went hunting for local Baathists to kill. In Najaf there were many army officers who had deserted, including Colonel Khafaji, who, with the encouragement of the Grand Ayatollah, set up a military committee to try to organize the thousands of Shia soldiers and armed young men milling about in the streets. The first government counterattack on Kerbala faltered when a battalion commander shot his chief security officer in the head and changed sides. "But the committee could not keep his unit together," confessed Colonel Khafaji. "We had to tell the men to change into their dishdashas [Arab robes] and go home."[22]

Paradoxically, it was the very sectarian nature of Saddam Hussein's regime, which had provoked the mutiny of Shia units and Kurdish Jash (locally recruited pro-government Kurdish militia), that now enabled him to survive. The Shia and Kurds—eighty percent of the Iraqi population— wanted to overthrow him, but the Sunni, despite recent disasters, did not want him ousted by the other two biggest communities in Iraq. The security services, the Baath party, and the elite Republican Guard units of the army were Sunni-dominated and had remained intact. Despite losses in Kuwait, the government still commanded a formidable force. According to a March 1991 U.S. Defense Intelligence Agency (DIA) report, seven Republican Guard divisions remained intact (compared to twelve before the war), of which three were armored, one mechanized, and three infantry. This was in addition to twenty-four understrength regular army divisions, of which eighteen were infantry. The DIA estimated the Iraqi army to be less than half the size it had been before its devastating losses in Kuwait, but it was still militarily strong enough to overcome the enthusiastic but unorganized insurgents.[23] These lightly armed rebels had no answer to the regime's tanks and artillery. If the insurgents had made a successful dash for Baghdad in the first moments of the rebellion, could this have led the badly battered regime to unravel? The Shia were the majority of the population in Baghdad.[24] They might have risen up, but it was not very likely. Saddam still had units on which he could rely. In any event, if there was such an opportunity, it was fleeting.

Saddam Hussein was always likely to survive unless the United States intervened and stopped him from using his tanks and artillery. After the intifada was savagely crushed, President George H. W. Bush was accused of encouraging the Iraqis to rise up and then doing nothing. On February 15, he had called on "the Iraqi military and the Iraqi people to take matters into their own hands and force Saddam Hussein, the dictator, to step aside." This was not exactly a starting pistol for a rebellion. It had begun not because of Bush's words, encouraging though they might have been, but because the defeat of the Iraqi army in Kuwait led to a military mutiny. This in turn provoked a civil rebellion. Once it began, it was reasonable for the Shia to expect U.S. help in finishing off Saddam. Bush, on the other hand, had hoped that the Iraqi military would get rid of Saddam Hussein on their own. He expected not a mutiny in the ranks but a military coup d'état at the top by senior army commanders. "We were concerned that the uprisings would sidetrack the overthrow of Saddam by causing the Iraqi military to rally around him, to prevent the break up of the country," Bush later explained. "That may have been what actually happened."[25]

Preventing "the break up of the country" was in effect a palatable code word for supporting the Sunni over the Shia and Kurds. The Shia were not, after all, trying to break up Iraq but rather to get their fair share of power within it. Using slightly different words, Zalmay Khalilzad, then director of policy planning at the State Department, wrote: "The partitioning of Iraq will not serve our long-term interests. Iraqi disintegration will improve prospects for Iranian domination of the Gulf and remove a restraint on Syria."[26] The Shia rebels on the ground soon noticed the impact of the American attitude. U.S. forces were close to Basra, Nassariya, and Samawa, but studiously avoided assisting the rebels. Insurgents saw Iraqi arms dumps containing weapons they desperately needed erupt in flames as American army engineers blew them up. The United States was suddenly showing a decorous sensitivity about interfering in Iraq's domestic affairs and offending its Arab allies. In Washington, Secretary of Defense Dick Cheney declared piously on March 5 that "it would be very difficult for us to hold the coalition together for any particular course of action dealing with Iraqi internal politics."[27] On the same day, U.S. Marine major general Martin Brandtner, deputy director of operations for the Joint Chiefs of Staff, said, "There is no move on [the part] of U.S. forces to let any weapons slip through [to the rebels], or to play any role whatsoever in fomenting or assisting any side."[28]

The evident intention of the U.S. forces to stay neutral while the rebellion was crushed was a frightening development for the people around Grand Ayatollah al-Khoei. Already they could see the Iraqi army using attack helicopters without impediment from the allied forces. They were the leaders of the Shia community insofar as it had any. Sayyid Majid, with the blessings of his father, set off together with Colonel Khafaji and a small group on March 9 to make contact with the allies. "Find out what are their ideas about us, what are they going to do," the Grand Ayatollah instructed his son. It was a frustrating journey as they drove south looking for allied leaders to speak to, knowing that Saddam Hussein was beginning to launch a devastating counterattack they could not hope to withstand. They met American forces outside Nassariya and explained their mission to its commander. He disappeared for ten minutes and on his return claimed he was out of touch with his headquarters. This did not seem very likely to Brigadier Ali, since American units were loaded down with communications equipment. The officer advised them to talk to the French eighty miles to the west. The French had heard the al-Khoei name and at first were helpful. A meeting with allied commander General Norman Schwarzkopf was promised but never took place. Finally the French explained the problem to Majid: "The Americans are worried about the Iranians. They asked who brought Khomeini's pictures into Iraq. I explained that I had seen no pictures of Khomeini in any of the cities I had passed through. I said that people were mistaking pictures of my father, Grand Ayatollah al-Khoei, for Khomeini, because both were old men with white beards."[29]

How far did the Iranians play a role in the uprising, as Baghdad furiously claimed and many in Washington quietly believed? Hussein al-Shahristani, the nuclear scientist and prisoner of Saddam Hussein who was to become Iraq's oil minister in 2006, denounces Iran for encouraging an uprising and then betraying it. Many in the opposition believed it was Saddam's men who put up pictures of Khomeini to scare the United States. "He sent his own *mukhabarat* to the south with pictures of Khomeini," the secular Iraqi opposition leader Saad Jabr told me. "The Badr

Brigade never came. We talked to the Iranians. They swear by the Koran they didn't send the pictures."[30] But in Basra and Amara, both close to the Iranian border, there were signs that Mohammed Baqir al-Hakim, the leader of the SCIRI, the political master of Badr, was intending to play a role. His picture appeared along with a statement saying "all parties working from Iranian territories should also obey al-Hakim's orders, no party is allowed to recruit volunteers; no ideas except the rightful Islamic ones should be disseminated."[31] There is no doubt that Iraqis who had lived for a long time in Iran did go back to Iraq, but not always to fight. There were, after all, one million Iraqi refugees in Iran. Sanaa Mohammed encountered one Iraqi returnee from Iran who had come to Kerbala to see what had happened to his property, which had been confiscated by the government. He was angry that his neighbors had not been more supportive.[32]

Colonel Othman, who played an active role in suppressing the uprising, was convinced that Badr, Dawa, and Iranian Revolutionary Guards were flooding into Iraq from Iran aided by the Shia *ulema* and used *husseiniyas* (Shia places of worship roughly equivalent to a small mosque) "as their bases and a place to store arms. Iran had a very major role in these events." This was the view of most of the Sunni community inside and outside the Baath Party. "Sunni mosques were turned into Shia *husseiniyas* and religious chants could be heard from them," recalls the colonel. "Badr, the Quds Organization of the Iranian Revolutionary Guards, and Islamic Dawa all passed through the border crossing point between Mehran and Badrah [towns on the Iran-Iraq border north of Kut and due east of Baghdad]. After assembling at *husseiniyas* they were guided by hawza members to camps and security headquarters of the Baath party, where they executed the officers and the soldiers."[33]

The most convincing account of the Islamic militant and Iranian role in the uprising is given by Hussein, a dissident Shia from Basra. He confirms that "during the war in Kuwait we had continual contacts with the Badr Organization, which had a secret headquarters in Kut city, which they reached from Mehran [a town just inside Iraq]. They played no part in igniting the uprising, which was a spontaneous reaction to the army's defeat in Kuwait and the reckless and foolhardy actions of Saddam. Mohammed Baqir al-Hakim and his people, supported by Badr, were supposed to come through Mehran to Kut, but they never came. This was one of the reasons for the hostility later between Sadrists and al-Hakim." The most likely explanation for the failure of al-Hakim to appear was that the Iranians stopped him. There was a hunger for known leaders among the victorious insurgents. "In Basra, when the province was taken over, there was a rumor that Mohammed Baqir al-Hakim had come to the city," says Hussein. "There really was a man wearing a turban in the [former] governor's car with half of his body sticking out of the open roof waving to the crowd. They ran after the car, but when they found it was not al-Hakim but a man well known in Basra, they were very angry."[34] The Iranians seemed to have been as surprised as everybody else by the uprising, and were fearful of offending the United States. If Badr, a well-equipped and well-trained military force, had aided the uprising, then the Iraqi army would have had to fight harder to regain control of southern Iraq. A week after the insurgents had seized southern Iraq, it was becoming grimly apparent that they could expect no help from the Iranians or the Americans.

Saddam Hussein was already certain he could crush the insurgency without provoking U.S. intervention. General Samarrai, the military intelligence chief, says the decisive information on the U.S. position came in the form of an intercept of two radio conversations between two Shia rebels somewhere near Nassariya. The fact that the intercept had been made, and was passed on by the listening station at Rashidiya north of Baghdad, shows that the Iraqi military machine was reconstituting itself. After a glance at the transcripts, Samarrai saw its significance and had a copy rushed to Saddam. Samarrai recollects that the conversation opens with one rebel saying: "We went to the Americans for their support. They told us, 'we are not going to support you because you are from the al-Sayyid group [Mohammed Baqir al-Hakim].'"

"Ask them again," responds the second speaker. "Go back and ask once more."

A second transcript contains the Americans' reply, which must have been devastating news to the rebels as it was the death warrant of the uprising. The first rebel leader reported back: "They say, 'We are not going to support you because you are Shia and are collaborating with Iran.'" Samarrai says this finally convinced Saddam Hussein, as he must have already suspected, that, for now at least, the Americans were not going to allow the Shia to overthrow him. "After this message," says the intelligence chief, "the position of the regime immediately became more confident. Now [Saddam] began to attack the intifada."

CHAPTER SIX

Saddam's Revenge

I saw the first signs of the Iraqi army offensive against the Shia rebels at a place called al-Aoun, east of Kerbala. On each side of the road were the blackened stumps of date palm trees, which had either been set ablaze by artillery fire or burned by soldiers to deny the insurgents cover for ambushes. The countryside and the outskirts of the city were unnaturally empty with few people about, apart from bored soldiers at the many checkpoints. The fighting had been fiercest in Kerbala itself, especially around the shrines of Abbas and Hussein. Just above the gateway into the shrine of Abbas, a rocket-propelled grenade had smashed into the blue-and-yellow tiling, exposing the brown bricks underneath. Inside one room in the corner of the rectangular buildings surrounding the inner court-yard, our guides showed us a gibbet in the ceiling and dark blood marks on the concrete floor, where Baathist officials had their throats cut. Outside the battered gates were three or four massive British-made Centurion tanks, captured by the Iraqi army during the first few victorious days of the Iran-Iraq war. Their long gun barrels pointed out over a wide empty space that separated the shrine of Abbas from that of Hussein four hundred yards away. Two months earlier this had been filled with small shops and twisting alleyways, which had been heavily shelled and then bull-dozed. I could see mounds of broken bricks and smashed woodwork on either side of the devastated area. I went with other journalists to see General Abdul Khaliq Abdul Aziz, a vigorous, confident-looking man who had been appointed governor of Kerbala. He viewed the city very much as conquered territory and tried to persuade us that the Iranians had been the driving force behind the insurgents in the city. He pointed to a few ammunition boxes and TNT charges that he claimed could only have come from Iran.

We drove south to Najaf, where, at first, the golden dome of the shrine of Imam Ali looked undamaged. When we entered the courtyard of the shrine itself, the flagstones covering the ground were pitted with little craters where mortar bombs and rocket-propelled grenades had detonated. The dome itself had been punctured by heavy machine-gun fire. Soldiers were nonchalantly guarding the gates. There was not a single pilgrim in the courtyard where once Shia from every corner of the world had gathered. A solitary attendant was sweeping up broken blue tiles from the side wall of the shrine itself. I went to see the governor of Najaf, Abdul Rahman al-Dhouri, who told the same tale as his colleague in Kerbala, about how the Iranian Revolutionary Guards had swept into Najaf only to be routed by the loyal forces of the Iraqi government. I left his office and walked back toward the shrine. Once again I was struck by the emptiness of streets that had once teemed with people: clergy in black turbans, intent-looking pilgrims, and traders with their carts selling cheap goods. I was walking slowly on the sidewalk, a row of closed shops with heavy metal shutters a few feet to my left, talking to another journalist. Somebody must have heard us. Suddenly, from behind a shutter, I heard a thin despairing voice in Iraqi-accented English say: "Help us! Help us!"

By that time many people in Kerbala and Najaf and the other cities that had risen against Saddam Hussein at the beginning of March were beyond help. The government counterattack was led by General Hussein Kamel, Saddam's cousin and son-in-law, who boasted of being the founder of the Republican Guards. His first probing advance had been blocked at al-Aoun, but the Republican Guards had swung south and circled behind Kerbala to cut off the city from Najaf. By March 12 his forces were entering Kerbala. "We started to hear the sound of helicopters overhead and tanks entering the outskirts," says Sanaa Mohammed, the local government employee who found the intifada anarchic and frightening. "They distributed leaflets ordering people to leave Kerbala. We fled to a farm on the edge of the city. We saw insurgents with ragged beards and clothes with bloodstains on them who shot at our feet." There was food in the farm, but all around Sanaa could hear the sounds of shooting and bombing. Her

brother brought news from the center of Kerbala, saying that many people had sought refuge in and around the shrines, thinking these would be
the safest places. Instead they found themselves trapped in the middle of a
savage battle that went on for over a week. As it died away Sanaa's family
decided to return to their house. "On our way home we saw corpses all over
the streets along with severed heads and burned-out buildings," she says.

Hussein Kamel issued an order to arrest all young men over the age of
fifteen. A story spread among the Shia that he had ordered the bombing
of the Imam Hussein shrine, declaring, "My name is Hussein and so is
yours. Let us see who is the strongest." Like the story of the tank gunner
who fired a round into a portrait of Saddam Hussein in Basra, this became
another iconic story of the uprising, but its truth is impossible to verify.
(Hussein Kamel is in no position to answer inquiries; he was shot to death
by his relatives in Baghdad after defecting to Jordan in 1995 and then
unwisely returning in 1996.) Sanaa Mohammed heard a nastier story that
reflects the terror felt by the people in Kerbala: An old man was walking
with his daughter when they encountered Hussein Kamel. The general
asked them "Who is better, me or the Imam al-Hussein?" The old man was
afraid and said "You," but the girl answered unhesitatingly "The Imam
Hussein." Hussein Kamel shot her and she died at once; the old man cried
so much because he had abandoned Imam Hussein that he became blind.
The story has the unreal feel of Christian tales of martyrdom for the faith
that were the staple of medieval Christianity, but the merciless revenge of
the Baath party on the Shia is very well substantiated and no atrocity can
be ruled out.[1]

By March 19, Kerbala was finally back under government control.
Troops immediately began a reign of terror. A young lawyer by the name
of Abu Muqtad says he saw soldiers throw a patient off the roof of the al-
Husseini hospital.[2] All men of military age were in danger. Shia were killed
simply because they were Shia. Colonel Othman estimated that 150,000
Shia were killed in Iraq during the intifada.[3] Accounts of what happened
next in and around Kerbala, Najaf, and Kufa resemble horror stories about
the roundup of Jews in Poland and Ukraine in the wake of the advancing
German army in World War II. Whole families were casually slaughtered.
In the aftermath of the 1991 uprising, tales of atrocities were collectively
convincing but individually difficult to prove. Then in May 2003, mass
graves containing the bodies of thousands of people killed at the end of
the uprising were found around al-Hilla and al-Mahawil, a former army

base twelve miles north of Hilla. In two mass graves alone, 2,300 bodies were unearthed. Many of those who had disappeared during the uprising were identified because their identity documents were found or some personal item, like a watch, was still intact. Often the dead had been arrested at random and later executed. A fourteen-year-old boy was sent by his mother to get water from the river and had been arrested by soldiers on a bridge; two men had gone to buy food in a nearby market; a lawyer and his student son had gone looking for a missing relative. Their bodies were all found twelve years later at al-Mahawil.

There is only one known survivor of the death pits of al-Mahawil, and his testimony is convincing. His name is Nasir Khadir Hazim al-Husseini and he was only twelve years old at the time. His story is worth telling at some length because it shows how Saddam's regime deliberately inflicted collective punishment on the Shia for the rebellion, regardless of whether or not they took part. Nasir came from the city of Hilla south of Baghdad, which is about seventy percent Shia and thirty percent Sunni. On March 16 his twenty-eight-year-old mother, Khulud Abud Naji, took Nasir, two other thirteen-year-old relatives, his uncle Muhanad Abud Naji, and his cousin Mohammed Yassin Mohammed to see their grandfather in another part of Hilla. On their way they were stopped by a soldier and accused of being looters. They were taken first to a school where they were kept in a classroom that soon filled up with other detainees. "They blindfolded us and bound our hands, and then they put us in Land Cruisers with shaded windows and a bus," says Nasir. "They took us to al-Mahawil military base." There was a perfunctory investigation by senior officers who wrote down their names. They received no food and were taken to a big hall. "We were sitting in [family] groups, me with my relatives and the others with their relatives. No one dared speak to other groups." Toward the end of the second day, on March 18, 1991, the detainees were taken outside and lined up in the courtyard of the compound where "they brought some blankets which they ripped and they tied our hands and blindfolded us with those," Nasir remembers. "They covered our eyes and put us inside some TATA buses looted from Kuwait." Some forty-five to fifty people were crammed together in the bus that drove down a dirt track. Nasir was sitting next to the window of the bus and could just see through a gap in his blindfold. He recalls an abandoned canal and a building, which he later saw was a brick factory.

The bus stopped and executions began immediately. A pit had already been dug and people were dragged off the bus and machine-gunned. "When they started taking us off the bus, some of us began reciting the *shahada* [Muslim declaration of faith]. My mother told me, 'Repeat the *shahada*, because we are about to die.' I heard the shouting of the children. We grabbed each other's hands—me, my mother, my cousin, and my uncle. They pulled us, we were all together." Nasir and his family were flung into a pre-excavated mass grave by one group of men while another group were firing with their guns. "When I fell down, there were so many bodies underneath me. I laid down on top of them. They started to shoot at us." After a time the shooting stopped but Nasir felt somebody pull at his clothes and say "This one isn't shot yet, shoot him." He heard shots but still was not hit. An order was given for a bulldozer to bury the bodies, but Nasir, still uninjured, was at the edge of the grave. As the bulldozer shovel got closer to him, he was able to crawl to one side of it. "I heard the man who was standing on the hill instruct the shovel driver to bury us more—he had seen that I was not yet buried—but the driver left the place and did not do it." Nasir heard the vehicles drive away and then crawled out of the grave, leaving his dead relatives behind. He made his way to the Baghdad-Hilla road and was lucky enough to meet four sympathetic Shia soldiers who helped him return home.[4]

The slaughter was mainly of people from the al-Hilla area who had been selected wholly at random, though most of the victims were young men. Among the dead were more than a dozen Egyptian laborers working near al-Hilla. Few of these were from Kerbala, Najaf, or Diwaniyah, suggesting that those who disappeared from these cities, where the resistance to government forces was far greater than Hilla, are buried somewhere else. Iskandar Jawad Witwit, a high-ranking air force officer based at al-Mahawil, said that the uprising in Hilla had been crushed by March 11, and was followed by a campaign of mass arrests of men, women, and children. "The executions happened every day," he says. "They killed thousands of people." Witwit was himself arrested on March 16, accused of sympathizing with the uprising, but his testimony is important because, as a soldier, he mixed with the perpetrators of the massacres. He identified them as being Baath party members, General Security, Special Security, the intelligence services (*mukhabarat*), and leading members of the pro-government Albu Alwan tribe, including its head sheikh. The involvement of the Special Republican Guard, the elite force recruited from Sunni tribes, is tellingly revealed by another soldier, Salim Murgan Hitban, returning from a three-day leave in Najaf with a cousin who was also a soldier. They were picked up at a Special Republican Guard checkpoint, held in grim conditions in a hall at the base, and the cousin was then shot. Hitban only survived because a major on "the execution committee" had once been his commanding officer in Mosul.[5]

How many people were killed at al-Mahawil? Sayyid Jabir Muhsin al-Husseini, a local farmer who witnessed the killings, says that the executions started at nine a.m. and ended at five p.m., with three groups of between 120 and 150 people being machine-gunned every day between March 7 and April 6, 1991.[6] This means that more than 10,000 were killed from the al-Hilla area alone, which makes Colonel Othman's figure of 150,000 Shia killed in total in southern Iraq seem credible. Butchery on this scale could only have taken place on the instructions of Saddam Hussein himself. The aim, if these mass killings had a rational motive, was to terrorize the Shia population of Iraq by inflicting on them a collective punishment so bloody that they would never rise again.

The army counterattack in Basra quickly retook the city after three days of fighting. Tanks from the 51st Mechanized Division, a unit that had not been involved in the mutinies, captured the road that overlooks the working-class areas of north Basra. Six weeks later, I could see where the heavy machine-gun bullets had penetrated the thin-walled brick houses and tank shells had destroyed a fire station that insurgents had used as a center for resistance. As in the rest of southern Iraq there were many atrocities. A man who had entered the city with relief goods on March 7 saw through his binoculars a column of twenty tanks heading toward the city center. "I saw that the tank that was leading had three children tied to its front," he said. "They did it because four hours earlier they had tried to attack in the same way, and a fourteen-year-old girl with explosives had jumped on the front of the first tank and exploded it [*sic*], forcing the whole column to withdraw."[7] I did not myself see damage on anything like the scale of Kerbala, which may have been because resistance fighters could escape to Iran. "I would say there were more than one thousand dead," Dr. al-Rawi told me at the Basra Teaching Hospital. "Basra General Hospital issued six hundred death certificates. It was a bad time. You could see dogs eating bodies in the streets."[8] Resistance continued in the suburbs and villages on the east side of the Shatt al-Arab until the end of March, because the bridges had been destroyed by allied aircraft in January and February and troops could not cross the waterway.[9] As government forces took each area there was the same merciless but haphazard detention of civilians, who were then shot or drowned in the river.

In Kurdistan, the highly successful Iraqi army counterattack against the Peshmerga (Kurdish fighters) had an unexpected result. The Kurds were terrified of Saddam Hussein's revenge, which had killed 180,000 of them in 1988–89. They fled in their millions to Turkey and Iran, leaving their dead and dying by the roadside, and their sufferings were shown on television screens around the world. At first President George H. W. Bush did not intend to do any more for the Kurds than he had for the Shia, but public pressure to help them became irresistible. A no-fly zone was declared by the United States, and the Kurds began the first stages of creating a semi-independent enclave in the northern three provinces of Iraq. The sufferings of the Shia were far less visible, and therefore provoked much less international reaction. Foreign journalists could interview refugees arriving in Iran or Saudi Arabia with terrible tales, but could not report firsthand while the fighting was still going on.

Surprisingly, film of the repression did emerge, and it was taken by the Baath party itself. The party had what amounted almost to a cult of cruelty, and apparently shot the film to encourage its supporters and frighten its enemies by showing their fate. These films sometimes fell into the hands of secret opponents of the regime, who smuggled them out of the country.

One such film, shot around the end of March by a Baath party cameraman, records two Baath leaders taking part in the search for insurgents in the marshy lands near the town of Rumaytha, about twenty miles from Samawa on the Euphrates northwest of Nassariya. The film was later given to me in London and shows what must have been a typical search-and-destroy mission against the insurgents. Clearly visible is the newly appointed interior minister Ali Hassan al-Majid, also known as "Chemical Ali" for his murderous Anfal campaign against the Kurds in 1988, in which poison gas was repeatedly used against civilians. At first I thought the video was only vaguely interesting, because it had no sound track, but then I found that by turning up the sound to full volume, it was possible to hear what was being said. Al-Majid, who had a reputation for savagery second to none in the regime, is heard instructing a helicopter pilot on his way to attack insurgents holding a bridge. "Don't come back until you have burnt them," he says. "And if you haven't burnt them don't come back." He is joined by Mohammed Hamza al-Zubeidi, soon to be made prime minister because of his reputation for ruthlessness. Zubeidi slaps and kicks prisoners as they lie terrified on the ground. "Let's execute one so the others will confess," he suggests. The four or five prisoners in bedraggled civilian clothes, who look like farm laborers, say nothing except for one who pleads softly: "Please, don't do this." Al-Majid always has a cigarette in his mouth as he interrogates prisoners, and there is the sound of gunfire in the background. Pointing at one prisoner, he says: "Don't execute this one. He will be useful to us." The soldiers, who appear to be Special Republican Guard, kick the prisoners, shouting "Pimp" and "Son of a Whore."

Members of the Baath party dared not be seen as less than enthusiastic in eliminating the enemies of the regime. Any young Shia man was liable to be detained and shot at any moment. In most cases the executioners showed no hesitation. But in one case in Basra, 150 young men, mostly students, who had been herded into a hall in an office block belonging to the Oil Tanks Department of the Southern Oil Company, were unexpectedly freed. While they were there they were visited by a Baath party veteran and friend of Saddam Hussein who was accompanied by his son Jassem. Jassem did not share his father's Baathist sympathies but felt safer with him while the army was picking people up at random in the streets of the city. He saw the students crying and begging to be released because they had done nothing. He also knew that Ali Hassan al-Majid was due to visit Basra the next morning and was likely to order a mass execution of the young men. In the middle of the night Jassem hit the single Baathist guarding the entrance to the hall with the butt of his pistol and opened the door. Holding up a hand in front of his face so they could not recognize him, he told the detainees to run as fast and as silently as they could. Jassem then went back to bed, confident that nobody would imagine that the son of such a stalwart Baathist as his father could have knocked out the guard and freed the prisoners. The story does not have a happy ending. "When the other Baathists saw the guard unconscious and the prisoners gone they panicked, because Ali Hassan al-Majid was coming expecting to order the executions," says a friend of Jassem. "The Baathists rushed out into the street and seized everybody they saw until the hall was full again with 150 people, who were executed as had been planned."[10]

CHAPTER SEVEN

The White Lion

Saddam Hussein reasserted his grip on power with surprising speed in the wake of his defeat in Kuwait and the uprisings by the Shia and the Kurds. Few other rulers could have survived the self-inflicted catastrophes of 1991, but Saddam had a sure knowledge of the Iraqi political landscape, its lethal pitfalls, and how to escape them. This was in sharp contrast to his ignorance of other countries, which led to his disastrous decision to invade Iran in 1980 and Kuwait ten years later. In the twelve years after 1991, no plot or second uprising came near to unseating Saddam despite several attempts. "We have got the worst of all possible worlds," an Iraqi friend said gloomily to me in 1992. "We have been completely defeated and we still have Saddam Hussein in power."

In successfully stabilizing his regime, the Iraqi ruler made one serious mistake. It was a strange and atypical error by a man who regarded even his closest aides and relatives with suspicion and slept in different houses every night to confuse potential assassins. For once in his career, Saddam trusted somebody too far. From the Shia Intifada he had drawn the lessons that the Shia masses detested the regime and that the Shia religious leaders such as Grand Ayatollah al-Khoei could not be trusted. Savage though repression of the Shia had been, he did not rely on it alone. After the death by natural causes of the ninety-three-year-old al-Khoei in August 1992, Saddam conceived a plan to install his own candidate as head of the Shia religious hierarchy. He would choose someone who was of Arab rather than Iranian origin like al-Khoei as paramount Marji' al-

Taqlid (supreme religious authority). He would be an Iraqi nationalist as well as a religious leader, and must back the regime in its confrontation with the United States. Persecution of the Shia community and their clergy was intense in 1991–92. Saddam Hussein himself was believed to have penned a series of anti-Shia articles in the Baath party newspaper *al-Thawra* in which they were accused of believing in "deviant" doctrines and not being fully Iraqi.[1] Many of the hawza were dead, imprisoned, or scattered; their schools and colleges were closed. It was Saddam's idea of a political masterstroke to relax this persecution and reconcile with the Shia community by co-opting a member of the al-Sadr family, who would be a cat's-paw of the regime in Baghdad. Saddam's nominee would have all the more legitimacy because of his blood relationship with the revered Shia martyr Mohammed Baqir al-Sadr, whom the regime had executed so brutally twelve years earlier.

The man Saddam chose to be religious leader of the Shia community was Mohammed Sadiq al-Sadr, a cousin, student, and senior aide of Mohammed Baqir al-Sadr. At the time he struck his deal with the regime in 1992, his family was well-known but he was not. He was highly intelligent, had an original mind, and was cunning enough to deceive the Iraqi *mukhabarat*, an organization devoted to smelling out treachery, into believing it could manipulate him in its own interests. He used the breathing space this gave him and his supporters to revive the morale and religious commitment of the Shia after the slaughter of the 1991 uprising and the oppression that followed. His mixture of Islamic revivalism, nationalism, and populism had a deep appeal to angry, alienated, but terrorized young Shia men. "He made us feel self-confident while before we were controlled by fear," recalls Ali Hussein Khidr, a pious seventeen-year-old from Nassariya who traveled with his teenage friends to see Mohammed Sadiq in Najaf in 1997. "We felt that a strong man was standing with us, so we were afraid of nothing."[2] As a religious leader, al-Sadr was interested primarily in reviving the faith among the Shia masses, addressing the immediate problems of their daily lives, and subtly undermining the propaganda of the regime. At first he expressed his real feelings indirectly, but they would have been clear to any Iraqi. He would begin Friday prayers, which he had introduced in a radical break with Shia tradition, by leading thousands of worshippers in the mosque in Kufa in chanting: "Yes, yes to Islam; yes, yes to the faith; no, no to injustice; no, no to Israel; no, no to America; no, no to the devil." There was nothing here that the regime could object to, but his congregation would have noticed that there was no call to support the Iraqi leader. Sheikh Yassin al-Assadi, who heard him speak, says: "What he said was an intelligent and deliberate contradiction of the regime's slogans such as 'yes, yes to the leader Saddam Hussein' and 'with our soul and blood we will sacrifice ourselves for you, Saddam,' and many others."[3]

There was a fundamental difference between Sadiq al-Sadr's approach and that of his mentor and relative Baqir al-Sadr. The new leader did not intend to make a direct attack on the state, trying to gain power by supporting a political party or through a coup. He seldom mentioned, at least at first, political issues in his fatwas (judgments). Mohammed Hassan Ibrahim, a seventeen-year-old from the impoverished Shia city of Kut, south of Baghdad, saw clearly the different approaches of the two al-Sadrs. "The first al-Sadr set up a political party linked to the elite of the hawza, while the second was immersed in the world of tribes and issues of daily life," he said. "The first wanted a political revolution, while the second aimed for a Shia cultural revival in which it was important what you saw at the cinema and the music you listened to. He wanted to establish an Islamic popular base strong enough to stand up to a murderous and tyrannical regime."[4]

Mohammed Sadiq was extraordinarily successful in his mission, given his own slender resources and the power of the Iraqi state. Today it is his face one sees on posters pasted on the walls in the Shia areas of Iraq. Pictured standing alongside his cousin Baqir al-Sadr and his son Muqtada, he looks older than his years, his features dominated by his long, straggly, silver beard, which led to him being given the nickname "the White Lion," *al layth al-abyadh*. In 1998 he began to wear a white shroud over his shoulders, a sign that he expected to be martyred. Observers did not have to be told who he thought would kill him. At about this same time he recorded a CD, widely distributed before and after his death, in which he gave details of his career. It is as if he wanted to set the record straight and rebut calumny from rival Shia religious leaders, who repeatedly denounced Mohammed Mohammed Sadiq al-Sadr as a police agent.

Mohammed Mohammed Sadiq al-Sadr was born in Najaf on March 23, 1943, the only son of his father, Sayyid Mohammed Sadiq al-Sadr. Confusingly, he was generally known by his father's name. He lived with his mother's father, Ayatollah Mohammed Reza al-Yassin, married young, and had four sons—Mustafa, Muammal, Murtada, and Muqtada—and two daughters. Intellectually precocious, he began his study in the hawza in 1954 at the age of eleven. There he was to meet and study under the men who were to reshape the Shia world in Iraq, such as his cousin Ayatollah Mohammed Baqir al-Sadr and the Ayatollah al-Khoei. He entered the Faqih college in 1960 and studied science and languages, gaining a working knowledge of English. He completed his studies under the future leader of Iran, Ayatollah Khomeini, and Sayyid Muhsin al-Hakim, then the most prominent member of another great Shia clerical family who were to become his fierce opponents. By 1977, Mohammed Sadiq became a *mujtahid* at the early age of thirty-four, which qualified him not only to interpret Shia law but to give judgments on political and social questions.

A decade earlier, these undoubted academic achievements, together with his membership in the Shia clerical aristocracy, might have opened the door for Mohammed Sadiq to enjoy a sedate and well-respected career in Najaf. There would have been spats and rivalries with other religious families, such as the al-Hakim, or religious notables, such as Ali al-Sistani. Clerical rivalries, whether Islamic or Christian, have a long tradition of extreme rancor at odds with the supposed otherworldly concerns of opponents. Even in as decorous a religious establishment as the Church of England in the nineteenth century, Anthony Trollope describes with accurate relish the fierce feuds of clergymen in their struggles for jobs, promotion, and power. In twentieth-century Najaf, as in nineteenth-century Barchester, the fictional English cathedral town where Trollope's novels are set, the fact that contestants had grown up together or rubbed shoulders for decades made their disputes all the more venomous. But after the Baath party staged its coup d'état in 1968, all parallels between the Shia clergy of Iraq and ecclesiastical hierarchies, in other countries and in Iraq in the past, ceased to be valid. Before this, Shia clergy led a cloistered existence in which it seldom faced persecution. The worst punishment faced by the *mujtahid* who had promoted the rebellion of 1920 against the British occupation was a short spell in prison and enforced or voluntary exile. All this was to change as Shia religious leaders entered an era during which they endured unrelenting persecution. From the beginning it was clear that the Baathists did not intend to share authority with anyone. They identified the Shia clergy, and above all those sympathetic to the Dawa party, as dangerous antagonists, and moved to crush them with the brutality that was their party's hallmark.

Mohammed Sadiq was arrested twice, the first time in 1972, when he was detained along with his cousin Mohammed Baqir al-Sadr and

Mohammed Baqir al-Hakim. His second arrest was in 1974, when he was tortured in the *mukhabarat* office in Najaf. When he protested against the brutal treatment of other prisoners, he was taken to another security office, this one in Diwaniyah to the south of Najaf, where he was tortured even more severely. His mistreatment had an understandably serious impact on his personality and his religious views. After his release from prison in 1975, he devoted himself so intently to prayers that he began to damage his health, and his teacher Mohammed Baqir was forced to ask him to moderate his religious observances. The young cleric remembered this as a time of isolation, because, although he was out of jail, he was under house arrest and few dared enter his home. When he was allowed a little more freedom, he was still closely watched by Iraqi security, and people were too frightened to say hello to him when he visited the Imam Ali shrine.[5] It was during this time that the first signs began to appear that his ideas were moving in a dramatically different direction from that of other *mujtahid*. He developed an interest in mystical Islam, explaining later that he was taught this by an ordinary worker in Najaf named Hajj Abd el-Zahra al-Gara'wi. This in itself was a surprising and telling admission for a member of a clerical class, whose knowledge and advancement came through tuition by scholars of proven learning and was acquired by years of study.[6]

In the 1980s, Mohammed Sadiq did little to draw attention to himself, but he developed original ideas about how Shia Islam and its leaders should respond to persecution by the state. Endurance and passive resistance, the traditional Shia recipe for surviving tyrannical governments, were not enough. He opposed the principle of Taqqiyya (dissimulation and concealment) when dealing with Saddam Hussein, arguing that, on the contrary, this was the moment for Shia religious leaders to stand up openly for their faith. He would later speak scornfully of the silent or pacific Marji'iyyah compared with the active or militant Marji'iyyah. Many of his ideas about the creation of an Islamic state he owed to Mohammed Baqir al-Sadr, but he gave priority to starting an Islamic cultural revolution that would precede seizing state power. The latter option was in any case impractical in the 1990s, given the disparity between the feeble resources of the Shia community and the strength of the Baathist regime. Sadiq al-Sadr believed that by withdrawing from the world the Shia hierarchy had abandoned their own people, whose sufferings, already great, had become a great deal worse after 1991. His plan was to persuade the regime that he was under its control so he could build a mass movement, making Shi'ism once more relevant to the spiritual, psychological, and economic needs of the faithful. His status as the successor to Mohammed Baqir, Sadr I, was reinforced by marriages between Sadr I's three daughters and Sadr II's three sons. Jafar al-Sadr, the son of Sadr I and principal assistant of Sadr II, says: "Muqtada married my youngest sister in 1994, Sayyid Mustafa the eldest in 1987, and Sayyid Muammal the second oldest in 1992."[7]

The Iraqi economy and society were collapsing under the weight of UN sanctions imposed at the time of the invasion of Kuwait in 1990 and not lifted until 2003. Millions of Iraqis saw their lives being ruined. This explains why they were so receptive to Sadiq al-Sadr's religious message. The severity of the sanctions and their devastating impact on ordinary Iraqis were never understood by the outside world. They were not like past sanctions, such as those imposed on South Africa or Rhodesia as a sign of international disapproval; they were more akin to a medieval siege— a siege, furthermore, that lasted thirteen years. They were supposedly aimed at denying the Iraqi government access to its oil revenues, but in reality it was the population and not the political elite who were hit hardest. The latter could increase their personal wealth through black-market operations and state-sanctioned smuggling. Sanctions were a disaster for ordinary Iraqis because so many of them were directly or indirectly employed by the government, which now had no money to pay them. Officials, teachers, army officers, and pensioners were all suddenly penniless. A friend of mine named Jawad, a much-qualified professor of engineering at Baghdad University, was unlucky enough to return to Iraq in the summer of 1990 in order to see a highly valued student through his Ph.D. When Saddam invaded Kuwait, Jawad found he was trapped because no country where he had previously held teaching jobs would give him a visa. He found his income had fallen to the equivalent of five dollars a month. By 1995, he was shyly asking me if I could find him a job as a driver with the UN office in Baghdad. The Iraqi currency collapsed after the invasion of Kuwait and savings were wiped out. When I first went to Iraq, a dollar was worth about a third of a dinar; by 1992, a single dollar would buy you two thousand dinars. When I changed a hundred-dollar bill with the money changers in Saadoun Street in central Baghdad, they would hand me a weighty black plastic bag full of greasy bundles of dinar notes held together by rubber bands.

Iraqis were bewildered and frightened by the ongoing catastrophe that so cruelly dislocated their lives and showed no sign of ending. Many had hoped up to the last minute that the war over Kuwait would be averted. Even the most pessimistic had not foreseen that in the space of a few days, bombs and missiles would wreck the infrastructure of power stations, oil refineries, telecommunications centers, and water treatment plants that had turned Iraq into a modern country over the previous half century. Some of the better-off had stocked up their deep freezes with meat to see them through the conflict. But when the electrical system ceased to work during the first days of the bombing in 1991, the freezers stopped working and the carefully stored meat began to rot. Soon there was a penetrating stench in middle-class neighborhoods because people were forced to throw out the maggot-ridden meat, only to find it was not collected by garbage collectors and was left on the ground. The garbagemen had no gasoline for their trucks because Saddam had not even taken the simple precaution of storing fuel in the weeks before the refineries were put out of action. When garbage removal eventually resumed after the war, the collectors made a discovery with sinister implications. Previously, one-third of what they collected had consisted of food scraps, but this was no longer the case. In a country where ever-more people were not getting enough to eat, nothing edible, not even the toughest melon rinds, was being thrown away.

The closest approximation to the disaster that befell Iraq and Iraqis in 1991 is the Great Crash of 1929 in the United States. In both cases the collapse was sudden and totally unexpected by its victims. In the three years between 1929 and 1932, unemployment in America rose from 1.5 million to 13 million. In Iraq there was full employment in 1990 and there were an additional one million Egyptians working in the country. Two years later, the Iraqi Ministry of Labor recorded that unemployment had risen to over fifty percent of the workforce. When U.S. troops invaded Iraq in 2003 and saw the miserable shantytowns on the road to Baghdad, they thought this was the normal state in which Iraqis lived; in fact, for many Iraqis, this grinding poverty was a new experience. In the 1970s, the Iraqi health system had been similar in quality to that of Greece. But when I visited a hospital on the outskirts of Baghdad in 1996, its parking lot was full of trucks on blocks because their wheels and engines had been cannibalized to keep a couple of vehicles going. While I was there, a child was dying because there were no more oxygen bottles available.

In fact, what happened to Iraqis in the 1990s was far worse than the experience of Americans in the 1930s. In the United States, the folk memory long persisted of hungry men and women forced to pick through maggoty trash in a desperate search for food. But it was a recollection of a disaster that was safely in the past and unlikely to be repeated. For Iraqis, there was no comforting sense that, if they endured a few years of deprivation, life would begin to improve. Sanctions would stay as long as Saddam Hussein governed Iraq, and there was no sign of his rule ending. Indeed, sanctions seemed designed more to keep Iraq weak than to remove him. For all the brutality and unpopularity of his regime, more Iraqis were dying because of UN sanctions in the 1990s than were being shot, tortured, and imprisoned by the regime.

At this time the Ministry of Information in Baghdad insisted that any foreign journalist traveling outside Baghdad should be accompanied by a "minder" from the ministry. I used to ask minders to take me to their home village, which they were always eager to do. Many were well-educated men who secretly blamed Saddam Hussein for forcing them into a job they considered below their talents. One day my minder and I went to a fruit-growing village in Diyala, a well-watered province northeast of Baghdad. Ten years later this area was devastated by tit-for-tat massacres between Sunni and Shia, but at this time the villagers here were doing better than most in Iraq. They grew their own food and sold fruit in the markets of Baquba, the provincial capital, and Baghdad. But their prosperity was only relative. "It looks as if we are well-off," Buhha'a Hussein al-Sayef, a local farmer, told me as we sat on the shady balcony of his house overlooking his groves of pomegranate trees and date palms. Then he went on to explain that their water purification plant had long ceased to work, so they were drinking polluted water from the canals that made many of them sick. Driving away from the village I saw people chasing after our car. It turned out they thought I was a foreign doctor. When we stopped I explained I was a journalist, but they still seemed to think I had medical expertise. Several people went back to their houses to get dusty old X-rays of their children, many of whom were ill. The X-rays had been taken years before, either in Amman, Jordan, or in a local clinic that was now closed. One man, Ali Ahmed Suwaidan, was determined that I should look at an X-ray of the head of his daughter Fatima, who was playing on the ground nearby. "There is something wrong with her balance," he said sadly. "She cannot stand up." He held the little girl upright for a few seconds and then removed his hands. She immediately crumpled at our feet.

The devastating impact of sanctions explains why Mohammed Sadiq's open hostility to the United States and covert opposition to Saddam Hussein spoke straight to the heart of millions of Iraqi Shia. They hated the regime in Baghdad but also detested an American government that they blamed for the sanctions that were destroying their lives and those of their children. I could see the terrible results of sanctions in the village and city streets. If further evidence was needed, there was the grim procession of medical reports and statistics. A survey of 2,120 children in Baghdad under the age of five was conducted by a foreign team in the summer of 1995. It showed that 29 percent of them were underweight compared to 7 percent in 1991. The number of children who were "stunted" had risen from 12 percent to 28 percent. The authors of the report said that only in Mali had they seen conditions comparable to Iraq.[8] One foreign medical delegation had reported watching with horror as Iraqi doctors tried to carry out an operation in which they could not even cut the patient's skin because the scissors they were using were too blunt.

The mass impoverishment of Iraqis, and the failure or inability of the government to do anything about it, was the essential precondition to the swift rise of Mohammed Sadiq al-Sadr in the early 1990s, and his son Muqtada after 2003. The Shia community was affected worse than the Sunni because it had always been poorer, and such well-paid jobs as did exist were likely to go to Sunni loyal to the regime. Saddam Hussein might have money to build palaces and mosques, but he no longer controlled revenues sufficient to buy off dissent. It was a tactic that, in common with the rulers of other oil states, he had used effectively in the past. In the first couple of years of his unpopular war with Iran, Saddam had rebuilt much of central Baghdad, using large loans from Saudi Arabia and Kuwait, partly in a bid to show Iraqis that the conflict was not stopping economic development. He gave jobs, contracts, cash, scholarships, cars, and houses to those whose cooperation he needed. After 1990, though, this was no longer possible. In 1989, Iraq's oil revenue was $13 billion. Three years later it was down to $400 million a year, derived from Turkish truck drivers whose smuggling of oil across the northern border was tolerated by the United States because Turkey and the Iraqi Kurds both benefited. One consequence of the state's lack of money and inability to supply services was a greater demand for the work of religious charities established by Sadiq al-Sadr and later by Muqtada. The oil-for-food program introduced in 1996 fended off starvation, if not malnutrition, but it did little else.

The United States, Britain, and other supporters of sanctions claimed for years, contrary to all evidence from international aid organizations, that the burden of sanctions on the Iraqi people was exaggerated. They argued that if they were being impoverished it was all the fault of Saddam for diverting money into his own pockets and wasting resources by constructing giant palaces. But in the three Iraqi provinces of Kurdistan, where Saddam had lost control after 1991, the impact of sanctions was as bad or worse than farther south. In 1996 I went to a village called Penjwin in Sulaimaniyah province in Iraqi Kurdistan. It was on the Iraqi side of the border with Iran and, because of its frontline position during the Iran-Iraq war, it was liberally sown with mines. In the village street I noticed that an astonishing number of people were missing hands or legs. Villagers explained dolefully that in order to feed their families they had to undertake one of the most dangerous jobs in the world. They would locate an Italian-made mine called the Valmara that jumped into the air, propelled by a small explosive, if you touched it. At waist height the main explosive would detonate, spraying hundreds of lethal ball bearings in all directions. People from Penjwin would defuse this lethal contraption in order to make a few dollars by selling the aluminium wrapped around the explosive. Some did not survive the operation and others, like those I had seen, were mutilated for life.

There were those who understood exactly what sanctions were doing to Iraqi society, but their warnings were ignored or derided in Washington and London. Denis Halliday, a fifty-seven-year-old Irish Quaker appointed UN humanitarian coordinator in August 1997, said simply that "the infrastructure is collapsing and it will take ten to twenty years to restore." After resigning in protest over sanctions a year later, he spelled out their calamitous long-term effects not just on health but on the fabric of Iraqi society: the great increase in crime, fewer marriages because people could not afford to marry, the bitterness and rage of young men without a future. He compared them to the orphans of the Afghan war who had formed the core of the Taliban movement. He saw a generation growing up in Iraq that was filled with hate. "What should be of concern is the possibility of more fundamentalist Islamic thinking developing," said Halliday prophetically. "It is not well understood as a possible spin-off of the sanctions regime. We are pushing people to take extreme positions."[9]

Mohammed Sadiq's brief but explosive career as a Shia religious leader illustrates the growing strength of fundamentalist Islam. It is a dramatic story that falls roughly into three unequal parts. He had been imprisoned after the Shia uprising like many of the Shia clergy. After his release, between 1992 and 1996, he appeared to cooperate with the regime, dwelling on social and religious topics and avoiding politics. Speaking, in an interview, on his relations with the government, he said: "They avoid harming us so long as we avoid harming them."[10] It was not a relationship that was likely to last long. Saddam and the Baath party were never able to tolerate allies who showed any degree of independence. "The regime was afraid of internal opposition so they were looking for a cleric they could control," says Jawad al-Khalasi, a cleric with extensive contact with the Sadrists. "They thought Sadiq al-Sadr was perfect, that he was weak and was easily controlled. But he tricked them."[11] His initial priority was to establish a network of preachers and organizers to revive Shi'ism among the Shia masses in Baghdad and southern Iraq. "He used very intelligent tactics by establishing a sort of truce [with the regime] in order to give himself space to operate," says Sheikh Yassin al-Assadi, who knew him during this period.[12] At times, his ambivalent relations with the authorities seem to have amused him. In the mid-1990s, at a time when they still trusted him, a senior Iraqi security officer offered him some bodyguards. Sadiq turned him down categorically, saying that to accept protection would destroy his credibility as a religious leader, and adding that many people "already consider me a government agent. If I accept this protection that means nobody will pray with me. Thank the president for his concern about my safety, but Allah is the one who will protect me and I accept God's will."[13] The moment of trust did not last long. The ever-watchful Iraqi security forces saw with dismay that their protégé was creating a mass movement, and they tried to rein him in. From about 1997, Mohammed Sadiq started to become more confrontational, and the government restricted his activities more and more, limiting the number of worshippers at the Kufa mosque where he preached and banning religious processions. This period of growing friction was followed by a few months at the end of 1998 and early 1999 when he became convinced that Saddam Hussein intended to kill him.

The attempt by the regime to co-opt Sadiq al-Sadr was part of its broader effort to use religion as cement to keep itself in power. The Baath party had been highly secular in the 1970s, but just before the opening of the war in Kuwait, *Allahu Akbar* (God Is Great) was inscribed on the Iraqi flag. In the wake of defeat there was a surge in popular piety among both

Shia and Sunni. Arab nationalism had been discredited by Saddam's costly military adventures and the failure of corrupt elites in other parts of the Arab world. The Iraqi leader now wanted to ride the wave of Islamic revivalism. He started his so-called Faith campaign in 1994. Restaurants along Abu Nawas Street, where I used to drink *arrack,* an aniseed-flavored liquor, and eat *mazgouf* fish from the Tigris, went dry. In 1996 I visited a favorite Lebanese restaurant called al Mudhif on Abu Nawas, which had formerly served wine and spirits. Knowing of the new "dry" policy, I brought red wine concealed in an anonymous flask with me. "Put it away," whispered a waiter who caught sight of it, and turning pale he pressed his wrists together to indicate that he feared being handcuffed. "Do you want me to go to jail." In the streets of Baghdad there were noticeably more women wearing the veil. Saddam, who carried everything to excess, announced that he would build a hundred new mosques, including one at the old Muthanna municipal airport, which would be the biggest in the world. It was to have a dome the size of a soccer field and would rise from the center of an artificial lake in the shape of the Arab world. My friend who had been a professor of engineering at Baghdad University—he only succeeded in evading a ban on resignations from official jobs by faking a heart attack—was a consultant on the design of the giant mosque. He lamented the absurdity of the project, which could never be completed because Iraq lacked the basic construction materials and equipment. "We do not have high-tensile steel, pile drivers, reinforcement bars, or additives for the cement," he said. The only part of the mosque to be completed was an elegant pavilion from which the self-appointed chief engineer of the project, Saddam himself, could view its progress.

Mohammed Sadiq later downplayed his cooperation with the authorities, but at first it was extensive. "They gave him money and the key to the school taken from Mohammed Baqir al-Sadr in 1980," says a former Dawa militant who is generally unsympathetic to him. "They also gave him the right to authorize residence visas for non-Iraqi Shia students and scholars in Najaf, which was a very important right because so many of them came from other countries." Mohammed Sadiq was allowed to speak and travel and to send his emissaries all over Iraq. His main platform for reaching ordinary Shia was Friday prayers, a central feature of Sunni Islam, but hitherto regarded as heretical by the Shia *ulema.* To a non-Iraqi, this introduction of Friday prayers may not appear a radical move, but when they

were instituted in the mid-1990s it was viewed by Sunni and Shia in Iraq
as an extraordinarily significant development. The theological justifica-
tion for not having Friday prayers was that to do so would be to recognize
the legitimacy of earthly rulers. It appeared that al-Sadr was now prepared
to do so. "We saw it as a sign that the Shia were reconciling with Saddam,"
recalls the Iraqi journalist Ghaith Abdul-Ahad, who was living in Baghdad
at the time. "I remember the dinar rose against the dollar as the news
spread."[14]

Mohammed Sadiq began to send out emissaries to all Shia areas of
Iraq, paying particular attention to the very poor and to the clans and
tribes. "Mohammed Sadiq's movement started in 1992 and was from the
beginning a mass popular movement which attracted the poor and
deprived," says Jafar al-Sadr, the son of Baqir al-Sadr, who was one of
Sadiq's chief lieutenants. He says this distinguished it from his father's
movement, which was more "intellectual, cultural and elitist."[15] Sadiq's
representatives tried to penetrate even to the most remote parts of the
country, such as the marshes of the south, notorious for bandits and dis-
ease. Iraqis identify strongly with their home districts, and the representatives were encouraged to go back to the areas they came from, where
they were known and trusted. Their arrival created great excitement, particularly among the young, and dismay among local Shia religious dignitaries. Mohammed Hassan Ibrahim was seventeen years old in 1996, when
missionaries from Sadiq al-Sadr arrived unexpectedly in Kut, an impoverished Shia city south of Baghdad, and announced they would hold Friday prayers. "The announcement that prayers were to take place was by
posters on the walls and by word of mouth," he remembers. "We went to
the prayers in an unknown mosque because all the mosques and *husseiniyas* [Shia houses of prayer] were strongly connected to each other and
all supported [Grand Ayatollah Ali] al-Sistani. There were a great many
people there and it was a beautiful scene. The prayers were important for
us and most of the sermon was about social problems."[16] Sometimes none
of the Shia mosques could be used. Ali Hussein Khidr, also seventeen years
old at the time and living in the large Shia city of Nassariya on the
Euphrates, says: "I was in Nassariya in 1997 when Friday prayers were
announced for the first time by loudspeaker. They were led by Sayyid
Muammal [Mohammed Sadiq's second son] and, because all the mosques
and *husseiniyas* were controlled by followers of Sayyid al-Sistani we gathered in Hbubi Street, the main street in Nassariya. People came to see this

strange event. They had not seen Friday prayers. Most of those who came to pray were young people who stood in lines and held hands with each other."[17]

What sort of topics did Sadiq al-Sadr's representative talk about? It was not merely to avoid confrontation with the authorities that they concentrated on social and economic rather than dangerously political issues. It was the Sadrist belief that the traditional Marji'iyyah had lost touch with life as it was really lived by ordinary Iraqis, and al-Khoei and al-Sistani dwelt in aristocratic isolation from the world of their followers. Given that, in the 1990s, most Iraqis were desperately trying to cope with a permanent economic crisis, there was a vigorous appetite for advice and counseling on how to survive. One former disciple of Mohammed Sadiq tells an anecdote illustrating his master's pragmatism. "One day, I was sitting with Mohammed Sadiq in his office, when a man came in to ask the price of tomatoes," he says. "The question infuriated me: I thought he had come to mock us. But al-Sadr, wiser and smarter than I am, gave him a detailed answer, giving him the price of different kinds of tomatoes. He had understood what the question was about. I caught up with the man as he left the office and asked him why he had asked the question. He replied: 'In selecting a *marji*' [a religious figure to emulate and whose rulings he would accept], I choose the one who knows my suffering, who is close to the poor and the disinherited.'"[18]

The Sadrists, as they were later known, sought to involve themselves in all aspects of life. The aim was less to establish an Islamic state than to restore Islamic beliefs and mores. Mohammed Sadiq set up a court that did not have penal powers but dealt with divorce and payment of donations to clergy. He issued rulings on tribal law covering questions that the *ulema* had previously avoided, like the payment of blood money after a killing or arranged marriages to prevent or end a blood feud. It was during this period that Sadrists became strong in areas that were to be their political and religious bastions under both Mohammed Sadiq and Muqtada. The most important of these was Sadr City, renamed in 2003 after Sadiq al-Sadr. With a population of two million people it was almost entirely Shia, impoverished and tribally linked to Maysan province in southern Iraq. Yassin Sajad, a young man from Sadr City, explains why its people followed Mohammed Sadiq: "Sayyid al-Sadr had a very good relationship with the tribes of Sadr City, which includes a large number from the south. When he held prayers we found him the only *marji*' who spoke directly and in public about the disintegration of Iraqi society as a result of the economic blockade. He also talked about services, electricity, water, and other things we were short of. Since he had a good relationship with the tribes, most of them followed him and did not follow [Grand Ayatollah Ali] al-Sistani because Sadiq al-Sadr talked to the poor and needy. This is what the Marji'iyyah did not do before."[19]

There was a social revolutionary element in Sadrism as it developed in the 1990s, all the more potent because so many Iraqi Shia had always been poor and many more were becoming so. "Sadiq al-Sadr's power base was well-defined, and Muqtada's present-day followers belong to the same social class," concludes a highly informed study by the Brussels-based International Crisis Group. "The relatively well-to-do, urbanized, educated or commercial classes eyed him [Sadiq al-Sadr] warily, viewing his plebeian, militant Shi'ism as a source of instability and a threat to their interests."[20] The former possessing classes of the Shia community were being destroyed by sanctions or were emigrating abroad. The highly educated could be seen standing for hours outside Arab embassies, clutching CVs showing they spoke three or four languages, hoping for some ill-paid teacher's job in Libya or Syria.

The Sadrists emphasized activism and missionary zeal. They persistently, and sometimes unfairly, contrasted their public campaigns for the Islamic faith and opposition to the authorities with the "quietism" of the followers of al-Khoei and al-Sistani. This militancy was not always well received. Sadiq al-Sadr sent a representative to the marshes around Basra to preach to the impoverished rice growers and buffalo breeders. He was traveling in a small boat when its owner asked him a question about a religious issue and, on receiving an unsatisfactory reply, promptly threw the representative into the water, forcing him to swim to safety. The man returned to Najaf bitterly complaining to Mohammed Sadiq about his treatment but was persuaded to return to the marshlands to try again.

Religious revivalism is often accompanied by self-righteous puritanism, and this was true of the Sadrist delegates. In Basra, the largest Shia city with a population of two million, prayers took place in the street because the mosques were not big enough to accommodate the number of worshippers. Ali Kassem, a local Sadrist militant, says the prayers were led by Sheikh Saleh al-Jizani, who gave a sermon in which "he called the Gypsies to repentance and he explained why the voice of Islam did not reach them and how they wallowed in their lusts and we must reform them by talking to them. In fact this is what happened: There is a street in Basra called Bashar, the Hayaniya district, and the Five Miles area, all of which have bad reputations, but soon there were less noisy dances and the brothels closed."

The Sadrists' greatest appeal was to the embittered Shia youth that was coming of age in the 1990s, as the UN representative Denis Halliday had forecast, without a future and without hope. Speaking about Kut, Mohammed Hassan Ibrahim says that eight or nine weeks after the first Friday prayers were held, there was "a sorting out between those who follow al-Sistani and those who follow al-Sadr. Truthfully, those who supported Sistani were more numerous, but the majority of the young were with Sayyid al-Sadr." The Sadrists consciously targeted the young. A high point of cooperation with the regime came in 1996 when it allowed them to publish a magazine called *al-Huda,* which was edited by Muqtada, Sadiq's youngest son. "The vast majority of al-Sadr followers were young, the oldest among them born in 1964," says Ali Hussein Khidr, the young religious enthusiast from Nassariya. "We were highly motivated by the revolutionary sentiments of al-Sadr and we had had enough of the submission and silence of Taqqiyya." There had always been a strong Messianic theme in Shi'ism in which the world would be put to rights by the return of the twelfth imam, the hidden Mehdi who has never died. But as with the return of the Christian Messiah, the postponement of revolutionary change on earth until the Mehdi's reappearance at an uncertain future date conveniently allowed the present generation to get on with their lives without having to trouble themselves too much about it. Mohammed Sadiq rejected this. Ali Hussein says approvingly: "Sayyid al-Sadr was telling us in his speeches that the Mehdi is not happy with this kind of Taqqiyya and we must create the right kind of conditions for him to reappear."

The content of the Sadrists' preaching was about restoring traditional Islamic customs or restrictions such as the prohibition on the sale or consumption of alcohol. His followers started telling taxi drivers not to pick up women if they were not wearing the veil. There was a fatwa forbidding people from watching the Shabab television channel, owned by Uday, Saddam's playboy son, which, though popular because it showed Western films, was considered a source of corruption (when the Americans took Baghdad in 2003, they thought Iraqis would be eager to see the latest Hollywood movies, only to learn that they had already seen pirated versions on Shabab).

Confrontation was inevitable. Under Saddam's rule, the date of the founding of the Baath party and a highly fictionalized account of its history were drilled into students in Iraqi schools, while there was nothing about the Shia imams and little about Islamic Iraq. Mohammed Sadiq was pushing Islamic and Shia culture as a direct antidote to Baathism. Soon there were menacing signs that Saddam was beginning to realize that his plan to install his own candidate as religious leader of the Shia had spectacularly backfired. One man had no doubts about the final outcome of the escalating struggle between the government and its erstwhile protégé. "It will all end with one bullet," predicted Mohammed Sadiq to his disciples.[21]

CHAPTER EIGHT

A Second Assassination

Students entering their classroom in the Najaf hawza at the beginning of the 1998 school year were greeted by a strange request from their professor. He asked them to remove and disassemble their turbans so they became just a long piece of cloth. When the students had complied with this curious demand their professor immediately asked them to remake their turbans and put them on again. Some, who came from religious families, speedily did so, but others, mostly those who had entered the seminary recently, struggled to rewrap the cloth so as to re-create the turban. The purpose of the exercise, recalls Sheikh Akram al-Assadi, who was a student in the hawza at the time, was to identify those students whose ignorance in the matter of turbans revealed that they might be police spies. "The government sent a hundred to a hundred fifty young security and intelligence officers to be students and teachers inside the hawza," says Sheikh al-Assadi. "Some of those who had important jobs in [Mohammed Sadiq] al-Sadr's office became students only after the uprising of 1991 and after al-Sadr himself became important. So many new and strange people were entering the hawza that we knew they were from the intelligence agencies."[1]

The unwrapping of the turbans might be taken as a symptom of the paranoid anxiety inevitable among people living in any police state. Sheikh al-Assadi's very high figure for the number of Baathist spies infiltrating the hawza is suspect since they could scarcely all have been so incompetent as to be readily identifiable. It is also true that in an author-

itarian state, security services spread rumors that their all-seeing eye is
everywhere in order to demoralize dissenters. But in Iraq, the state had a
multitude of informants, easily recruited through cash payments, fear of
arrest, and favors granted or withheld. Saddam would not have started so
risky a tactic as devolving power over the hawza to Sadiq al-Sadr and
allowing him to appoint prayer readers in hundreds of cities and towns
without monitoring his actions closely.

Right up to the moment that security agents ambushed and killed al-
Sadr and his two elder sons, Mustafa and Muammal, at a traffic circle in
Najaf on February 19, 1999, many of his Shia opponents openly denounced
him as a collaborator with the regime. After his death, when they saw Sadiq
al-Sadr's vast popularity among the Shia masses, these critics were deeply
embarrassed by their previous allegations. There was an unseemly scram-
ble to suppress denunciatory pamphlets and articles by the exiled groups,
notably the Tehran-based SCIRI of Mohammed Baqir al-Hakim and the
remnants of Dawa, by now divided into several different factions. Today
these documents are difficult to obtain, closely guarded by their authors,
who are reticent about the republication of their ill-timed criticism of a
man whom many Shia regard as having semidivine attributes. Among the
Sadrists there lingers a bitter sense of betrayal by other Shia religious leaders, a belief that, while they were fighting Saddam and dying, others, like
Grand Ayatollah al-Sistani, stood by in silence or lived comfortably in exile
like al-Hakim in Tehran or Sayyid Majid al-Khoei in London.

The feuds of the Shia religious parties are important because the divisions and hatreds stemming from events in the 1990s are vital to an understanding of the men who, a decade later, had come to dominate the Iraqi
government. By 2007 the leader of Dawa was Nouri al-Maliki, no longer
a hunted exile in Damascus but the prime minister of Iraq, who spoke by
video phone to President George W. Bush every fortnight. The most powerful party within his coalition of Shia religious parties was SCIRI. Their
sometime ally and frequent opponent within the Shia community was
Muqtada al-Sadr, by now leader of a movement whose Mehdi Army militia was identified by President Bush as one of the greatest threats to the
United States in Iraq. Grand Ayatollah Ali al-Sistani, whom Mohammed
Sadiq denounced as a pawn of Sayyid Majid al-Khoei, retains immense
influence over the Shia community.

The allegations against Sadiq al-Sadr are worth looking at in greater
detail, because they illustrate the subtle as well as the crude methods used

by Saddam Hussein to shore up his authority during his last decade in power. Sheikh Akram al-Assadi explains the case against al-Sadr, though he says he does not necessarily believe all the charges. The essence of this is that Sadr was the creature of the Baathist regime when they released him from prison in 1991, three months after the uprising. He was naïve, often changed his mind, was easily influenced by those around him, and had made a full confession to his interrogators in 1972 and 1974. In 1991 he first supported the uprising, but he later criticized it when it failed. The regime wanted to use him to control the hawza, so it gave him control of all religious schools, and all new students had to have his authorization. Only he was able to obtain residence visas for the many students from elsewhere in the Shia world. The Iraqi authorities funded him and allowed him control over what religious books were published in Najaf. It was further claimed that Rokan Ghafour al-Tikriti, the nephew and aide-de-camp of Saddam, acted as liaison between the regime and Sadiq al-Sadr through his eldest son, Mustafa. By 1998, SCIRI in Tehran was saying in pamphlets that militants should be very careful in dealing with al-Sadr and "not reveal their real names because he was surrounded by members of the security and intelligence services."[2]

Mohammed Salem, a student of Mohammed Sadiq, rebuts these and other charges, saying that "Sayyid al-Sadr wanted to exploit the weakness of the regime after the uprising, though he was absolutely against the government. He was waiting for his moment to fight the regime, but first he needed a truce with it." Salem agrees there were security agents among Mohammed Sadiq's students though he contends this was also true of other clergy. As for Rokan Ghafour al-Tikriti, one of whose jobs was liaising with the southern Shia tribes, Mohammed Salem says he only came to see Sadiq al-Sadr once, at the end of 1998, and this was to tell him to stop his Friday prayers. Sayyid al-Sadr's response was to put the head of his brown walking stick on Rokan's chest and say defiantly: "Tell your master I will not stop prayers as long as I am alive."[3]

Whatever Saddam Hussein and his security forces expected from Sadiq al-Sadr, he betrayed them. This was why they assassinated him and his two elder sons. There were obviously police agents in his entourage, as there were everywhere else in Iraq. But Mohammed Salem argues convincingly that not many of al-Sadr's representatives can have been double agents, since "more than 120 imams and preachers who followed al-Sadr were arrested or executed before or after his assassination." At the same time,

Mohammed Sadiq, for several years at least, must have convinced the Baathist authorities, some of the most suspicious men in the world, that he was genuinely cooperating with them. The rumor about Rokan's contacts with Mustafa is interesting because Rokan played a central role in another Saddam tactic, this one aimed at securing his power during the 1990s. The plan was to cultivate the Shia tribes of southern Iraq, both urban and rural, pay off their leaders, and use them as one more instrument of government control. Saddam knew the Iraqi state machine was getting weaker because of lack of money, and that the Shia tribes, whose power the Baath party had previously sought to eliminate, were getting stronger. Instead of opposing this process he sought to bring it under his control so his authority would be strengthened. At an early meeting with the Shia tribal sheikhs, Saddam even apologized for land reforms that had destroyed their feudal power. Where there were no sheikhs to cultivate, or where they were hostile to the regime, new ones were appointed. These were known contemptuously among Iraqis as "Taiwan sheikhs" because they were deemed fake or secondhand copies, like cheap products made in Taiwan.[4]

I used to see these sheikhs from distant provinces staying at government expense in the al-Rashid Hotel. They were known to hotel staff as "the flying sheikhs" because they were fascinated by the hotel elevators, which they had never seen before. Accompanied by their heavily armed bodyguards they would take the elevators up and down for hours with evident enjoyment. But though despised as hillbillies by the staff of the al-Rashid Hotel, the Shia tribal leaders had real authority. The differing levels of financial compensation for victims of violence is revealed in an agreement signed by four clans in Baghdad at this time: "For physical assault with the bare hands ID [Iraqi dinars] 75,000; for an assault with a wooden club causing no bleeding ID 100,000–150,000; for an assault with a sharp instrument which involves no loss of leg or limb ID 200,000–300,000. If death is caused the blood money runs into millions depending on the victim's gender, age or work."[5]

Much of Mohammed Sadiq's missionary zeal was directed toward the tribes, particularly those in the slums of what was then known as Saddam City (now Sadr City), in Baghdad. The laws and customs of the tribes were often at odds with those followed by the traditional Shia clergy. This made them particularly open to the Messianic revivalism of Sadrist prayer leaders. "The integration of Iraqi tribalism and Shiite puritanism has yielded a potent and cultural force," suggests Mahan Abedin, an analyst of Iraqi and Iranian politics. "It is partly for this reason that the government sponsored Mohammed Sadiq al-Sadr. In his controversial book *Fiqh al-Asha'ir* (Tribal Jurisprudence), Mohammed Sadiq al-Sadr has sought to reconcile tribal customs with *Sharia* and conferred upon tribal leaders the right to administer religious law."[6] Saddam saw the role of Mohammed Sadiq as being one way of securing his authority over the poorest and most tribal of the Shia who had revolted in 1991.

For people like Mohammed Sadiq, living on their nerves because violent death is always around the corner, petty disputes become magnified out of all proportion. Friction with other Shia religious leaders is evident in episodes witnessed by his students and is sometimes captured in tape-recorded remarks. At one point Mohammed Sadiq issued a fatwa permitting smoking during fasting, and was asked why other members of the hierarchy made an opposite ruling. He replied impatiently: "Habibi, go and ask the others why they permit the chewing of gum [during fasting]. Are they only forbidding smoking because al-Sadr is in favor of it?"[7] A tape recording made by Mohammed Sadiq in 1998 refers to a quarrel with the al-Hakim family over rights to control a school in Najaf, and their questioning of his scholarly credentials. He says he wanted to settle the quarrel but his overtures were rejected. When al-Sadr visited al-Sistani in his home, he was wounded by the failure of the Grand Ayatollah to address more than a few cursory remarks to him or accompany him to the door to say good-bye. Elsewhere Mohammed Sadiq wonders what right Sayyid Majid al-Khoei, by then running the al-Khoei Foundation in London, had to spend funds donated because of the great prestige of his father.[8]

Looking at these squabbles it is easy to forget that opposing Saddam Hussein in Iraq while he was still in power was an act of great courage. Death and detention were never far away. Nor was this courage confined to the Sadrists. Many of those in exile had lost members of their families. Of Mohammed Baqir al-Hakim's eight brothers, six had been killed by Saddam. The so-called quietist clergy following al-Khoei were not immune. More than one hundred of them, including al-Khoei's son-in-law, had disappeared during the mass arrests in 1991. His son Mohammed Taqi was killed in what the al-Khoei family believe was a government-arranged car accident between Najaf and Kerbala on July 21, 1994. These deaths were in keeping with the Shia tradition, stretching back to Imam Hussein, of martyrdom in opposing tyranny.

Furthermore, many of the issues furiously debated by Shia spiritual leaders are not unique to Iraq. They have been at the core of religious and philosophical dispute in other countries down the course of history. The al-Sadr family advocated direct political involvement by the Islamic clergy in defense of the people and against Saddam Hussein. Grand Ayatollahs al-Khoei and al-Sistani opposed it, arguing that they must remain above the political fray or the purity of religion would be sullied and discredited. Their attitude was not so very different from that of Jesus two thousand years earlier when, asked by opponents of the Roman occupation of Palestine about paying tribute to the authorities, he famously retorted: "Render unto Caesar that which is Caesar's."

Relations between Mohammed Sadiq al-Sadr and the regime in Baghdad reached their high point in 1996 and then began to sour. The immense numbers attending Friday prayers alarmed the Iraqi security services. They were also beginning to suspect that al-Sadr's cooperation was temporary and tactical, and that he was, in practice, one of Saddam Hussein's most dangerous enemies. This revelation was slow in coming and Mohammed Sadiq tried to put off a final confrontation, which he correctly assumed would lead to his own death, as long as possible. "He realized that with Friday prayers he could fight the oppressor indirectly by confronting him ideologically and building a mass base," says Sheikh Yassin al-Assadi, a contemporary eyewitness in Najaf. "He was wary at first of saying a word that the authorities could use as evidence to arrest him, and his criticism of the authorities was only by means of hints."

Friday prayers led by Mohammed Sadiq only started in Kufa in 1998, but in other southern governorates they were initiated earlier. In Kut they began in 1996,[9] and al-Sadr issued a fatwa inaugurating them in al-Thawra in Baghdad in 1997.[10] He was also eager to resume the ritualized pilgrimages to Kerbala and Najaf, which were so central to the popular Shia religious tradition. These had been banned or curtailed over the years. Mohammed Hassan Ibrahim from Kut heeded a call by al-Sadr to take part in the walk to Kerbala in 1997 to celebrate the birthday of Imam Mehdi. What followed shows that neither the authorities, al-Sadr himself, nor rival Shia religious leaders were quite ready for a confrontation. Mohammed Hassan recalls that the Baathist officials rejected al-Sadr's request for the march to be authorized because "they feared the march would turn into an Islamic political demonstration against the regime.

Al-Sadr ordered the marchers, who had already started the pilgrimage, to stop and go home in order to prevent bloodshed. I was among the marchers. It was wintertime and the weather was cool. Sometimes we would walk in the main road and at others we would go through the farms where people would hide us from the police or disguise us as one of themselves. Sometimes we saw police in plainclothes walking with us, but they did not do anything to us, just collected information." Despite hearing al-Sadr's order to stop the march, Mohammed Hassan continued walking to Kerbala with two friends. He stayed on in Kerbala to go to a sermon delivered by Mohammed Sadiq, who "hinted clearly that the regime in Baghdad had done a service to colonialism and the colonialists and Zionists when it stopped visits to the Imam Hussein shrine." He went on to attack the passivity of the leaders of the hawza on the question of the march. Al-Sadr said: "One notices that on the question of the march and the ban on the march the traditional silent hawza or their representatives said nothing, as if they don't know what is happening in Iraqi society."

By the following year, Mohammed Sadiq was addressing hundreds of thousands of people gathered in and around the mosque in Kufa. It is worth giving at some length the story of Ali Hussein Khidr, the seventeen-year-old from Nassariya, whose account conveys the enthusiasm of young Shia teenagers for the Sadrist movement. He and his friends went repeatedly to Kufa to attend Friday prayers. "We traveled on Thursday afternoon by car to Kufa," he says. "In winter we slept at friends' homes or sometimes somebody working with al-Sadr found a place for us to sleep despite the very large number of people in the same situation. In summer we either slept in the mosque or in the street. We were prepared to endure the hot weather in order to see al-Sadr. The regime began harassing young people in Nassariya traveling to Kufa. The Baathist authorities gave the driver of a bus a piece of paper that was meant to make it easier to enter Kufa, but when he handed it over to the guards at the entrance to the city [there were always checkpoints on roads leading into Iraqi cities and towns] they arrested him." This cut down the numbers going to Kufa but only marginally, and Ali Hussein and his friends would simply hitch rides in private cars or go in vehicles owned by committed Sadrists. He says the number of arrests was not large "because the regime did not want a clash with so many people, especially with the youth, after the uprising."

Ali Hussein describes typical Friday prayers as delivered by Mohammed Sadiq in the great mosque in Kufa. "There were very large throngs of people singing songs and shouting slogans to welcome him. He got out of an old Mitsubishi car, dating from 1982, accompanied by his sons Muammal, Muqtada, and Mustafa. They had difficulty getting into the mosque because of the immense crowds. Once inside he would retire to a small room, close the door, and nobody saw him again until he mounted the podium and began his speech. He would first pray to the Prophet and then start a topic without preamble. Once, when he delivered the second of his sermons, I saw people trying to touch his cloak and kiss his hand. He was wearing a white shroud and leaning on a brown stick. During his walk he saw a small child with a beautiful face and walked with him to where he would speak. He then thanked all those who were attending the prayers and asked the security and intelligence officers observing them to also join in the prayers. He repeated his well-known slogans starting with 'No, no to America,' 'No, no to Israel.' Then he delivered a sermon aimed at ending differences between Sunni and Shia, and invited Sunni to pray in Shia mosques and asked Shia not to refuse to pray before a Sunni prayer leader."[11]

All the while his tone was getting sharper and his opposition to the regime less discreet. For instance, in October 1997 there was a referendum, the result carefully fixed in advance, on the position of Saddam Hussein as a leader. The regime's slogan was "Yes to Saddam Hussein." But in a sermon delivered on October 15, 1997, Mohammed Sadiq said: "*No!* Yes is just for God."

The personality of Mohammed Sadiq is elusive because those who came to talk to him in Najaf or Kufa mostly saw him as a living saint. Many of these were young men who found him approachable, modest, and willing to discuss matters they found embarrassing to talk about, such as "temporary marriages." His approach was deliberately democratic, and his sermons were delivered using common Iraqi speech, whereas his lectures to his students were in more complex Arabic. This may explain why his opponents accused him of naïveté and simplicity. He succeeded in giving his followers, often very young, confidence in themselves. "When we entered Najaf city we felt as if al-Sadr was telling us that we are the owner of the land," recalls Ali Hussein Khidr. "It was as if he was saying you are Shia, you are one of Imam Ali's followers, you are strong."[12]

For most of his short public career Mohammed Sadiq focused on the practical issues immediately facing the Shia community. Avoiding political questions was also part of his effort to postpone confrontation with the state. At the same time, he believed that the active and militant Marji'iyyah must prepare the way for the twelfth imam, the return of the hidden Mehdi who would end oppression on earth. In the longer term, his support for an Islamic state ruled by the learned jurist (*Wilayat al-Faqih*) was in the tradition of Mohammed Baqir al-Sadr and Ayatollah Khomeini. He did not see this spiritual primacy as being exerted over all Muslims, as did the Iranian leaders. The question was in any case theoretical in Iraq under the iron rule of Saddam. It was also going to remain theoretical in the future, since Iraq may be sixty percent Shia but it is also forty percent Sunni if Sunni Arab and the Kurds, who are overwhelmingly Sunni, are taken together. The complete primacy of a Shia religious leader was never feasible. But when al-Sadr proclaimed his leadership over the Iraqi Shia, the move was deeply resented in Iran. His offices in Iran were immediately closed and his representatives expelled. "All ties were broken as soon as Mohammed Sadiq proclaimed his *Wilayat al-Faqih* because . . . it contradicted Ali Khamenei's *Wilayat al-Faqih*," said one of Muqtada's representatives. "I think that is the reason why Iran shut down al-Sadr's offices in Iran at the time."[13]

The escalating confrontation between the Sadrists and Saddam in 1998 took place against a background of ever-increasing pressure on Baghdad by the United States. The crisis over the access of UN inspectors looking for Iraq's supposed weapons of mass destruction (WMD) finally boiled over on December 16, 1998, when the United States launched Operation Desert Fox. Once again bombs and missiles fell on Baghdad and other Iraqi cities. Iraqi officials guessed that the brief bombardment was a diversionary tactic by President Bill Clinton as impeachment proceedings began in Washington over his affair with Monica Lewinsky. But the international crisis over WMDs made the regime nervous. Its tolerance of al-Sadr was already wearing thin. A more repressive policy toward the Shia was presaged by the mysterious assassinations of two leading ayatollahs—Ayatollah al-Gharawi and Ayatollah Burujurdi—earlier in 1998. These killings were universally blamed on the regime by the Shia community. The UN reported that twenty-five hundred people had been executed in Abu Ghraib prison since the end of 1997, including some who had taken part in the 1991 uprising.[14]

The regime was impatient at Sadiq's equivocations concerning overt support for Saddam Hussein. It wanted him to praise openly the Iraqi leader at Friday prayers. It ordered him to cancel the march to Kerbala at the end of 1998 and to limit the vast congregations attending his prayer meetings. According to Sheikh Yassin al-Assadi, Mohammed Sadiq realized that an open breach with the regime was now inevitable and would end with his death. He therefore "refused to invoke Saddam's name at Friday prayers despite the insistence of Saddam and his aides who said it was a political necessity because of U.S.-British aggression."[15] In a sermon on February 12, 1999, he called for the release of the 101 clergy and students arrested at the same time as Grand Ayatollah al-Khoei in 1991. As he shouted this demand, the vast audience of tens of thousand in the Kufa mosque echoed back his words, chanting: "Immediately! Immediately! Immediately! We want! We want! We want!" Al-Sadr's aides reportedly said that he had been telephoned by Saddam himself asking him to withdraw the demand, and when he refused, the Iraqi leader slammed down the phone.[16] Even if Saddam did not make the call himself, he sent a series of intimidating messengers, such as Mohammed Hamza al-Zubeidi, the notoriously brutal Baath governor of the mid-Euphrates region who had been videotaped mistreating Shia rebels in 1991. He told Mohammed Sadiq: "There is a presidential order forbidding Friday prayers this week." Al-Sadr responded: "I will pray, I will pray, I will pray."

The government was also worried by signs that for the first time since 1991 Shia militants were switching to armed resistance. The most serious outbreak was in Nassariya. Ali Hussein Khidr, a committed follower of Mohammed Sadiq, gives an account of an abortive Shia uprising that took place at this time. "I was with Sheikh Abdel Karim Ismail with groups of Sayyid [Mohammed Sadiq] al-Sadr's followers who planned to overthrow the government. Its agents knew of our plan, ambushed us, and arrested Sheikh Abdel Karim with a group of young people. There were violent clashes in Nassariya and the governor's headquarters [was] attacked with rockets. The government lost control of the city for several days. I fled with family to the villages so as not to be arrested or executed like other young people. We were in a village whose people were from the clan of Jouber and the village had the same name. Mohammed Hamza al-Zubeidi deployed the Republican Guard. But the village and the clan were well armed with antiaircraft and antitank weapons supplied by the Badr corps in Iran. When al-Zubeidi came to the village he completely destroyed it: he cut off the water supply and bombed and executed many villagers, including women and children. My family and I miraculously escaped because we were some distance from the village. We heard the sound of the bombs, the shooting, and the screams until they died away. The situation was very difficult in the city and all the cities of the south."[17]

People in Najaf saw ominous signs that the regime was preparing to act against Mohammed Sadiq. Dr. Hassan Mustafa, about thirty years old at the time and now a professor at Najaf University, came from a religious family that had good relations with the hawza. He was an attentive witness to the last days of al-Sadr. He says the atmosphere in the city was very tense. When Sadiq al-Sadr entered the Kufa mosque, an official approached him and told him not to hold prayers. He rejected the advice. Security forces were very visible in the mosque, says Dr. Mustafa: "We knew the faces of most of them, but this time there were more of them and they looked hostile. None of them were from Najaf, and from their appearance they appeared to be from the west not the south of Iraq." (In other words they were light-skinned men from the overwhelmingly Sunni Anbar province that covers western Iraq and not darker men from the Shia south.) In Najaf, checkpoints began to spring up every 150 to 200 yards, manned by soldiers from the Hammurabi Republican Guard division. This started a week or ten days before the assassination, and then the faces at the checkpoints changed again: "There was a special force called the Fedayeen Saddam, brutal people trained to murder and sabotage, known for their ferocity and frightening appearance." The regime was also sending fresh troops to Shia areas like al-Thawra (now Sadr City), Hurriya, and al-Bai'aa areas in Baghdad as well as Kufa and Najaf. It had offered Mohammed Sadiq guards but Sadiq refused them. There is evidence from another source that Mohammed Sadiq knew what was about to happen. Around February 15, Mustafa al-Khadimi, an ex-Dawa militant then living in London, got a message from Mohammed Sadiq via Jafar al-Sadr, the son of Mohammed Baqir and a senior lieutenant of Mohammed Sadiq. It was to be passed on to Ahmed Chalabi, one of the leaders of the Iraqi opposition. The message read simply: "I need help. Saddam is going to kill me."[18]

On February 19, Mohammed Sadiq was returning to his house with his two elder sons, Mustafa and Muammal, and their driver. By Dr. Mustafa's account, as they were entering the 1920 Revolution traffic circle, a second car, later identified as an Oldsmobile, was waiting. It was filled with gunmen armed with machine guns. They riddled al-Sadr's car, killing his sons and the driver immediately. Al-Sadr alone remained alive but was badly wounded in the head and legs. He was taken to the Saddam Hospital, about two miles away. "I was with one of my friends and they stopped us from going through the main gate of the hospital, so we tried and failed to get in through a side entrance," says Dr. Mustafa. There were security men everywhere, from other parts of Iraq but not from Najaf. Outside the gates a crowd was shouting and trying to get in. Staff in the hospital later told Dr. Mustafa that these men kept doctors from entering the room where Mohammed Sadiq and his two sons had been taken. "One of the doctors said that Sayyid al-Sadr was alive when they brought him into the hospital, but they let him bleed to death."

In al-Thawra and in other Shia cities of southern Iraq there was an explosive reaction as news of the assassination spread. Nobody had any doubt who was behind it. The regime was prepared for an angry popular reaction to the murder, but even so it must have been aghast at the extent of the outbreaks of violence. The willingness of so many people to die or face arrest while making hopeless protests shows the extent to which al-Sadr was seen as a Messiah. "I was one who loved Sayyid al-Sadr," says Sajad Ali, thirty-six, from Sadr City, "because he was the only man who tried to assist poor and needy people, especially the young, at a time when there was widespread unemployment, the economic blockade, and injustice by the authorities." Protestors gathered around the Muhsin mosque in al-Thawra and chanted: "Down with the regime." They called for revenge. The clashes between the demonstrators and the security forces there lasted for hours. Fifteen of the latter, including a major, were killed and several of their cars burned. They opened fire indiscriminately, killing and wounding numerous demonstrators. Sajad Ali said four hundred people died in the hail of bullets. Foreign diplomats estimated that the number was forty to eighty dead, and an Iraqi government official privately told a foreign aid official that the true figure was fifty-four.[19] "When I heard the news of his [Mohammed Sadiq's] death I was shocked (I was twenty-eight at the time), and I went with my friends to the mosque to ask for weapons to resist. But at the mosque we agreed with its imam Sheikh Ali al-Ka'abi to hold prayers as a protest the following Friday, when he chanted and shouted against the regime. Afterward there were clashes and Sheikh Ali al-Ka'abi was arrested. They said they would release him if he agreed not to criticize the government, but he refused. At the time of his arrest he hit one of the investigators, so he was held for a long time and severely tortured." Surprisingly, he was released, but he continued his attacks on the government and was arrested again and finally executed.

The courage and determination of Sadiq al-Sadr's supporters is astonishing. On the second Friday after the killing his followers returned to the Muhsin mosque. They were determined to die. Sajad Ali says: "This time we tied our feet and ankles together with strong rope so we could not escape when the security forces attacked us and we would continue to pray until martyrdom. Instead they beat us with sticks that gave us electric shocks that did not kill us but stopped us praying." Some of the worshippers in the mosque, however, were shot and killed. "The authorities would only return the bodies to their families if they paid for the bullets that killed them and promised not to perform mourning ceremonies."[20] Repression was finally effective. Resistance ebbed away because of the mass arrests and executions of the very young. Sajad Ali makes a surprising admission for a man so committed to Sadiq. He says that even in al-Thawra, opposition to Saddam was not total because "in many houses, though not in all, there was a brother and sister who was a Baathist."

A month after these first outbreaks of spontaneous violence there was an ill-coordinated uprising that became known as the al-Sadr intifada. It was not on the scale of the 1991 rebellion, and the regime crushed it so swiftly and ruthlessly that little news of these bloody events surfaced outside Iraq. A general uprising in all the cities of southern Iraq was originally planned for February 28, but instead the outbreaks took place one after another. The most serious revolt was in Basra on March 17, 1999, when, at night, groups of armed men attacked government buildings, intelligence headquarters, and Baath party offices. There was heavy fighting in which at least forty Baath party members were killed.[21] Jassem, then a thirty-six-year-old Sadrist sympathizer and one of the few survivors of this little-known episode, says that the uprising was the work of a mixture of groups. "There were about 168 students from the Faculty of Engineering in the University of Basra," he says, as well as a group from Hezbollah (an Iraqi movement not connected to the Lebanese movement of the same name) and the Badr Corps. "There was meant to be a simultaneous uprising in all the southern provinces." The rebels waited for the arrival of the ten-thousand-strong Badr Brigade stationed in Iran, its participation essential if there was to be any chance of success, because they were well-trained and well-armed professional soldiers. Jassem says the leaders were to be Karim Mahmoud, a famed guerrilla leader from Amara who was also known as the Lord of the Marshes and led the Hezbollah group; Sheikh Saleh al-Jizani from Basra; and Sheikh Abdel Karim Ismail, also from Basra. But at the last moment Mohammed Baqir al-Hakim, the leader of SCIRI, who controlled the Badr group, postponed the uprising. "We don't know the reason for the delay to this day, but we felt let down," says Jassem. The rebels went ahead with the plans anyway and "many martyrs fell during their attack on the party and security headquarters, where we killed large numbers of the security forces including senior Baathists and intelligence officers." Jassem says that they gained control of the center of Basra for two nights before troops from the 3rd (Iraqi army) Corps and the Baathists retook it.[22]

Government vengeance was savage. A four-page document listing 120 men who were executed was found by looters in the office of the General Security Directorate after British troops took Basra in 2003. The youngest victim was sixteen and the eldest was thirty-six. Some were executed by the families of Baathists who had been killed in the uprising, according to notes on the list. The bodies were buried in mass graves by Basra Airport. The executions were carried out under the authority of Ali Hassan al-Majid, who was in charge of southern Iraq. He summoned Shia clan and tribal leaders to a meeting where he furiously berated them, saying those who went to Friday prayers were criminals, claiming a fatwa had been issued by Shia clerics allowing brothers to marry their sisters, and demanding that they cease helping the Sadrists and cooperate in hunting them down.

Mohammed Baqir al-Hakim probably called off Badr support for the uprising because he could see it was doomed. The Iranians, who had veto power over his actions, are also likely to have forbidden Badr troops from crossing into Iraq from Iran. But the failed intifada and the assassination of Sadiq al-Sadr himself, the very man whom al-Hakim had been denouncing as a police agent, deepened the hostility that amounted at times to hatred between the Sadrists and the exiled groups. This had significant repercussions after 2003, when the Shia leaders began to assert themselves as the new leaders of Iraq.

There is a final, dramatic episode in the story of Mohammed Sadiq, which illustrates the cultlike devotion he attracted among ordinary Iraqis. It took place in Qom, the Iranian holy city, where there were thousands of Iraqi refugees, guerrilla fighters from Badr, and religious students from Iraq. They heard the news of al-Sadr's murder the day after it had happened. Horrified, many of them immediately rushed to the house of his representative in Iran, Sayyid Jafar al-Sadr, the son of Mohammed Baqir al-Sadr. It was Jafar who had relayed the message from Mohammed Sadiq to London a few days earlier, saying that Sadiq expected Saddam to kill him. "The masses gathered in front of his house and in the street to express their pain and sorrow at what had happened," recalls an eyewitness. "They chanted against Sayyid Mohammed Baqir al-Hakim and Saddam, and some scuffled with those who had criticized al-Sadr, but the situation did not get out of control."[23]

The murder of Mohammed Sadiq by the Iraqi leader put both al-Hakim and the Iranians in an embarrassing position. The former had publicly denounced him as a collaborator, and the Iranian government had closed Jafar's office when Mohammed Sadiq had declared himself the supreme leader of the Iraqi Shia, thus contesting the claim of Ali Khamenei, the Iranian supreme leader. In a conciliatory if hypocritical gesture, the office of Khamenei arranged for a mourning ceremony at the A'azum mosque, one of the largest in Qom. It was filled to overflowing with Iraqi exiles, Iranian officials, and Shia clergy, so latecomers had to stand outside the mosque. Al-Hakim unwisely decided to attend. As he took his seat the crowd in the mosque began to shout: "Long live al-Sadr! The al-Hakim family are traitors!" The preacher pleaded with them to drop this slogan, but without success. Jafar al-Sadr, who had been receiving delegations, then tried to calm the congregation, but was also ignored. "Some people began to throw their shoes, cigarette packets, and anything that came to hand at Sayyid al-Hakim to express their anger and even their hatred," said an Iraqi observing the scene. "He decided to leave the mosque as soon as his car and security guards arrived. While he was moving towards the car more shoes were hurled at him."

The explosive growth of the al-Sadr movement, the assassination of its leader, and the "al-Sadr intifada" that followed were, taken together, the most serious domestic crisis faced by Saddam's regime between 1991 and 2003. It was an extraordinary achievement for Mohammed Sadiq to have created such a powerful mass movement under the eyes of the Iraqi authorities. His blend of Islamic revivalism, populism, and Iraqi nationalism had a strong appeal to the mass of Shia. Depleted by death, flight, and mass arrests, his movement went deep underground but did not disappear. It was to reemerge after the fall of Saddam with Sadiq al-Sadr's youngest son, Muqtada, at its head. The most convincing explanation for his rapid rise, according to a member of the Dawa party, is that "Muqtada's movement was built by his father. All he did was help it to evolve and continue the process initiated by Mohammed Sadiq al-Sadr."[24]

CHAPTER NINE

Muqtada Survives

Muqtada was lucky to survive. He probably owed his life to the hypocrisy of the regime, which pretended that it had nothing to do with the assassination of his father and his two brothers Mustafa and Muammal. Government officials brazenly attended the mourning ceremonies in Najaf to commiserate with him. Muqtada, now responsible for his mother and his brothers' wives and children, was careful to play along with the pretense and sent a letter formally thanking the government for its sympathy. Even so, an office he set up to receive condolences from more credible mourners was swiftly closed by the *mukhabarat*.[1] The regime produced its own unlikely explanation of what had happened. The official government newspaper *al-Jumhuriyah* described the killings as "among the many conspiracies against Iraq" and an effort to "disturb internal security" but reassuringly added that several suspects had been arrested. The Iraq News Agency, on April 6, 1999, announced that two clerics, Sheikh Abd al-Hassan Abbas al-Kufi and Sheikh Ali Qazim Hajman, and two religious students, Ahmed Mustafa Ardebili and Haidar Ali Hussein, had been executed for the crime. The statement said the four men were "foreigners," implying they were Iranians. In other media the regime blamed paid intelligence agents who were part of an American-Zionist plot. The claims impressed few people inside or outside Iraq. One of the men, Sheikh al-Kufi, had been arrested in Najaf on December 24, 1998, and could not have taken part in the assassination.[2] "Baghdad television," says Dr. Hassan Mustafa, "showed the confession of the detainees, who were dressed as Shia clerics, in which they spoke of the assassination of al-Sadr and his two sons, Mustafa and Muammal. But the confessions were obviously made in a torture chamber and did not fool anybody, or obscure the fact that Saddam's regime was responsible."[3]

This clumsy cover story had the advantage, from Muqtada's point of view, that, after claiming to have caught the assassins of his family, the regime could not easily move to kill him as well, though, going by Saddam's history, it would have done so if its security men had suspected he posed the slightest threat. In later years, Western news agencies were to use the cliché "firebrand cleric" to describe Muqtada, but the phrase, implying spontaneous and ill-considered militancy, is highly misleading. On the contrary, his success in Iraqi politics has often been due to his ability to make swift retreats, politically and militarily, when faced with an adversary of superior strength. His politics might be radical, but he would scarcely have survived after 1999 unless his behavior had been carefully calculated not to arouse any suspicion on the part of the *mukhabarat* that he was a danger to the regime. He neither accused the Iraqi security services of murdering his father and brothers nor did he play any role in the sporadic uprisings that followed. Saddam may have feared that the murder of another al-Sadr could transform these outbreaks into general Shia rebellion. "The government balked at killing Muqtada al-Sadr because it feared this would provoke a popular uprising," says Sheikh Ali, the nom de guerre of one of Muqtada's aides and later a leader of the Mehdi Army. "Members of the Marji'iyyah, senior religious figures, advised Muqtada to stick to attending religious classes and to reduce the number of people he met to a minimum so as to preserve his own life. They pointed out that there was nobody left in his immediate family, just himself and his surviving brother, Murtada, who did not have an important position." (Murtada is variously described as being sick or a recluse and to have died around 2005.)

Muqtada's low profile over the next four years was not just a matter of choice. His every action was closely monitored. "The security forces tracked his movements even inside his own home," recalls Sheikh Ali. "Everybody and everything had to be inspected before it was allowed into his house, which was surrounded by security men."[4] The regime's excuse for this close surveillance was that it was intent on protecting Muqtada from the same dire fate as his relatives. One commentator suggests that the permanent stress under which Muqtada lived during these years "may have psychologically scarred the young cleric."[5] Certainly, these years of living under such close scrutiny, never knowing if he would end the day in prison or be killed by the regime like all his close relatives, explains Muqtada's continual wariness and suspicion of those around him.

Muqtada is the fourth and youngest son of Mohammed Sadiq al-Sadr. He was born on August 12, 1973, which would make him twenty-five years old when his father and brothers were assassinated. He married a daughter of Mohammed Baqir al-Sadr in 1994, but they have no children. His many enemies were later to claim that his father paid little attention to him and did not rate his talents highly,[6] though this is strenuously denied by his followers. Mohammed Sadiq al-Sadr operated very much through his three politically active sons, who were his closest aides. Ayatollahs normally rely on their sons as their political lieutenants, but Sadiq was doubly dependent on them because of his need for tight security, as he double-crossed the regime while claiming to be its ally. His eldest son, Mustafa, was much better known among Shia than Muqtada himself, and Sadiq was sometimes called Abu Mustafa (father of Mustafa). But Muqtada still played a number of crucial roles. In late 1997 or early 1998, when the Baath regime had its greatest confidence that the Sadrist movement was working in its interests, it had made the unprecedented decision to allow the Sadrists to produce their own Islamic magazine. This was called *al-Huda* and Muqtada was its editor in chief. It published his father's speeches and fatwas, decisions on what was *al-haram* and *al-halal* (forbidden and permitted), as well as articles by Shia scholars. "It sold out quickly," says a witness, "because it was the only nongovernment magazine issued in that era of political persecution and intellectual monopoly. It was bimonthly and we were working to make it a weekly when Sayyid al-Sadr was assassinated."[7] The role of Muqtada was to oversee contributions, printing, and distribution.

Muqtada had various other jobs. Sheikh Ali says he was responsible for his father's security, particularly when Mohammed Sadiq was addressing vast crowds at the mosque in Kufa, when "two guards were placed in front of him and three behind." He was also dean of a religious university set up by his father in Najaf. Most important of all, Muqtada was responsible for al-Thawra (later Sadr City) in Baghdad, which was to become the main bastion of his strength. Several men who later became his lieutenants, such as Mustafa al-Yaqubi, were appointed by him. Exact details of Muqtada's biography are contentious because of the adoration and hatred he was to inspire after the fall of Saddam Hussein, but there is no doubt that politically he was highly experienced and well connected by the time his father and brothers were assassinated.

Supporters of Muqtada admit that his isolation under house arrest prevented his leading any Sadrist underground in the four years following his father's death. He did cautiously seek to contact religious sheikhs, but the *mukhabarat* surveillance was too great to hold meetings. Persecution of the Sadrist remnants was intense, and it was difficult and dangerous even to visit his father's tomb in Najaf without courting arrest. Many of those who had been leaders of the movement, like Ali al-Ka'abi in al-Thawra, were dead, in prison, or had fled abroad. There were attempts to hold commemorative prayers for Mohammed Sadiq in Diwaniyah and the Baghdad districts of Shu'ala and Khadamiyah in 2000, a year after his death, but those who turned up were immediately detained.

Muqtada continued his theological studies, which were essential to his rise in the clerical hierarchy. He had started these under his father, studying alongside Mahmoud Hassan al-Sarki, Sayyid Hassan Husseini, and Qassem al-Ta'i. He had entered the hawza in 1988 but never got beyond pregraduation research, which was interrupted when his father was killed. Asked what Muqtada did in the 1990s, Jafar al-Sadr, Sadr II's chief lieutenant, simply says: "He was working hard in his father's office."[8] It is a rule of the hawza that studies have to be continued under the same teacher in order to progress to the next clerical rank. Muqtada transferred to Mohammed Ishaq al-Fayadh, an Afghan ayatollah living in Najaf whom his father had recommended as a man to be consulted, though al-Fayadh was closer in belief to the quietism of Grand Ayatollah Ali al-Sistani than to the militant activism of the Sadrists. Still, they considered him "a generous and good-hearted man but far from political life."[9] As his official successor, or rather as a man whose words he had advised his followers to heed, Sadiq had appointed Ayatollah Khadim al-Ha'eri, who was an Iraqi by origin but had lived in Qom in Iran for two decades. In practice, neither man had the energy or the experience to play a leading role in Iraq's complex and violent politics.

Muqtada was keen to burnish his religious credentials and, despite his much enhanced status after the overthrow of Saddam, came back for further study under Ayatollah Fayadh. His opponents later criticized him for his lowly place in the Shia religious hierarchy, implying that he lacked intelligence or academic ability. The next four years showed that Muqtada was a highly astute politician, but his enemies, both Iraqis and Americans, persistently underestimated him. His lack of the right religious qualifications mattered little in the turmoil of post-Saddam Iraq. In any case, the Sadrist movement under Muqtada's father had always had an anticlerical strain, accusing the Marji'iyyah of failing to do anything to alleviate the misery and oppression of ordinary Iraqis. Muqtada's very youth was an advantage, because it meant that he had grown up in the 1990s, in the wake of the Iraqi army's defeat in Kuwait, the merciless crushing of the Shia uprising, and the destruction of the Iraqi economy and society by UN sanctions. His very lack of official status as a member of the Marji'iyyah made him all the more attractive to many impoverished young Shia who were distrustful of all religious and political authorities. They found it easier to identify with Muqtada, who had stayed in Iraq, than to trust people like Sayyid Majid al-Khoei, who had lived for twelve years in London, or Mohammed Baqir al-Hakim, the leader of SCIRI, who had spent twenty-three years in Iran. Muqtada himself was very conscious of the status that his continued presence in Iraq gave him. In an interview in June 2003, he acknowledged that he had not reached the rank of *mujtahid*, but claimed the right to leadership because of the sacrifices of those "who never left the country and remained with their people in Iraq to share their burdens."[10]

Muqtada's greatest strength was that he was the son of Mohammed Sadiq al-Sadr and the son-in-law and cousin of Mohammed Baqir al-Sadr, the two great martyrs in the modern history of the Shia. He spent a large part of his time while under house arrest, between 1999 and 2003, archiving their work and speeches. When he was asked in later years to define what was meant by the "Sadrist Movement," he denied it was a political party. He said it was simply made up of people who followed the teachings of Mohammed Sadiq al-Sadr (known as "the Second Martyr" or Sadr II). He added that in a broader sense, the movement included anybody who honored the "Speaking Hawza" and followed the teachings of Ayatollah Baqir al-Sadr ("the First Martyr," or Sadr I). Both wanted an Islamic society that would prepare the way for the return of the Imam Mehdi, the redeemer who would end the rule of tyrants and establish justice in the world.[11]

At times, Muqtada seemed to merge his identity with his revered and martyred relatives. He not only articulated their theology, he imitated their personal behavior. His manner of giving a speech was clearly modeled on that of his father, each word emphasized by the same abrupt gestures until, as one observer put it, "he makes you feel dizzy." Where he differed from Mohammed Sadiq was that he was unwaveringly serious, in contrast with his father, who often lightened his conversation with jokes. In public, Muqtada cultivated an image of melancholy gravity, as if to rebut charges that he was a youthful lightweight, while in private discussions he is described as businesslike, moody, and, at times, short-tempered. "He can't endure any question or fact to be repeated," comments one of his supporters. "And if the topic has deviated from the topic under discussion he will return to the main point quickly. His own comments are short."

Groping to describe Muqtada, Western commentators often note that he is "charismatic" (occasionally that he is "uncharismatic"), and for once the cliché has a kernel of truth, though the word now tends to mean little more than that a person has glamour, charm, and allure. The original meaning of the word *charismatic* suggested that the person so described had a special kind of holiness or semidivine grace. And this was certainly true of Muqtada, who acquired a cultlike status and whose followers believed he had a special relationship with God. This belief was never shared by a majority of Shia, but there was a core of people around Muqtada who saw him as the true redeemer for whose return the Shia had prayed for over a thousand years.

The Sadrists, a religious movement in a country in which secular politicians had to struggle to get a hearing, were surprised by the scale of support for them as Saddam's regime fell apart in early April 2003. Like every other Iraqi group, they underestimated the extent to which ordinary Iraqis were suspicious of returning Iraqi exiles. Class differences were very deep in the Shia community, and only they represented the millions of laborers and unemployed. At the same time, they may have been too conscious of their own weakness since, although they had many sympathizers and a limited number of militants on the run, they had no real political structure. Right up to its final collapse on April 9, Saddam's regime was fearful of a repeat of the Shia uprising of 1991. Its security forces were everywhere on the alert. The only action carried out by the Sadrists, by their own account, was the organization of protests in October 2002 after Saddam had declared a general amnesty for all prisoners except those imprisoned for political reasons. "Women, children, and the elderly took part in peaceful demonstrations demanding the release of prisoners linked to the Sadrist movement," recalls one Sadrist militant. "The authorities did not stop such demonstrations because they were peaceful and there were no slogans against the regime."[12] Foreign journalists in Baghdad at the time were astonished to find these demonstrators standing outside the Ministry of Information in central Baghdad calling for the release of their relatives. Wider protests took place in what was to become Sadr City. "These demonstrations were the first sign of the unexpectedly strong movement that was developing behind Muqtada," the Sadrist militant adds.

There was never any likelihood of a second Shia rebellion. Unlike 1991, the regime was forewarned. Its security men had large-scale maps of every district in Iraq on which the houses of potential opponents were marked in black ink. A Shia shopkeeper from Baghdad who fled to Kurdistan told me in early March 2003: "If there is any sign of weakness on the part of the government there will be an uprising." But the Shia remembered the terrible price they had paid for the failed rebellion in 1991 and were cautious about risking a second failure. The U.S. ground offensive had started on March 19, and there seemed to be no point in an Iraqi risking his or her life if the Americans were going to overthrow Saddam Hussein regardless of what Iraqis did or did not do.

I spent the weeks of the initial invasion of March/April 2003 in Kurdistan. I knew the government in Baghdad was not going to give me a visa because it was offended by a book I had coauthored with my brother, Andrew, titled *Out of the Ashes: The Resurrection of Saddam Hussein,* which was an account of how Saddam survived defeat in the first Gulf War. I had heard that the regime was particularly angry about the chapters dealing with the Shia and Kurdish uprisings, as well as the murderous activities of Saddam's family. For a time I feared I would be unable to reach Iraq before the war started, but in February, Hoshyar Zebari, later Iraq's foreign minister and then spokesman for the Kurdistan Democratic Party, called me in Washington to say jubilantly that he had persuaded the Syrian government to let me cross the Tigris from northeast Syria into Iraqi territory controlled by the Kurds.

Four days after the start of the war I spoke to two Shia soldiers, Haider Abdul Hussein and Abdul Hassan Ali, who had deserted from the Iraqi army in the north. "I heard the war had started [by listening to] a little radio the size of a cigarette packet we had smuggled into my unit, although radios were forbidden," said Haider. "I did not want to die for Saddam."

He did not expect a Shia uprising, pointing out that the one in 1991 had only happened because the army had already broken up.[13] The Americans were, in any case, against action by Iraqi armed resistance. The one Iraqi city to be taken by Iraqi insurgents opposed to Saddam was Amara, two hundred miles south of Baghdad, which fell on April 7. It was captured by guerrillas led by Karim Mahmoud al-Mohammedawi, nicknamed "Abu Hatem" and also "Lord of the Marshes," who had taken part in the failed uprisings in 1999 after the assassination of Mohammed Sadiq al-Sadr. But no sooner had he captured Amara than he was ordered out by the CIA, with the implied threat that he would be bombed if he did not withdraw.[14]

Muqtada moved more quickly than anybody else in Iraq to organize his supporters as the regime began to crumble. On April 8 he was deputized by Ayatollah al-Ha'eri, whom his father had appointed as his official heir and who lived in the Iranian holy city of Qom, to act as his representative in Iraq and issue fatwas to his followers. None of his rivals were as energetic. He had a web of supporters who could be quickly activated. Many of them were very young. In al-Thawra, the vast Shia slum, a twenty-three-year-old cleric and local leader, Sayyid Ali al-Rawawi, said the Sadrist movement was able to take control of the area with just ninety trainee clerics. He had a letter from Muqtada appointing him his *wakil,* or representative. Mosques and *husseiniyas* were used as meeting places and centers for organizing neighborhoods. Within a couple of months the Sadrists controlled ninety percent of the mosques in Sadr City and had taken over schools, hospitals, and welfare centers. Much of this happened in the first few days after the fall of Saddam Hussein. A week after he fled, the Sadrists claimed to have fifty thousand volunteers organized in predominantly Shia east Baghdad, collecting refuse, directing traffic, and distributing hospital meals.[15]

The euphoria and anarchy in Sadr City during those first hours of freedom is captured in the account of a highly committed young Sadrist militant named Abbas. "We believed Sadr II [Mohammed Sadiq al-Sadr] was like the Prophet Mohammed because he did so many things for our community," he says. "We, his followers, had a sense of failure and guilt that we had not been able to stop him being killed, so we felt it our duty to support his son and complete his work." He says nobody organized his activities or those of his friends: "We knew that the regime had fallen on the morning of April 9 when we found that people had started to rampage and loot. We heard people running through the streets screaming hysterically:

'Saddam has fallen! Saddam has fallen!' After a few hours the crowds began to disappear and we thought they had gone to celebrate, but unfortunately they were looting. In the afternoon they came back carrying stolen objects, large and small. This situation went on for a few days and then we, the young men, organized ourselves and volunteered, without anybody leading us, to guard public property. Communications were cut so we did not know what was happening in other provinces. We guarded the power stations, transformers, and electricity cables, so if there was any electricity at all in Baghdad after the fall of Saddam it was because of al-Sadr's followers."[16]

Muqtada never doubted his right to lead the Sadrists despite challenges from important lieutenants of his father such as Mohammed al-Yaqubi, more senior than him in the Shia hierarchy, who was to set up his own party, Hizb al-Fadhila, which later won control of Basra. After the murder of Mohammed Sadiq there were disputes between Muqtada and Yaqubi over the control of donations and the official stamps from Sadiq's office. Generally, the followers of Muqtada gained control of villages, towns, and city districts where his father had also had many followers. One difference, however, was that Muqtada was more reliant than his father on the impoverished urban masses, whom his opponents denounced and feared as a dangerous, criminalized mob.

Muqtada succeeded in asserting his authority over swathes of Shia Iraq in a few days because of his own abilities and the legacy of his father, in terms of both prestige and organization. But he was also riding a wave of Shia self-assertion that was as overpowering as it was unexpected. Suddenly there were pictures of Sadr I and Sadr II and other Shia religious notables pasted on every wall. The new post-Saddam Iraq had no secular heroes. More surprisingly, there were traditional signs of Shia identity everywhere. Shia waved green date palm leaves and green banners, symbolizing Imam Ali. People held up clay tablets known as *turba* made from soil taken from Najaf. These were placed in front of the worshipper so that, as he prayed, his forehead would touch the sacred earth of the city where Imam Ali was buried. As Saddam's statues were torn down, Shia demonstrators would beat their chests in a ritualized sign indicating their Shia identity. "By God we swear never to forget Imam Hussein," chanted the vast crowds, and "No God but Allah." It was already evident that the future belonged to the Shia religious leaders, and a struggle was already beginning as to which of them would come out on top.

CHAPTER TEN

Murder in the Shrine

The enemies of Saddam Hussein always attributed the extreme violence in Iraq to him and his regime. They optimistically imagined that once he was overthrown, Iraqis would be able to resolve their differences peacefully. But within twenty-four hours of Saddam's fall on April 9, 2003, one of his ablest and most important opponents, Sayyid Majid al-Khoei, the son of Grand Ayatollah al-Khoei, was hacked to death by fellow Shia after being dragged, hands bound, from the Imam Ali shrine in Najaf. It was further alleged that he had not been accidentally killed by an out-of-control mob but was instead deliberately murdered on the instructions of Muqtada al-Sadr as part of a long-running family feud. The death of al-Khoei, a charming and intelligent man, was an early sign that the new Iraq was going to be just as dangerous as the old, possibly even more so. The Shia leaders wanted to use the overthrow of Saddam by the United States to displace the Sunni as rulers of Iraq, but the savagery of the attack in Najaf revealed the bitter divisions within their own community.

I last saw Sayyid Majid four months before he died, at a rancorous conference of the Iraqi opposition in London in mid-December 2002. As Londoners held pre-Christmas office parties in the Metropole Hotel on a rain-swept Edgware Road, they could not have guessed that they were rubbing shoulders with Iraqis engaged in the first battles to decide who would succeed Saddam. I saw Sayyid Majid—an alert, good-looking forty-three-year-old in a black turban, short dark beard, and flowing robes—sweep through the hotel lobby, attracting curious glances from partygoers sipping their margaritas. He had a slightly amused smile on his face, his normal expression, which suggested that he was not going to be surprised by anything that happened at the conference. I had first met him a decade or so earlier. On fleeing Iraq in 1991, after trying and failing to get American support for the Shia uprising, he had come to London. When his brother Mohammed Taqi was murdered in 1994, he became head of the al-Khoei Foundation, an influential and well-funded Shia charity with its headquarters in north London. He gathered a group of very able Iraqis around him and cultivated good relations with the British Foreign Office and the U.S. State Department. I saw him often. He would say that the Shia had made a mistake in 1920 by rising against the British occupation, enabling the Sunni to take power in their stead. This became something of a cliché later, but I first heard it from Sayyid Majid, and it represented an important political truth. The Shia community, a majority of Iraqis, was not going to oppose a U.S. attack on Iraq to overthrow Saddam. Sayyid Majid was also openly scathing about clerical supremacy in Tehran, though distressed when his criticisms of the Iranian regime appeared in print.

That December conference in London was all too accurate a guide to the chronic disunity of Saddam's opponents in the years to come. In fact, it had almost failed to convene at all. I had seen Hoshyar Zebari, then a leading member of the Kurdistan Democratic Party and later Iraqi foreign minister, a few days earlier in the hotel where he was staying in Knightsbridge. I had known him when he was a student at Essex University, twenty years earlier, and had always been impressed by his energy, ability, and unquenchable optimism in the worst of circumstances. But on this occasion even he, slumped in a hotel armchair, was sounding depressed. "If we can't discuss things democratically between ourselves now, what will it be like when we are part of a [post-Saddam] government?" he asked gloomily—and, as it turned out, prophetically.

It was a good question. Many of the differences that were to cripple future Iraqi governments were already surfacing. The delegates at the conference were overwhelmingly Kurds or Shia Arab. There were very few Sunni. The Tehran-based SCIRI of Mohammed Baqir al-Hakim—its members secretive, well-organized, and effective—wanted to be accepted as the main representative of the Shia community. The Sadrists were not present, and nobody at the conference supposed they still existed as a significant force. The U.S. envoy to the conference was Zalmay Khalilzad, a suave and experienced diplomat who was later to be U.S. ambassador to

Baghdad. He sought to unite the opposition in public but steered away from allowing it to form a provisional government or promising it real power. It is easy, in retrospect, to deride the delegates as naïve, but at the time their main fear was that the United States would balk at the last moment at overthrowing Saddam. There was also an unspoken anxiety among the Shia and Kurds that Washington would double-cross them by removing Saddam and his clique but sustaining Sunni Arab dominance under American tutelage. This would be a repeat of the old British formula for controlling Iraq. Khalilzad had to deny that the United States wanted "Saddamism without Saddam." I wrote, somewhat cynically, that the most ominous sign at the conference was the absence of smoke-filled rooms. Most Iraqis in Iraq were and are chain-smokers, seldom without a cigarette in their mouths—understandable given the strain under which they live. Few of the delegates at the conference were heavy smokers. They had been in exile for years, living in cities like New York, Chicago, and Los Angeles, where smoking is frowned upon. In other words, they had very little experience or knowledge of present-day Iraq.

Few realized how deeply Iraqis inside the country had changed since 1991 as a result of the crushing defeat in Kuwait, the Shia and Kurdish uprisings, the savage repression that followed, and the deadly weight of UN sanctions, which had destroyed the economy. Sayyid Majid was eager to remove the American suspicion of the Iraqi Shia as pawns of Iran. He was heavily influenced by his experiences in 1991, when he had seen the Americans so decisively shy away from aiding the Shia rebellion in the attempted overthrow of the Baathists. He said that, at that time, the United States was full of people who were "scared to shake hands with a man in a black turban." After talks with politically active Americans a few months previously, he told me he found them more open to the idea of Shia predominance in Iraq, and even a separate Shia state in the south. He was commonly described in the press as "a pro-American" cleric, but his pro-Americanism had the very practical intention of making the Iraqi Shia acceptable to Washington. He underestimated the extent to which many Iraqi Shia hated the United States and its friends just as much as they did Saddam Hussein.

The United States was eager to see Sayyid Majid back in Iraq. The U.S. State Department and the CIA liked him. On March 28, 2003, he flew with a group of supporters and friends from Gatwick Airport to the U.S. military base in Bahrain. With him was Abdul Hassan al-Khafaji, also known as Abu Tariq, the former Iraqi army colonel who joined the uprising in 1991 and had accompanied Sayyid Majid on his agonizing journey across southern Iraq in a vain search for American aid. As an ex-military man he was in charge of security for the group. Other members of the party included Ma'ad Fayadh, a journalist from *Asharq Al-Awsat* newspaper; Maher al-Yasseri, a Shia cleric from Detroit; and Hazem al-Shalaan, later a highly controversial Iraqi defense minister. On April 3 they boarded a U.S. military plane that flew them to Nassariya. The road north to Najaf was deemed unsafe, so the group was flown there in a U.S. helicopter, but thereafter they refused American protection. "People in Najaf were amazed to see him," says Ma'ad Fayadh, the Iraqi journalist who was also a friend of Sayyid Majid. "Some abandoned their cars in the middle of the street so they could greet him." But there were also signs of suspicion of the returning exiles as people who had lived in luxury abroad, on the payroll of foreign intelligence services, while Iraq sank into ever deeper misery. Fayadh heard people ask: "Who is this coming from London?"[1]

Early on, some members of the group had raised the idea of Sayyid Majid visiting Muqtada al-Sadr, who was also in Najaf. Fayadh, who does not conceal his loathing for Muqtada and blames him for the bloody events that were about to happen, says nevertheless: "It was clear that he was a power in Najaf. He was supported by all the people who were Fedayeen Saddam [a militia force established by Saddam. Opponents of Muqtada routinely accused him of recruiting them but never produced evidence that he did so]. They were all the poor and the unemployed, and they had Kalashnikovs in their hands. They shouted at us: 'Muqtada is our imam.'"[2] The long feud between the al-Khoei family and the al-Sadrs played a role in Sayyid Majid's fatal decision not to see Muqtada and try to resolve their quarrels. In a tape recording from 1998, one can hear Mohammed Sadiq al-Sadr, Muqtada's father, denounce Sayyid Majid publicly as not being worthy of a place in the Marji'iyyah, the Shia hierarchy, and question his right to control the al-Khoei Foundation funds. Presumably, Sayyid Majid believed that as the scion of a revered clerical dynasty he was untouchable. "We said 'Muqtada has power. Talk to him,'" says Fayadh, recalling that the conversation took place on April 7. Sayyid Majid retorted grandly: "Why should I? Who is this Muqtada?" Members of his group noticed black-clad supporters of Muqtada, possibly precursors of the Mehdi Army, shadowing them through the streets of Najaf, but they were not too worried. None of them thought they were in danger. "They looked at us like enemies, but we never supposed they would attack us," says Fayadh.[3] Colonel al-Khafaji, who was in charge of security, recalled that at first people in Najaf were nervous on seeing them. "They were frightened that Saddam might come back and said, 'maybe the same thing will happen as in 1991.' But day by day the number of people coming to the shrine with us increased."[4] Sayyid Majid distributed $350,000 to the poor from al-Khoei Foundation funds; his staff later denied rumors circulated by his political rivals that he had ever received $13 million from the CIA.

On the morning of April 10, al-Khoei took a dangerous step, much riskier than he supposed. As part of his campaign to reconcile different factions in Najaf, he went to the house of one of the most unpopular men in the city, Haidar al-Rufaie al-Killidar, and asked him to come to the shrine. Haidar came from a family in Najaf that for centuries had been hereditary custodians and key-holders of the shrine of Imam Ali. It was not an easy job. Radwan Hussein al-Rufaie, a cousin of Haidar, said, "I turned it down because I was against the regime and my brother took it over, but he disappeared in 1991, accused of plotting against Saddam. Haidar, on the other hand, was seen as completely affiliated with the government. He appeared on television talking with Saddam Hussein and was a member of the Iraqi parliament."[5] Haidar, a portly man with a plump face, had sensibly not been to his office in the shrine since the war began. Though visibly nervous, he now allowed himself to be persuaded by Sayyid Majid that he should return.

Leaving Haidar's house, Sayyid Majid and his party went at about 8:45 a.m. to the shrine and entered the spacious wood-paneled office of the custodian. Surviving photographs show Sayyid Majid in a long dark robe sitting on a sofa and smiling gently but confidently at his companions, unaware of any impending danger. On the wall above his head is a painting of Imam Ali and Imam Hussein. An hour passed before there were any signs of hostility, but a crowd had begun to gather in the courtyard outside the office, and there were shouts of "Long life to al-Sadr" and "Give us Haidar or we will kill you." A few moments later a window was smashed. At first, Sayyid Majid tried to calm the crowd, which by now numbered some four hundred, but the microphone he picked up did not work. By one account the cable had been cut. As he stood in the door of the custodian's office somebody lunged at him with a knife and he jumped back for safety. Al-Khafaji told me that the first shot was fired into the air by Maher al-Yasseri, the cleric from Detroit, where there is a large Iraqi community: "He became frightened and fired a shot. Many of the crowd ran away, but only to get their own guns." A gunfight started. There were two Kalashnikovs and two pistols in Haidar's office. The party trapped inside started to shoot back even though they had little ammunition. Al-Yasseri was mortally wounded by a bullet and fell down. Al-Khoei took off his turban and pressed it to the wound in the chest of the dying man, shouting as he did so: "Don't shoot! This young man is dying! He is a Shia! He is a Muslim!"

The shooting went on for ninety minutes. Ma'ad Fayadh, who fired a pistol at someone trying to get through the door, describes the last desperate moments of the fight: "Somebody threw a grenade," he says. "I heard Sayyid Majid call out, 'I am hurt.' One of his fingers had been blown off and another was hanging by a piece of skin." Fayadh tried to stanch the bleeding with a towel. There was no sign of help coming. Colonel Khafaji had managed to get away, and those remaining in the custodian's office believed he would call the Americans on his satellite Thuraya phone. "I do not understand to this day what happened," says Fayadh. "He [Khafaji] left early, returned to the house [where they had been staying] and did not call the Americans." Even had he done so it is unlikely that U.S. forces would have entered the shrine, one of the holiest of the Shia faith. The alleged inaction of Colonel Khafaji was a source of bitterness and recriminations afterward. The siege ended when al-Khoei's group ran out of ammunition and one man went outside with a white shirt and a Koran to surrender. Some of the crowd burst into the office and tied the hands of those inside behind their backs.

What happened over the next hour was to spawn almost as many different versions as the Kennedy assassination. Sheikh Salah Bilal, one of those who was tied up, says his captor told him: "We are taking you to Muqtada al-Sadr to pass sentence."[6] Ma'ad Fayadh, whose own hands were bound, says that Riyadh al-Nuri, the head of the Sadrist movement in Najaf, said: "I am from Muqtada and you are the hostages of Muqtada." They were then led out of the room and through the gate of the shrine in the midst of an angry, jostling crowd, many of whom were armed with guns, swords, and knives. Ma'ad Fayadh recalls: "The first thing I saw was swords and knives flashing in the sun. I thought, 'Oh my God, that's it.'" Within moments he saw Haidar al-Rufaie, the hereditary key-holder, hacked to death in front of him and al-Khoei repeatedly stabbed with knives. While the attention of the crowd was on its two main victims he was able to slip away.

Muqtada's house was a few hundred yards away, down a narrow lane crowded with small shops. Sayyid Majid was badly wounded though his dark robe hid the bloodstains. He slumped down by the door when they came to Muqtada's house. "Most of his body was bleeding and he lay down on one side," says Sheikh Salah Bilal. "I put his head on my leg." After some minutes, he says, a message came from Muqtada that said: "Don't let them sit by my door." Sayyid Majid, Sheikh Bilal, and a man called Hamid al-Timimi took refuge in a sewing-machine shop in the same street. The owner of the shop tried to save them by telling the crowd that Sayyid Majid was dead, but they did not believe him. After a few minutes they smashed down the door, dragged Sayyid Majid out, and shot him at the end of the street. His lifeless body lay where it fell for some hours, until it was claimed by his in-laws, who washed and buried him. Muqtada, denying any responsibility, attended the mourning ceremonies claiming that he had sent men to help Sayyid Majid.

Over the following months stories multiplied among Muqtada's many enemies about how his senior lieutenants had mocked Sayyid Majid as they dragged him from the shrine, and that Muqtada had directly and publicly ordered his execution. These accounts are dubious. It is unlikely that so cautious a man as Muqtada—and anybody who survived Saddam had well-honed survival instincts—would have openly incriminated himself by issuing instructions before witnesses for the murder of a rival. At the same time, there is overwhelming evidence that the mob that besieged and then stormed the office in the shrine was led by Sadrists. Riyadh al-Nuri, Muqtada's office manager, was identified as taking Sayyid Majid away. The siege went on for an hour and a half, and if Muqtada did not know that al-Khoei was being done to death, it may well have been because he did not choose to know.

The Sadrists' version of what happened in the days after Sayyid Majid arrived in Najaf and during his last bloody few hours at the shrine makes sense on most points, but it is not quite convincing concerning their complete lack of responsibility for his death. According to Sheikh Ali, Sayyid Majid had returned to Najaf at a time when nobody controlled the city. His account largely confirms the story of the survivors of Sayyid Majid's group. He says: "Majid al-Khoei came to Najaf on the back of an American tank. He was with Haidar al-Killidar, who was a Baathist and a member of parliament. Followers of al-Sadr were in the shrine at the time performing their religious duties when they saw an agitated mob surround Majid and Haidar, so they interfered to protect Majid and tried to get him out of the shrine. What happened was that one of Majid's bodyguards fired a shot from his gun, killing one of the crowd. When people saw this they killed them with their knives." The shot he refers to was probably fired by Maher al-Yasseri, the young Shia cleric from Detroit. Sheikh Ali also argues that Muqtada himself had only just been released from prolonged house arrest by Saddam's security services a week before the murder of Sayyid Majid. "Sayyid Muqtada did not know him and did not meet him. Sayyid Majid al-Khoei came [to the shrine] the day after the fall of the regime; how could Muqtada have had men ready to kill him, since he had been under house arrest for so long? The main point is that the people were furious and wanted to retaliate against any Baathist they could get their hands on. Al-Khoei's visit was badly timed because law had broken down and nobody controlled Najaf." This may have been true of the original riot at the shrine, but it does not explain why a desperately wounded Sayyid Majid was turned away from Muqtada's house, dragged out of his last refuge in the sewing-machine shop, and killed in the street.[7] As I discovered at a Mehdi Army checkpoint in Kufa a year later, the Sadrist movement contained many violent young men loyal to Muqtada but only loosely under his control. It was a convenient excuse for the Sadrists in the coming years that they were not responsible for much of the violence carried out in their name.

CHAPTER ELEVEN

Seizing the Moment

Muqtada's dramatic rise to prominence immediately after the fall of Saddam mystified the outside world as well as many Iraqis. His most important advantage was that he was the son and son-in-law of the most revered Shia martyrs. He was also ideally placed to take advantage of the political vacuum in Iraq as the old regime collapsed on April 9. The exiled parties were still out of Iraq, unfamiliar with their country after years abroad, and suspected by Iraqis of being pawns of the United States or Iran. The tragic fate of Sayyid Majid al-Khoei underlined the dangers exiles faced if they did not carefully prepare the ground for their return. The Grand Ayatollah Ali al-Sistani had immense prestige, but a central theme of his theology was that the clergy should avoid direct political involvement. Saddam's *mukhabarat* had long ago destroyed the secular opposition parties, and his own ruinous wars had discredited secular Arab nationalism. The triumphant U.S. military forces, having made no coherent plans about what to do after overthrowing Saddam Hussein, were still on the sidelines. The way was open for the Sadrists to step into the gap and seize as much power as they could.

Muqtada was highly active. His resources were limited but he deployed them with energy and skill. Abbas, the young Sadrist militant in Sadr City, says Muqtada was in touch with about twelve to fifteen religious sheikhs on legitimate matters during the last days of Saddam.[1] This gave him a nucleus of local leaders on whom to rely. He swiftly appointed others such as Sheikh Mohammed al-Fartousi, who became his representative in the

Rusafa, or eastern side of Baghdad. Fartousi immediately set up a Sadrist office in a building until recently occupied by the Baath party in Sadr City. Committees were established in an attempt to restore normal life. Sadrists picked up where they had left off at the last high point in Shia political activism, before state repression intensified following the assassination of Sadr II four years earlier, in February 1999. In Sadr City people reopened the Muhsin mosque, which had been closed since the day Shia worshippers were arrested there. "Immediately after the fall of Saddam," says an eyewitness, "people broke all the locks and opened the doors of the Muhsin mosque, cleaned it, and brought out the headdresses and shoes that belonged to those who had been praying for the last time before they were arrested."[2]

Muqtada himself did not come to Baghdad until July, but on April 11 he gave his first Friday sermon in the Grand Mosque in Kufa (this small city, unlike Najaf, was dominated by Sadrist supporters), where his father had so often spoken. "There were many people in Kufa who came from all of the southern provinces to hear him speak," says Abbas. "He talked about the fall of Saddam and the collapse of his regime and urged people to obey al-Ha'eri's orders. He also urged them to make the Arba'in pilgrimage to Kerbala because it had been banned by the old regime. Sadr II had called for it just before he died but then canceled it, fearing the cruelty of Saddam. This ritual was revived in memory of him and his son. It was at this time that we changed the name of al-Thawra to Sadr City [after Mohammed Sadiq al-Sadr] and there were pictures of Muqtada everywhere."[3] As we saw, up to one million Shia—some authorities claim three million—obeyed Muqtada's instructions and ignored the dangers of travel in wartime to make the pilgrimage to Kerbala.

The weekend of April 11–12 saw the mass looting of Baghdad and all other Iraqi cities and towns. Any building remotely connected to the government or the Baath party was fair game. Looting was an Iraqi tradition born of tribal raiding and poverty, and it should not have come as a surprise. After the invasion of Kuwait, the Iraqi army had systematically looted everything of value, from bulldozers to hotel cutlery. In the Shia uprising of 1991 looters had promptly ransacked the factories as well as state institutions. During the Kurdish civil war in 1996 some five thousand cars had been stolen in a single day in Arbil. There was a social revolutionary ferocity in the robbery and destruction that now swept across Iraq. Houses of the Baathist leadership were targeted in acts of political revenge and on the wholly correct supposition that it was there that the richest pickings were to be found. It was not only the impoverished masses of Sadr City who saw their opportunity. Government officials seized ministerial cars, computers, and photocopiers. The destruction often seemed driven by hatred of the powers-that-be and all their works. In the Natural History Museum in the Wazzariyah district of northeast Baghdad looters systematically smashed with the butts of their Kalashnikovs the display cases showing Iraqi wildlife. Only a stuffed white horse, given, when alive, to Saddam by the king of Morocco remained intact, for no obvious reason. Outside in the museum forecourt were enormous model dinosaurs that the looters had sprayed with machine-gun fire. One of them had even shinned up the long sinuous neck of a dinosaur to lop off its concrete head. A Sadrist militant from Sadr City explains that this apparently senseless vandalism was born of a new sense of empowerment and freedom from fear. "When people started to steal and destroy state property," he says, "they wanted to demonstrate to themselves that fear was gone and there was no longer any authority to watch, trap, and kill them. When a young man smashed up a police car he was really saying: 'This is the Saddam state and I am destroying it.'"[4]

The looting posed a dilemma for the Sadrists. On the one hand, it was deeply offensive to pious and puritanical young Sadrists like Abbas. On the other, the mass of the looters were the very same poor and angry young men who were the main support of Muqtada. Sadrism was a social as well as religious movement, though it was also true that Sadr City had long been famous for its thieves' markets. Abbas was proud of what he and other self-appointed guardians of order achieved, though his claims are a little too good to be true. "We guarded the hospitals from thieves after many things had been stolen," he says, "and we got the telephone numbers of doctors from the remaining staff and contacted them to get them to come back to work. We guarded them when they were treating people and we turned some of the mosques and *husseiniyas* near looted clinics into medical facilities. We directed traffic in the streets because there were many cars and no traffic policemen. We did all we could to regulate and direct social life." An appeal was made from the mosques for the return of loot, and many stolen objects were returned. "I personally was responsible for the electricity sector," he adds proudly. "Thousands of electricity transformers were returned and until now the Electricity Ministry is grateful for what we did for them. We were astonished when we saw people returning wads of dollar bills."

This was hardly typical behavior, but the Sadrist clerics did try to recover some of the stolen property. One woman went with a friend, also female, to a house in an alleyway in Sadr City, where two men in turbans were in charge of receiving loot, such as fittings from streetlights, that was being returned. "The two clerics wrote down what was given back, but they did not thank the young men who were returning stolen goods," she says. "They were upset by our presence and insisted that we wear the *abaya* [long black cloaks], which were borrowed from a neighboring house." Enough electrical equipment was returned for the electricity in Sadr City to be switched back on on April 16, a week after the fall of Saddam, an event immediately marked by young men rushing into the street and firing their machine guns into the air in celebration.

Muqtada was more ambivalent on the question of loot than Abbas supposed. The looters became universally known in Iraq as *al-Hawasim,* meaning "the finalists." The term was a derisive reference to Saddam Hussein's claim that an American invasion of Iraq would provoke "a final battle." In May, Muqtada issued what became known as the *al-Hawasim fatwa,* saying that looters could hold on to what they had expropriated so long as they made a donation (*khums*) of one-fifth of its value to their local Sadrist office. Many, including Sadrist supporters, found this deeply shocking. Sheikh Ali claims that the original fatwa was issued by Ayatollah Ha'eri, the nominal head of the Sadrists, in far-off Qom, and that Muqtada loyally issued the same instruction. This is difficult to take seriously. Given that Ha'eri complained that his orders were routinely disregarded by Muqtada, it is unlikely that he would have singled out this instruction to obey. The impact of the instruction was to frighten and alienate the Shia establishment and property-owning classes from the Sadrists; many of the better-off Shia began to see Muqtada as a dangerous Islamic Bolshevik and demagogue leading a mob of robbers and thieves. Four years later, Dr. Ahmed, who does not want his full name published, a supporter of Sistani living in Najaf, gave his opinion that "most of the followers of the Sadrist trend are thieves and I was convinced of that after the fatwa by their Marji'iyyah permitted the stealing of public property that turned them from poor people into rich people overnight."[5]

There were other reasons for the hawza establishment to be frightened. They were shocked by the murder of Sayyid Majid al-Khoei, the first time that the rivalry between the leading Shia clerical families had ended in killing. In the aftermath of the murder in the alleyway near Muqtada's house, pro-Sadrist mobs besieged the house of Sistani, who was of Iranian origin, and Ayatollah Mohammed al-Fayadh, who was Afghan, demanding they leave Iraq and return to their own countries. Sistani called on local tribes to provide fifteen hundred armed men to protect him and the other ayatollahs. The incident showed that the so-called quietist Shia leaders could mobilize support if they had to. The news of the siege of Sistani's house was spread by radio, and the response by the Shia showed that the Grand Ayatollah still had great popularity and moral authority. "I was sleeping in a village near Basra that night," recalls Hussein al-Shahristani, the nuclear scientist. "Suddenly I saw the villagers grabbing their guns and preparing to rush to Najaf, hundreds of miles away. 'Sistani is under attack,' they told me. That was all they needed to know. The same thing happened all over Iraq."[6] The rift between Muqtada and Sistani was evident, but it was not complete, and in the anarchic conditions of post-Saddam Iraq the Sadrists could disclaim with some credibility the excesses of their supporters. In Samawa, on the Euphrates south of Najaf, at a rally on April 16, demonstrators carried pictures of both Grand Ayatollah Sistani and Mohammed Sadiq al-Sadr. They chanted, "No to colonial occupation, no to America, blessed be Iraq."[7] They denied there was any division between Sistani and Muqtada and said both should be honored. The demonstration is interesting because it showed that Muqtada, despite his youth and lack of religious qualifications, was regarded with reverence almost equal to that for Sistani. Within a week of the fall of Saddam Hussein, Muqtada had successfully identified himself with Sadr I and Sadr II.

The high tide was soon reached for the Sadrists. They had moved faster and more effectively than other opposition movements, but their organized support was spread thin. The hawza was at first caught by surprise when its authority was challenged, but then began to reassert itself. For all their religious rhetoric, the Sadrists relied on religious students and followers of Muqtada's father who had not achieved high religious rank. Courts established by the Sadrists in Baghdad were imposing their own interpretation of Islamic law by arbitrary arrests, closing video shops, attacking liquor stores, and insisting that women wear the veil. "We had some imams saying women will be beaten in the streets if some of their hair is showing and liquor stores burned down," al-Fartousi told a reporter. "This is not what we are about. Gentle advice to such women or a tap on the shoulder should suffice."[8] This was hardly reassuring. The Sadrists might claim they were trying to control anarchy, but for many Iraqis, including almost all the middle class, they were the anarchists. Other opponents of Saddam began to return to Iraq. Mohammed Baqir al-Hakim, the leader of the Supreme Council for Islamic Revolution in Iraq (SCIRI), arrived in Iraq on May 10, 2003, with four hundred guards in a convoy from Iran. His reappearance had been advertised for several days by loudspeakers in the mosques. He was greeted by vast welcoming crowds as he passed through Basra, Samawa, and Diwaniyah. But the crowds noticeably diminished in size as he moved north, and in Najaf, where local leaders including Muqtada went to see him, there were only three hundred to four hundred supporters to greet him.[9] Soon, however, al-Hakim was leading Friday prayers in the Imam Ali mosque in Najaf in competition with Muqtada, who was doing the same thing a few miles away in the Grand Mosque in Kufa.

The bitter rivalries of the past did not diminish. The Sadrists remembered with anger al-Hakim's past denunciations of Sadr II as a Baathist. But al-Hakim had a powerful asset in the shape of the Badr Corps, which at this time had about four thousand to eight thousand well-trained and armed men. These returned to Iraq without fanfare, leaving their heavy weapons and artillery behind in Iran so as not to alienate the United States. The Sadrists pointed out that Badr, the one professional military Shia force, had failed to cross into Iraq to fight in support of the Shia uprisings in 1991 or 1999. Muqtada did not mince his words. Before al-Hakim returned, Muqtada was quoted as saying al-Hakim "betrayed the people of Basra and the south when he urged them to fight [in 1991] and didn't help them, causing the intifada to fail."[10] Baqir al-Hakim's men had fought on the Iranian side during the Iran-Iraq war and were believed by many Iraqis to have savagely tortured Iraqi prisoners. "Hakim does not represent Iraq," said Mohammed al-Fartousi, Muqtada's representative in Sadr City, soon after Hakim's return. "He represents outside forces and works with Iran, the U.S., and Israel. We need someone from inside who suffered with Iraqis and represents the people's voice. We don't want an Iranian state."[11]

It was bizarre that President George W. Bush was to claim repeatedly over the next four years that Muqtada and the Mehdi Army were Iranian pawns when SCIRI and Badr, by now allied with the United States, were demonstrably Iranian creations. The lack of U.S. criticism of SCIRI was because it had shown itself ready to work with the United States after the occupation. SCIRI had started cooperating with the United States in the mid-1990s and took part in the opposition conferences, notably the one in London in December 2002 described in the previous chapter. Mohammed Baqir al-Hakim was opposed to permanent U.S. occupation, but he was prepared to aid it in the short term. SCIRI joined the U.S.-appointed Iraqi government when it was set up in July 2003, and took part in all local elections. Unlike Muqtada's movement, SCIRI was well organized and well disciplined; it had a clear strategy of becoming the representative of the Iraqi religious, political, and tribal establishment. It intended to conciliate the Americans, and this aim was all the easier to achieve since Washington quickly came to detest SCIRI's rivals, the Sadrists. SCIRI always had limited popular appeal, but it was expert at infiltrating the institutions of the new Iraqi state, notably the Interior Ministry, the police force in the south, and, after the provincial elections of January 2005, the local government.

SCIRI usually moved in the shadows. The extent to which it still took orders or advice from Iran was a question often asked by Iraqis and Americans alike over the coming years, but never convincingly answered. Was SCIRI the ungrateful child of Iran that had transferred its affections to America? This interpretation was open to the challenge that it had started cooperating with the United States in the 1990s, when it was still based in Tehran and was very much under Iranian control. It was possible that Iran had decided to bet on all possible contenders for power in Iraq so it would win no matter who came out on top. Covertly supporting its enemies as well as its friends was a devious but traditional Iranian approach. An experienced Iraqi Shia commentator who was hostile to Iran told me dolefully a year later that, after traveling widely in southern Iraq, he had concluded that "it is impossible to oppose Iran because they are paying all the pro-Iranian parties—and they are paying all the anti-Iranian parties as well."

Muqtada could have gone on playing the anti-Iranian card, but it was a measure of his growing skill as a politician that he did not. For all his astonishing success in the first month after the fall of Saddam Hussein, he had also acquired an impressive list of enemies: the United States, the hawza, SCIRI, and Dawa. The secular middle class found his black-clad militants frighteningly like the Taliban in Kabul. In June 2003, Muqtada first went on the *hajj* to Mecca, and on his return traveled to Iran, the overt reason being to consult with Khadim al-Ha'eri, the nominal leader of the Sadrist movement. According to another Sadrist leader, Muqtada also talked about the idea of starting his own militia, to be called the Mehdi Army.[12] But his most important meetings in Iran were not with Ha'eri but with the Iranian supreme leader, Ayatollah Ali Khamenei, and, reportedly, also with Qasim Suleimani, the commander of the Quds Brigade (a special foreign department of the intelligence arm of the Iranian Revolutionary Guards).[13] Iranian journalists in Tehran at the time were perplexed as to why their government was devoting so much time to supporting a young man whose staying power in Iraqi politics seemed so uncertain. Four years later, President Bush was to denounce the Mehdi Army as an arm of the Quds Brigade in Iraq. His accusation sounded like an Americanized version of the Iraqi habit of seeing the sinister hand of Iranian intelligence behind everything that happened in Iraq. Much of this was paranoia, and allegations of significant Iranian involvement in Iraq were seldom backed by evidence, but Iran did provide a useful safe haven and potential source of supplies and money for the nascent Mehdi Army.

The attraction of Muqtada for the Iranians was that he was vigorously opposed to the U.S. occupation from the beginning. It was only grudgingly, at the end of 2003, when his movement was weak, that he had described them as "guests." This sharply distinguished him from the other important Shia political and religious leaders, all of whom either supported the occupation or were prepared to cooperate with it. From the first day of the occupation after the overthrow of Saddam Hussein, Muqtada said "the smaller devil has gone but the bigger devil has come." Other Shi'ite clerics made the same point during the first days of the occupation. "We thank the Americans if they have come here to liberate us," said Ali al-Shawki in Sadr City. "But if they are here to colonize us, we will regard them as enemies and fight them with all means."[14] This was in keeping with the vigorous Iraqi nationalism of Muqtada's father and was central to the Sadrists' appeal. In the summer of 2003 there were still many Shia who were uncertain about what benefits the U.S. occupation might bring, but within months they were becoming soured by the failures of U.S. rule.

These developments were not quite so obvious at the time as they appear in retrospect. The United States set up the twenty-five-member Iraqi Governing Council (IGC) on July 13, but it had little real power, and its members were widely regarded as corrupt American stooges. Muqtada was to benefit from being excluded from this body, while SCIRI, Dawa, and secular Iraqi leaders were discredited by joining it. From the beginning he denounced its legitimacy, saying: "The government is the result of an illegitimate order by the IGC, which in itself is illegitimate because it was appointed by an illegitimate occupation." He concluded: "We do not recognize it, directly or indirectly, since it exists contrary to the wishes of the Iraqis." The IGC was "a U.S. toy." These words resonated with Iraqis because by the end of 2003 and 2004, the Americans and the IGC were increasingly unpopular. They were also widely heard because Muqtada's speeches were being carried on al-Jazeera, the Arab satellite channel.[15] One of the big changes in Iraq at this time was that rooftops were blossoming with satellite dishes, which had been forbidden under pain of six months in jail under Saddam Hussein's regime.

On July 18, a few days after it was formed, Muqtada told thousands of worshippers in the Kufa mosque that IGC was made up of "nonbelievers." He said he was setting up a religious army, to be called the Mehdi Army, and called for "a general mobilization to fight the American and British occupiers." He was careful to stress that his army was going to use "peaceful means" and that he condemned armed attacks on coalition soldiers, but it was evident that these could not be ruled out in the future.[16]

At first, the Mehdi Army was very amateur. Most Iraqi men have guns, and know how to use them, and many had been drafted into the Iraqi army and received some military training there. "At the beginning the Mehdi Army was weak and had no real units such as companies and divisions, but was just groups of armed men," says Sheikh Ali, later one of its leaders. "The only condition for somebody who wanted to be a soldier in the Mehdi Army was to be a believer and perform prayers. You registered at the mosque, *husseiniya,* or a Sadr office in any part of Iraq. The applicants had to be recommended by well-known people and all followers of the Marji'iyyah could join, though no one came apart from followers of al-Sadr."[17] The Mehdi Army's first battalion graduated in Basra on October 6, 2003.

These new initiatives by Muqtada all worked to his advantage over the next year, but this did not happen immediately. On the contrary, at the height of the scorching Iraqi summer of 2003 there were fewer and fewer portraits of Muqtada pasted on walls in southern Iraq. Observers dismissed the Mehdi Army as a paper force. The great majority of the Shia leaders were intent on their original strategy of forcing the United States to hold elections, which the Shia were bound to win as the majority of the population. They feared that Muqtada's confrontational approach would alienate the Americans, whom they were so carefully cultivating. Among the Shia population as a whole there was less unanimity about cooperating with the United States. American political and military leaders seemed to be doing everything possible to discredit themselves, but they had not quite succeeded yet. On August 13, for instance, a U.S. helicopter stripped a Shia banner from a tower in Sadr City, provoking widespread protests. The U.S. military at first denied that the incident had occurred, only to find that it had been recorded on video.

The United States was absorbed in combating the developing threat of guerrilla war by the Sunni community, but on August 29 a suicide bomb killed Mohammed Baqir al-Hakim, the founder of SCIRI, and 125 people who were with him. There were allegations that the Sadrists might be behind the attack, but it turned out that the bomber was Yassin Jarad, the father of the second wife of Abu Musab al-Zarqawi, the *salafi* (bigoted anti-Shia ultra-orthodox Sunni) leader of the suicide bombing campaign and the founder of al-Qaeda in Iraq.[18] This was one of the first attacks planned by Zarqawi and showed that the Sunni insurrection was going to be directed against the Shia community as a whole, and not just against the Iraqi government and U.S. forces. This inability of the U.S. or Iraqi government forces to provide effective security against Zarqawi was to be a great recruiting device for the Mehdi Army. It also undermined Grand Ayatollah Sistani's strategy of patient endurance in the face of the *salafi* attack while the Shia took power through the ballot box.

In the second half of 2003, Muqtada overplayed his hand several times, and his support began to look uncertain even in Sadr City. On October 10 he announced he was setting up a shadow government with its own ministries of interior, finance, justice, information, and foreign affairs. A few days later on October 15, his supporters tried and failed to take over the shrines in Kerbala, and dozens were killed in the shooting. The control of the shrines was important not just because they were a potent religious symbol, but because they received large donations from the faithful. There were angry denunciations of the Mehdi Army in Najaf. One furious circular read: "The [Mehdi] army is composed of suspicious elements, [including] individuals from the extinct regime and its security officers and members of the [Baath] party who have wrapped their heads with white and black rags to mislead people into believing that they are men of religion when in truth they are only devils. . . . We do not need your army which you have slanderously and falsely called the Mehdi Army. . . . The

Imam [al-Mehdi] is in no need of any army made up of thieves, robbers and perverts under the leadership of a one-eyed charlatan."[19]

In Sadr City, the United States installed a handpicked group of men to replace the Sadrist council. The Sadrists had promised a massive street demonstration to protest the U.S. action. I went along to see if the support for the Sadrists was on the wane compared to earlier in the year. Security for the protest was well organized, with lines of men politely searching all those attending to weed out any suicide bombers. But the number of worshippers attending Friday prayers at the al-Ahrar mosque in Sadr City was only ten thousand. Prayers were to be followed by a march on Sadr City town hall, which was guarded by American soldiers and tanks. The sermon by Abdel-Hadi Daraji, one of Muqtada's senior aides, was a mixture of religious and nationalist appeals, but the crowd chanted "Yes, yes to Muqtada!" without much conviction. After prayers were over, only about three thousand people were prepared to march. A few days later, in early November, Muqtada announced that the coalition forces were "guests" in Iraq and that the main enemy were survivors of Saddam's regime. His retreat was a little humiliating after his previous denunciations of the occupation, but he was already showing a sure instinct for the swift tactical retreat when confronting an opponent of superior strength. It was a talent that was to prove essential for his survival over the coming year.

CHAPTER TWELVE

The Siege of Najaf

In early March 2004 I went to visit the office of *al-Hawza*, Muqtada's newspaper in Baghdad. There were only a few members of the staff there but they were relaxed and friendly. I talked to a young man named Hussein who was a student in the French department at al-Mustansariya University on Palestine Street near Sadr City, which was increasingly under Sadrist control. He was explaining the Sadrist positions on various questions when he was interrupted by the roar of an explosion nearer to the center of the city. I said I would have to cut short our talk to go to the nearest hospital to talk to the injured. It was almost impossible to get to the site of a bomb blast in central Baghdad unless one was very close by when it happened because the explosion immediately caused immense traffic jams. I had discovered that the best way to find out what had happened was to go directly to the hospitals receiving the casualties and talk to survivors and their friends. Hussein wanted to see them, too, but said he had no car and asked if we could give him a lift. We drove to al-Kindi Hospital, but the uniformed policeman at the gate said he was under strict orders not to let anyone in. Hussein, who was sitting in the backseat, leaned out the window and said quietly: "We are from the office of Sayyid al-Shahid [the Office of the Martyr, named after Sadr II but in practice Muqtada's office]." The policeman froze for a second and then ran to open the gates for us, saying in an awed voice to the other police as we drove through, "they are from the Sayyid's office." Clearly, the popularity and influence of the Sadrists in Baghdad had increased markedly since I had gone to the ill-attended protest march in Sadr City four months earlier.

I thought of this small incident when, a few weeks later on March 28, the U.S. viceroy and head of the Coalition Provisional Authority (CPA) Paul Bremer closed *al-Hawza* for sixty days. I suspected that the U.S. officials in the Green Zone were going to get a bigger reaction than they expected. The reason for the closure of the newspaper was that it had carried a sermon from Muqtada praising the 9/11 attack on the World Trade Center in New York as "a miracle and blessing from God," though the letter handed to the editor said only that it had broken the law on fomenting violence.[1] "Close the rag down," Bremer had said to aides when he read a translation of the offending issue. In his account of his disastrous year ruling Iraq, Bremer shows extreme animus toward Muqtada, describing him as "a rabble-rousing Shi'ite cleric" and even comparing him to Hitler. As early as June 2003 he quotes himself as thinking: "Muqtada al-Sadr has the potential of ripping this country apart. We can't let this happen."[2] In the second half of 2003 Bremer repeatedly portrays himself as decrying the timidity of the U.S. military, the CIA, and the British, all of whom hesitated before confronting Muqtada. Their fears were understandable and, as events soon demonstrated, wholly justified. Given the escalating armed resistance by the Sunni community it did not make sense to provoke a Shia uprising at the same time.

For months Bremer hovered on the edge of ordering the arrest of Muqtada and his closest lieutenants for the murder of Sayyid Majid al-Khoei. Iraqi judge Raad Juhi had even issued an arrest warrant for Muqtada in November, saying that he had two eyewitnesses who said they had heard Muqtada give the order for al-Khoei to be killed (the pretense that there was an independent Iraqi judiciary operating at the time was never going to cut much ice with Iraqis). Bremer held two beliefs that were dangerously contradictory. For him, Muqtada was at one and the same time a powerful and menacing figure capable of tearing Iraq apart, and so weak that he would tamely submit to arrest, while his following would be too small to make effective protests. Iraqi ministers were struck by the degree of Bremer's hatred and how much he belittled Muqtada. They were told not to refer to the "Mehdi Army" but to call it "Muqtada's militia." Ali Allawi, the highly intelligent independent Islamist who was a member of the Iraqi Governing Council, once tried to explain to Bremer how the Sadrists were the political representatives of the millions of Shia poor. Bremer furiously retorted that he "didn't care a damn about the underclass and what they [the Sadrists] represented."[3]

Though Muqtada and the Sadrists were not strong enough to stand on their own against the United States, their support, which had dipped in the second half of 2004, was growing once more. This was principally because they were the only Shia movement against the occupation, the unpopularity of which was increasing by the day. Not only was there friction with U.S. soldiers on the street, but the U.S.-led Coalition Provisional Authority (CPA) was manifestly failing to restore services and provide jobs. Teachers and civil servants were paid more, but the vast "underclass" that Bremer so despised was seeing few benefits from the overthrow of Saddam Hussein. Some seventy percent of the population was unemployed according to the Ministry of Labor. SCIRI and Dawa were members of the Iraqi Governing Council, which brought them little real power and did them political damage because they were seen as pawns of the occupation. The murders of Mohammed Baqir al-Hakim and Sayyid Majid al-Khoei also removed the two most active scions of the Shia clerical aristocracy who might have competed with Muqtada.

Yet the Sadrists were still a minority movement. The Shia might not much like the U.S. occupation, but most were still far from wanting to fight it. The most prestigious and influential Shia leader was Grand Ayatollah Ali al-Sistani. The Sadrist distinction between the politically active and inactive Marji'iyyah was always an oversimplification. Sistani might not want the clergy to actively take part in politics as in Iran, or seek to create their own clerical government. But this did not mean that he believed in a legal division between church and state as in the United States and France, or wanted a secular Iraq. He was not so much apolitical as acutely conscious of the corrupting effect of political power on the Shia clergy, as evidenced by Iran. He kept his distance from the CPA and would meet none of its officials. This lack of personal contact combined with distortions of Sistani's views when passed on by self-interested go-betweens led Bremer and the CPA to underestimate the determination of the Marji'iyyah to force elections, which the Shia community was bound to win, and to insist on a new constitution in which Islam was the primary source of legislation. On June 26, 2003, Sistani issued a crucial fatwa that said bluntly: "First of all there must be a general election so that every Iraqi citizen who is eligible to vote can choose someone to represent him in a foundational Constitution preparation assembly. Then the drafted Constitution can be put to a referendum." This was a recipe for revolutionary change. If it happened then Iraq, which had been part of the Sunni order in the Middle East for hundreds of years, would become a Shia state. Sistani's position was immensely powerful because of his own great influence on the Shia. For a few months after the overthrow of Saddam Hussein, Washington and its emissaries in Baghdad had an arrogant and self-deceiving sense of being in control of Iraq. As the Sunni insurrection began to take off, the Americans became more and more desperate for local Iraqi allies. They could not afford to fight the Sunni and offend the Shia at the same time. If Sistani's limited cooperation was rebuffed then the alternative to him would be Muqtada, who was against the occupation root and branch.

Muqtada had come close to an all-out fight with the CPA in August and October when Bremer was eager to order his arrest but was always frustrated at the last moment. Bremer optimistically hoped that the arrest itself would be carried out by the Iraqi police—something that was unlikely to happen. The coalition military force outside Najaf at this moment was Spanish and had no intention of entering the holy city to snatch Muqtada.[4] Muqtada himself went on denouncing the occupation, but was chary of a direct military confrontation with the U.S. army. This was a pattern we were to see twice in 2004, during the Mehdi Army's battles with the U.S. military. Muqtada adopted similar tactics in 2007 when he stood down the Mehdi Army in February at the start of the U.S. "surge," and in September, when he declared a six-month cease-fire after fighting with the police and Badr Organization during the 15 Sha'aban pilgrimage to Kerbala. For all his white martyr's shroud and Messianic rhetoric, he was a cautious man.

Bremer's errors are glaring in retrospect, and in later years his superiors were swift to hold him responsible for much that went wrong for the United States during the first catastrophic year of occupation. This was unfair or misleading, since it was evident in Baghdad at the time that U.S. actions were determined by the Washington political agenda, and above all the upcoming presidential election in 2004. Bremer also got disastrously poor advice from the returning Iraqi exiles, senior members of SCIRI and Dawa, and from Shia clergy hostile to Muqtada, all of whom had their reasons for wanting to see the United States dispose of a dangerous rival. The animosities between the different Shia leaders and groups were very evident to American officials in the Green Zone, but, confusingly, the divisions could suddenly be replaced by solidarity in the case of a common threat. Failure to see this was a principal reason why they were outmaneu-vered by Muqtada and failed to eliminate him. In their hearts the Shia Islamists, whether SCIRI, Dawa, Sadrist, or just supporters of Sistani, knew that the United States disliked not only Muqtada but all the Shia religious parties that were led by, or were under the influence of, black-turbaned clerics. At critical moments the Shia leaders saw that, however much they detested one another, they would be wise to hang together if they did not want to hang separately. There were signs of this on the street. In October the Mehdi Army had fought guards loyal to Sistani for control of the shrine in Najaf, but by January 2004 supporters of both had united to take part in marches in Baghdad called by Sistani to demand direct elections for the next Iraqi parliament. Enormous chanting crowds, waving their banners, carried portraits of Sadr II and Muqtada along with those of Sistani.

Bremer was probably right in thinking that Muqtada was at his most vulnerable in the last half of 2003, though he was not nearly as vulnerable as Bremer supposed. He still controlled the great Sadrist fortress of Sadr City, and this alone made him an important political player in Iraq. An area of twenty square kilometers of close-packed housing in east Baghdad with a population of 2 to 2.5 million, it was routinely described in the media as "a suburb of Baghdad," but it was a lot more than that. If it had been a separate city it would have been the second-biggest city in Iraq, larger than Basra or Mosul. It was always obscure how big it really was because Saddam Hussein's regime, the CPA, and succeeding Iraqi regimes found the existence of such an area, covertly or openly hostile to the powers-that-be, intimidating. Its population was almost entirely Shia, many of them from Amara, the province in the south from which they had fled in the 1950s to escape the tyranny of the feudal landowners. But as Ali Allawi points out in a description of the area based on unpublished Iraqi government studies dated 2004, "All the main tribes of the south, that is, up to 164 different tribes and clans, were represented [in Sadr City]. The power of the local tribal leaders, numbering over 300, was gen-erally acknowledged, but with the rise of the Grand Ayatollah Mohammed al-Sadr [Sadr II], who had specifically reached out to the inhabitants of Sadr City, most of the tribal elders had deferred to his overarching author-ity." Following the fall of Saddam, the religious, tribal, and professional leaders in the area gave their backing to Muqtada.[5] By the summer of 2003 some ninety percent of the mosques in Sadr City were under Sadrist con-trol. Islamic mores were enforced in institutions such as orphanages run by the Sadrists. Boys and girls were separated and girls were forced to wear the veil. Even so, the latter said they preferred the orphanage to the danger of the streets.[6] "The growing power of the clerics means that the chief of a clan has less influence in Sadr City," says Fadhel Mohammed, a professor of sociology and an expert on the area. "The big change since 2003 had been the growth of religious parties and groups such as the Mehdi Army, SCIRI, and Dawa, but the strongest of these is the Sadrist movement. Thousands of young men belong to these organizations, so the clans have lost authority over them. When there is a dispute the clans themselves ask for a sayyid or a sheikh to be the judge."[7]

Enforced Islamic puritanism became the norm. Gypsy villages, to give one example, were seen by the Sadrists as centers for prostitution and came under attack. Munawar Mashelah, who now works as a guard in a building in central Baghdad and disguises his Gypsy origins, recalls how a dozen or so young men in five sedans approached his village (known as a *kawliya*). They shouted warnings to leave by the following morning. "As soon as they left, families fled quickly," Munawar recalls, but they didn't know where to go, so some hid in the Rashid military camp. Those who stayed were attacked and one woman in each family was killed. As so often happens when it comes to violence attributed to the Sadrists, it is impossible to make a precise distinction between their actions and those of freelance and criminal gangs. It is a measure of the failure of the CPA and Iraqi government to provide personal security that the surviving Gypsy families thought their only chance of survival was "to pay large bribes to join and take the names of well-known tribes and clans who would then protect them in central and western Iraq."[8]

There was a further reason why the political tide favored Muqtada in the first months of 2004, ensuring that he was going to be a more dangerous opponent than Bremer imagined. The sectarian bombing campaign orchestrated by Abu Musab al-Zarqawi showed that the United States was incapable of providing security to ordinary Shia. On March 2, millions of Shia marched and prayed to celebrate Ashura, the most important event in their religious calendar, commemorating the battle of Kerbala in AD 680, when Imam Hussein and his seventy-two companions were massacred. It was a peculiarly triumphant moment, and the first Ashura to be celebrated since the fall of Saddam, at which ancient rituals could be performed openly without fear of arrest. Men slashed their scalps with swords so blood ran down their faces in memory of the death and suffering of

Hussein and those with him. People cried "Hussein! Hussein!" and beat their chests in ritualized grief. The walls of the shrine in Kerbala were decorated with scenes from the battle fourteen hundred years earlier: Hussein's half brother Abbas fighting his way to the bank of the Euphrates to bring water to the thirsty but refusing to drink himself; Hussein's infant son pierced in the neck by an arrow while clasped in the arms of his father; the severed head of Hussein stuck on a pike by the victorious Umayyad army. These modern-day Shia mourners felt a sense that, so many centuries after their historic defeat, they were finally on the winning side. Outside Kerbala a group of Sadrists chanted warnings against those who might try to deny the Shia their victory. "The oppressors tore apart your land, my people," they cried. "The envious ones sowed discord among you, but do not attack us to the sound of your drums or we will crush you—Iraq! Iraq!"[9]

At about ten a.m., a series of bombs exploded near the shrines in Kerbala and Khadamiyah in Baghdad. Some 270 people were killed and 570 wounded. Limbs torn off by the blast and mangled and bleeding body parts were placed in a heap in the inner courtyard of the Khadamiyah shrine. Zarqawi's bombing campaign had been sectarian from the start, but earlier attacks, such as those on Shia police recruits and the killing of Mohammed Baqir al-Hakim along with 125 worshippers in Najaf in August 2003, had some military or political motivation. The Ashura bombings were aimed at killing as many Shia civilians as possible simply because they were Shia. They bloodily demonstrated that the United States and the nascent Iraqi government security forces could not provide protection for the Shia masses, enabling the Mehdi Army to justify its existence and rapid expansion as a Shia self-defense force.

Bremer and the CPA could scarcely have chosen a worse moment than March 2004 for a confrontation with Muqtada. His newspaper *al-Hawza* had a circulation of only about fifteen thousand (Bremer seems to have been one of its few assiduous readers), but within days there were demonstrations by as many as twenty thousand people in Baghdad demanding its reopening. Muqtada deliberately decided to make an issue of its temporary closure. The inflammatory tone of his speeches and those of his lieutenants give the impression that he believed this would be a good moment and a good issue on which to confront the occupation authorities. "We fought Saddam and now we're fighting the Americans," said

Sayyid Hazim al-Araqi, Muqtada's representative in Baghdad. "Listen, America, Britain and Israel, there's a man named Muqtada al-Sadr and he gives resistance fighters their courage." Al-Araqi's denunciation of the occupiers was an interesting mixture of Iraqi patriotism, Islamic fervor, a defense of tribal mores, anti-Baathism, and anger at the failure of the United States to improve living standards. He accused the United States and its Iraqi proxies of creating "streets full of thieves, carjackers and rubbish." By cracking down on honor killings they had encouraged adultery, and by dismissing only top-level Baathists they were preparing the ground treacherously to reconcile with the Baath party.[10]

What happened in the next few days was as much a sign of the CPA's weakness and poor judgment as of Muqtada's strength. On March 31 a convoy carrying security guards from the U.S. security firm Blackwater was ambushed in the main street in Fallujah, a stronghold of the Sunni resistance. After killing four guards the insurgents ran off, but day laborers who normally stood beside the road waiting for work dragged the bodies of the dead Americans out of the burning vehicles and savagely hacked at them with their hoes and shovels, then hanged the charred remains of two of them from the steel girders of the bridge over the Euphrates. It was the sort of public humiliation shown on U.S. television, akin to the notorious pictures of the body of a dead American helicopter pilot being dragged through the streets of Mogadishu in 1993, to which Washington was bound to respond. The Sadrists were sharp enough to see that U.S. resources and attention would be largely focused on the spreading Sunni insurrection in Fallujah and the Sunni heartlands. Astonishingly, even after the killings in Fallujah, Bremer went ahead and escalated his confrontation with Muqtada by arresting his senior aide Mustafa al-Yaqubi, a Sadrist militant from Sadr II's time, on April 3.

The Sadrist response to the arrest was swift and exceeded in scope and violence anything U.S. officials in the Green Zone could have imagined. At midday on April 4, Bremer was just congratulating himself on the arrest of Yaqubi when he received an urgent and alarming phone call from the U.S. commander General Ricardo Sanchez. "All hell is breaking loose with Muqtada," he said. "We're getting reports from a lot of different sectors, Sadr City, Najaf . . . al-Kut. Demonstrators flooding the streets. A lot of them carrying AKs and RPGs [rocket-propelled grenade launchers]."[11] To the horror of the CPA, the Mehdi Army swept into cities and towns across southern Iraq without meeting much resistance. The fledgling Iraqi police had no intention of stopping them. The security in important cities in southern Iraq was in the hands of Italian, Polish, Ukrainian, Salvadoran, and Spanish troops who had been sent there at the high tide of U.S. success in 2003 and whose governments had never expected them to fight. A few weeks earlier I had been in Kut, the fly-blown city on the Tigris that was the site of the great British defeat at the hands of the Turks in 1916. Local people did not have a high opinion of the Ukrainian contingent, who were the only armed representatives of the coalition. "They are even poorer than we are," said a friend in the city. "You can bribe them to let your car through a checkpoint by handing them a few cigarettes." Sadrist gunmen were briefly able to occupy Kut and announced that the Ukrainians held nothing except the bridge in front of their headquarters. In Nassariya the Sadrists seized part of the city from the Italians, though the latter swiftly regained control amid accusations from the Sadrists that they had reneged on an agreement to withdraw. Meanwhile, the lethal anarchy that was spreading across Iraq had an important political advantage for the CPA and Washington. Rory Stewart, the adventurous former British diplomat who was senior adviser in Dhi Qar province, the capital of which was Nassariya, makes a significant point in his memoir that the situation had become too dangerous for the media to turn up to find out what was happening. "Then and later," he writes, "the world press were unaware that we were losing control of a city of 600,000."[12]

The spectacular Sadrist gains on the ground during the first week of April far exceeded what they could hold and, in most areas, they were soon on the retreat. There were, in fact, just three cities that the Sadrists needed to occupy permanently. These were Sadr City, their main political and military base; Kufa, where Muqtada delivered his Friday sermons; and Najaf, the spiritual capital of the Shia in Iraq and around the world, which the Sadrists knew the U.S. Army would be reluctant to assault because of the danger that they would damage the holy shrines and thus provoke a wider Shia uprising. The Sadrists were not particularly popular in Najaf, the seat of the hawza Muqtada so often criticized. The 500,000 population of the city were loyal to Sistani and also feared that their city would be turned into a battle zone, but with the Mehdi Army in control there was nothing, for the moment, that they could do about it.

Muqtada chose this moment to start a religious retreat in the mosque in Kufa, which was very difficult for U.S. troops to storm, but, before doing so, issued a direct call to arms. "Make your enemy afraid, for it is impossible to remain quiet about their moral offenses," he said. "I beg you not to resort to demonstrations, for they have become nothing but burned paper. It is necessary to resort to other measures, which you take in your own provinces. As for me, I am with you, and I hope I will be able to join you and then we shall ascend into exalted heavens. I will go into inviolable retreat in Kufa. Help me by whatever you are pleased to do in your provinces." For a man on religious retreat, Muqtada was surprisingly voluble and seemed to relish confrontation with the United States. He issued a statement saying: "The U.S.-led forces have the money, weapons and huge numbers, but these things are not going to weaken our will because God is with us." On April 5, Dan Senor, the spokesman for the CPA, announced that several months earlier a warrant had been issued for Muqtada's arrest, and implied that it might now be implemented. When Bremer subsequently called Muqtada an "outlaw," Muqtada responded: "If Bremer means that I am an outlaw according to the American legal code, then I take pride in it."[13]

Mehdi Army reinforcements from Sadr City poured into Kufa and Najaf. They were untrained and violent but highly committed young men who, as described at the beginning of this book, came near to shooting me, Haider al-Safi, and Bassim Abdul-Rahman at their checkpoint outside Kufa on April 19. One of the militiamen who came to Najaf from Sadr City was a twenty-three-year-old laborer named Ali Ahmed. "Frankly, the Mehdi Army wasn't prepared for such an uprising," he said. "It wasn't even divided into companies and battalions, but was in the form of groups who heeded the call for the coming battle against the Americans, the defense of the holy sites, and to ensure that the Sadrist current survived. The biggest concentration of our forces was in Najaf. People had either their own weapons or ones they had taken from the old regime. Some people were selling what they owned in order to buy weapons so they could fight with the Mehdi Army. Very few weapons and ammunition were supplied to us." Ali Ahmed noticed that one advantage in the first stages of the fighting was that "there were U.S. troops in Diwaniyah and Hilla provinces, but we mostly faced Spanish soldiers." These Spanish troops were in the process of being withdrawn by the newly elected Spanish socialist government, which disapproved of their deployment. Overall, he said, "We didn't fight because of the closure of the newspaper or the arrest of al-Yaqubi, but because we thought our religion was in danger."[14]

It was the strength of Muqtada that he could mobilize the Shia masses, the millions of angry and very poor young men whom nobody else in Iraq represented. His weakness was that he could not control them, and he knew the risk of being denigrated as a dangerous and destructive trouble-maker. As the uprising began to run out of steam he called on his follow-ers to obey the instructions of Grand Ayatollah Ali al-Sistani, who had called for a political solution and negotiations. The Americans were send-ing emissaries to Sistani to persuade him to give them permission to enter Najaf in pursuit of Muqtada (his exact location was unclear, and it was easy for him to move between Kufa and Najaf, which are only a few miles apart). On April 7 Muqtada issued an interesting statement to his follow-ers, justifying the uprising but also admitting that "a rebellious faction has infiltrated your [Mehdi Army] ranks and deliberately attempted to fan the flames of turmoil by plundering and looting government offices and money changers. They shut the doors of the universities and seminaries in such a way as to distort the image of Islam and of Muslims and of the Mehdi Army." He said that he was heeding the call of religious, tribal, and political leaders for a cease-fire and ordered an end to military operations and demonstrations.[15] His intention was to portray Bremer and the United States as the aggressors in the eyes of the Shia community. The last thing the CPA wanted to do was negotiate with Muqtada because its aim was to eliminate him. Bremer, once again overplaying his hand, said that there were just three choices facing Muqtada: surrender, arrest, or death.

Militarily the Mehdi Army was increasingly hemmed in in central Najaf. U.S. troops had replaced the Spanish forces in the middle of April. Ali Ahmed and the militiamen he was with moved into the vast cemetery of Wadi al-Salaam, where millions of Shia lie buried, "because it is large, difficult for the enemy to enter, and we knew its layout." The cemetery was a good place for guerrillas to hide and fight because it is a labyrinth of nar-row lanes between earth walls partitioning off compounds where the dead are interred. "The number of fighters in each group was between fifteen and seventeen. We moved cautiously at night by the light of torches because we were afraid to reveal our positions. We used snipers, mortars, and Katyusha rockets; we were not able to sleep at night and our food, when we could get it, was very simple." For all their bravery there was lit-tle the black-clad militiamen could do against American airpower and armored vehicles. "They destroyed the shops and buildings so Najaf became like a city of ghosts. The street fighting was very intense with the American troops staying inside their tanks while we tried to hit them from all directions." These fights were very uneven, with heavy losses among the militiamen and few American soldiers killed or wounded. On April 26, for instance, the militiamen outside Najaf attacked an M1 tank with rocket-propelled grenades. During the battle that followed, AC-130 gunships, capable of hosing the ground with machine-gun fire, were used against the Mehdi Army. The United States said it had killed fifty-seven gunmen, and there was probably more truth than was usual in the claim since ten local Najaf hospitals confirmed that they had received the dead bodies of thirty-seven young men of military age.

Muqtada, dressed in his usual dark robes and turban, moved secretly through Najaf to inspect his militiamen. Ali Ahmed recalled how careful he was in making sure his enemies never knew where he was. "No one knew where he was going in the dark alleyways of the city," he said. "He used to give misleading hints about his movements to confuse the enemy, who unfortunately were not only Americans." As the weeks passed the Mehdi Army's military situation grew weaker, but Muqtada's political position was becoming stronger. Shia politicians in Baghdad and the Marji'iyyah wanted to bring the siege of Najaf to an end by negotiations and were desperate to avoid an American assault on the shrine. The CPA abandoned its earlier demand for the arrest of Muqtada and, crucially, the disarmament and dissolution of the Mehdi Army. Muqtada, for his part, agreed to withdraw his men from the shrine and from Najaf.

Another development deeply alarmed the CPA and the U.S. military commanders at this time: cooperation was growing between Shia fighters in Najaf and Sunni fighters in Fallujah. Military supplies came to the beleaguered men of the Mehdi Army from Fallujah through Kerbala. "Fighters came from Fallujah though there were not many of them and it was toward the end of battle," said Ali Ahmed. "They were useful because they had also fought the Americans and were experienced in street-fighting tactics."[16] The cooperation was brief, but it was an important incentive for the United States to bring the long-running crisis in Najaf to an end. Losses among his men were heavy, but Muqtada had emerged the winner because he had challenged the U.S.-led occupation, held off their greatly superior army for weeks, and survived without making concessions that would have weakened him permanently.

CHAPTER THIRTEEN

The Fall of Najaf

On August 6, 2004, Abbas Fadhel, a twenty-four-year-old member of a Mehdi Army company, volunteered with a group of other fighters in Sadr City to go to Najaf to take part in the second battle for the city. It had started three days earlier, and shells and bombs were beginning to destroy much of central Najaf as U.S. Marines fought their way toward the Imam Ali shrine. Abbas had some military training because "when the Mehdi Army was set up we used to train in the open agricultural countryside on the eastern outskirts of Baghdad and pretend that we were hunting." In addition, he had fought in the resistance against Saddam Hussein some years earlier in Amara and Nassariya provinces, "so I knew how to use a Kalashnikov and a PKC [Russian-made light machine gun]."

Abbas and his companions, who belonged to Mehdi Army's Ahmed al-Sheibani company, named after the imprisoned representative of Muqtada in Basra, drove in a car on what is normally a two-hour drive from Baghdad. They could see U.S. aircraft bombing groups of young men traveling in the same direction as themselves on the assumption that they were going to join Muqtada's forces. The crashes of the explosions unnerved the young men in the car. "Some got out and disappeared into nearby farms or took lifts in passing cars going back to Baghdad," says Abbas. As they arrived at al-Aoun, a village surrounded by date palms just north of Najaf where Shia insurgents had briefly fought Saddam Hussein's Republican Guard to a standstill in the uprising of 1991, the driver of the car finally lost his nerve. Though he was a follower of Muqtada, he suddenly announced that he was going no farther and was returning to Baghdad. His fear infected others among Abbas's remaining companions, who took their last chance to avoid fighting in a battle in which they knew they were very likely to die. (These defections are striking because they show that the militiamen in Sadr City were not all fanatical fighters carelessly willing to become martyrs for Muqtada and Islam.)

The flight of the driver left the four remaining members of the party that had set out from Baghdad a few hours earlier standing disconsolately beside the road. "We four walked on foot to the Haidaria region using an unpaved dirt track because we were frightened of the American bombardment," recalls Abbas. "We came across a small saloon car whose driver said, 'Get in and I will drive you to Najaf.' I do not think he was entirely in his right mind, though he was not completely crazy, either. As he drove he kept yelling at people beside the road, saying 'You are cowards and agents of the occupier.' We stayed silent and did not speak to him. The situation was very dangerous because we were twice targeted by American snipers and we were very exposed because there were no other cars moving on the roads. He drove us by streets he knew until we were close to the Imam Ali shrine, and would not take any money when he dropped us off, saying, 'This is my work.' Najaf was a ghost city, with all the shops closed and there was nobody to be seen apart from Sadrist fighters." During a bombardment, Abbas, by now reduced to a single companion, took refuge inside the shrine.

When the shelling stopped, the two young men left the city again to rendezvous with a company of Mehdi Army fighters near the so-called Sea of Najaf, a lake just to the west of the city. "They trusted us when we showed them our identity cards, which were given to us in Baghdad, proving that we belonged to the Ahmed al-Sheibani company. We began shooting from a long distance at an American convoy. We never saw American soldiers on foot. They were always in tanks or armored vehicles, even inside the city, and also there were strikes by helicopters." The Mehdi Army militamen were very conscious of their military inferiority compared to the far better equipped U.S. Marines, who could kill them without suffering any equivalent losses. They did what they could to combat American armor. Abbas says that a man named Karim Dra'am, who repaired cars in Sadr City, came to Najaf and modified Katyusha rockets and mortar bombs so they would destroy an American tank, but he was killed in action.

Suffering heavy losses and under continual bombardment, the militiamen were ordered to retreat to the Wadi al-Salaam, the Valley of Peace, the largest cemetery in the world, some six miles by two miles in size, where at least two million Shia are buried, eager to have their final resting place close to the shrine of Imam Ali. Wadi al-Salaam is more of a necropolis or a City of the Dead than a cemetery, and spreads out in a great semicircle around Najaf. A few of its streets are wide enough to drive a car down, but most are winding lanes; only the grave diggers really know the layout. Even under Saddam Hussein, when the Iran-Iraq border was officially closed, pious Shia in Iran and elsewhere would pay border tribes to smuggle the bodies of deceased relatives across the frontier to be buried in Wadi al-Salaam. There are also larger tombs belonging to rich families, which look like small mosques or shrines, their walls painted a vivid pink or green. On the tombs there are sometimes photographs of the dead—aging sheikhs in Arab headdresses and young men in jackets and ties. Many members of the Mehdi Army who had been killed in the April battles were interred in the Wadi al-Salaam in plots bought by Muqtada, and they were soon to be joined by more of his militiamen.

"We fled to the cemetery and stayed in the crypts and fought from there," relates Abbas, who is very open about his terrifying experience. "The bombing continued day and night. We saw the graves being demolished and our companions killed. We buried the martyrs without washing them because they were martyrs and the weather was hot [Muslims traditionally wash their dead before burying them, but in Wadi al-Salaam there was little water and bodies rapidly decomposed in the heat]." At night the surviving fighters received water and food from the people of Najaf. "The water came in bottles and our food was biscuits twice a day, though in that situation we did not have much appetite. I saw two cars come from Fallujah with humanitarian aid and Muqtada thanked them. We found that there was food on top and weapons underneath. I don't know how they were able to get past American checkpoints. One morning a rumor spread that Sayyid Muqtada had been killed, and some fighters retreated, but others fought even harder. Then in the afternoon Muqtada came and visited the fighters, his hand wrapped in a white bandage. He fought with us and we saw him hold an RPG [rocket-propelled grenade launcher] and fire it at the American tanks. He was always turning up during the battle, though he kept his movements secret."[1]

*   *   *

A second round in the battle for Najaf was always predictable. In the April crisis Muqtada had, surprisingly, emerged as the outright winner in the confrontation that Paul Bremer and his Coalition Provisional Authority had half provoked and half tumbled into in their clumsy and counterproductive attempt to eliminate Muqtada as a political force. They achieved the exact opposite of what they wanted, elevating Muqtada into a major player as the world watched the Mehdi Army stand up to the U.S. assault for almost a month. Muqtada had been extremely lucky, or had chosen his moment superbly well, in that his uprising coincided precisely with the crisis in Fallujah. Thanks to extraordinary bungling by the CPA, the Sunni insurgents had acquired their own semi-independent capital half an hour's drive west of Baghdad. This diverted U.S. attention and made the U.S. Army nervous about fighting a two-front war against both Sunni and Shia. The CPA made a humiliating retreat from its threat to arrest Muqtada and disarm and disband the Mehdi Army. In any event, many of the militiamen did not even leave Najaf, as its leaders had pledged. "Muqtada gave an order saying everybody had to go back to his family," recalls Ali Ahmed, who took part in the April uprising. "But many of our men stayed inside Najaf saying that the truce was just a lie, and they also moved into nearby regions such as Mashkab, Haidaria, and Abbasia."[2]

By August the authorities in Baghdad were stronger than they had been in April. An interim Iraqi government had been installed with Iyad Allawi as prime minister on June 28, 2004, and sovereignty had in theory been transferred back to Iraq. There was a great deal less in this than met the eye. The United States had total control over security policy. Freshly raised Iraqi military units were incapable of fighting anybody. The new regime resembled many authoritarian regimes already existing in the Middle East, but unlike them, it did not even have its own security service or control of its own army. The Iraqi National Intelligence Service under General Mohammed al-Shahwani was openly funded by the CIA. Iyad Allawi had long been close to the British intelligence service MI-6 and the CIA. His defense minister, Hazem al-Shalaan, had a personal interest in getting rid of Muqtada, as he had been part of Sayyid Majid al-Khoei's party who had made the fatal journey to Najaf in April 2003. But he had not been prominent in the opposition to Saddam Hussein and, along with the new interior minister, Falah al-Naqib, was a long-term exile with very limited experience of Iraqi life. Both of these security ministers vehemently denounced Muqtada and the Mehdi Army as cat's-paws of Iran during the coming crisis. Such declarations were a joy to the ears of the administration in Washington, but they were untrue or grossly exaggerated. Despite the lessons that should have been learned in the April crisis, the United States and its Iraqi allies still underestimated Shia solidarity and the mass support for Muqtada. This was a serious weakness because the key to destroying Muqtada and his movement was to isolate him from the hawza, the Shia political parties, and the Shia community as a whole.

Muqtada's position was both stronger and weaker than four months earlier. He had solidified his grip on Sadr City and he still substantially controlled Kufa and Najaf. The Mehdi Army could, in areas like Sadr City, deliver on security in a way the police could not, by telling gangs of criminals and dealers to get out or be killed. In Kut, Sadrist militiamen provided backup for the local police. Class division within the Shia community usually determined attitudes toward the Sadrists. The laboring poor and unemployed revered him, and the middle class of shopkeepers and merchants regarded him with fear and contempt. "The Mehdi Army was created to maintain security and give Iraqis their freedom, so the duty of each of its fighters is to work alongside the police and the civil defense corps," claimed a Sadrist cleric in Kut named Sheikh Mohammed Fadhil al-Musawi piously. But the shopkeepers in Kut felt like Muneer Ahmed, a follower of Grand Ayatollah Ali al-Sistani, who declared himself skeptical, saying: "The fighters of the Mehdi Army were the cause of the riots that happened a few months ago—and now they're acting like good people?"[3]

Militarily, the Sadrist militiamen were better trained and equipped in August than a few months earlier, when they were no more than bands of religiously inspired gunmen. By now they were organized into companies and battalions with specialized crews for mortars and machine guns. "We tried to avoid the mistakes we had made in the first battle by studying their causes and finding solutions for the problems we faced," says Abbas Fadhel. He reckoned the army had "4,000 to 4,500 very well trained fighters."[4] Opponents of the Mehdi Army have a simple explanation as to why this happened. Writing toward the end of 2004, one well-informed commentator wrote that Muqtada "commands not a ragtag militia of dispossessed Shi'ites, but increasingly, a well-armed, well-trained force of insurgents. The transformation of the Jaysh al-Mahdi lies not in Iraq, but across the border in Iran." He goes on to repeat the claim of the London-based newspaper *Asharq Al-Awsat* that the Quds force of the Iranian Revolutionary

Guards had established three military training camps at Qasr-e Shirin, Ilam, and Hamid on the Iranian side of the Iran-Iraq border and were training between eight hundred and twelve hundred of Muqtada's militiamen.[5] Such claims of Iranian involvement by newspapers and governments in the Sunni world should be treated with caution. Saddam Hussein had denounced the Shia insurgents in 1991 as pawns of Iran, though the Iraqi Shia opposition to Saddam was bitter that Tehran, for all the bellicose rhetoric, had not helped them. The U.S. and British governments soon joined the chorus of attacks on Iran, claiming it was the hidden hand behind the Mehdi Army.

On the battlefield there was never much evidence that training and better equipment was transforming the Mehdi Army. Its militiamen were no more able to take on the U.S. Marines in August 2004 than they had been able to do in April. They did not have missiles capable of destroying American armored vehicles, as the Hezbollah guerrillas in Lebanon (whom Iran was also accused of arming) were able to do when they were attacked by Israeli tanks in the summer of 2006. The most striking feature of the Mehdi Army was its ability to take massive punishment without disintegrating, but it never attained the military proficiency of the Sunni guerrillas fighting the United States in Iraq, who were led by experienced professional soldiers. The Mehdi Army also had the disadvantage that, in Najaf and Sadr City, it was defending fixed positions that the U.S. military could locate and destroy with its massive firepower.

Muqtada had told his men to react quickly to any provocation.[6] There were signs in the first days of August 2004 that the expected crisis was imminent. Muqtada's representative in Kerbala, Sheikh Mithal al-Hassnawi, was arrested, and demonstrators in Najaf demanded his release. U.S. Marines passed close to Muqtada's house in Najaf, and the Sadrists alleged that they planned to arrest him. When eighteen policemen were kidnapped by Sadrists, the U.S.-appointed governor of Najaf, Adnan al-Zurufi, accused the Mehdi Army of working for Iran and called for U.S. military support. Heavy fighting started with U.S. forces in Najaf and Sadr City, and with the Italians in Nassariya. This did not at first look very different from previous clashes over the summer, but suddenly the political situation was transformed by a dramatic and unexpected event. It was well-known that Grand Ayatollah al-Sistani, like other grand ayatollahs, rarely left his house. But on August 6, after secretly leaving Najaf, he arrived in London seeking treatment for a heart ailment. It was evidently not a medical emergency, since he visited friends in Beirut on his way to London, where he did not immediately enter the hospital; and when he did, no surgery was required. Iraqi observers interpreted his swift and secret departure from Najaf as tacit permission for the United States to advance into the city: Sistani was no longer prepared to allow Muqtada to use his presence to shield the Sadrists from American attack.

As news spread that Sistani was in London, Muqtada issued a number of defiant statements. But he was cautious enough to have somebody else read his sermon in his father's mosque in Kufa. His absence underlined his fear that his enemies intended to kill him at the first opportunity. "America is the greatest of Satans," he told worshippers, and accused it of being responsible for the collapse of law and order. "I blame the occupier for all the attacks going on in Iraq, such as the attacks on the churches and the kidnapping," he said. As in the past he foreshadowed his own death: "Heaven does not come without a price. Don't wait for me to get up in the pulpit and give you directions. I, certainly, will be gone because the enemy is looking for me everywhere. Don't let my death divide you."[7]

Muqtada's words were accompanied by the rattle of gunfire in the background. As in so many other U.S. military actions in Iraq, the marines deployed immense firepower and underestimated the anger felt by Iraqis at the destruction and number of dead. When the marines claimed that they had killed three hundred Mehdi Army militiamen on the first Thursday and Friday of the battle, Iraqi television viewers noticed that some of the bodies scattered in the street were those of women. The slaughter appalled the Iraqi vice president and leader of the Dawa party, Ibrahim al-Jaafari, who said: "I think that killing Iraqi civilians is not a civilized way of building the new Iraq, which is based on protecting people and promoting dialogue, not bullets."[8] The attempt by the United States and Iyad Allawi to isolate Muqtada from the Shia community was already beginning to fray. A sign that the Iraqi government was nervous came when Allawi suddenly announced that "I invite Muqtada al-Sadr to take part in the elections next year."

People streamed out of Najaf to escape the fighting. The main market had already been pulverized and reduced to rubble. The scene was vividly described by my friend Ghaith Abdul-Ahad: "The wholesale food market, the size of a football pitch, had been reduced to a pile of warped metal. Everything had been incinerated, and each part of the market reeked with its own stench. The smell of burnt potatoes, figs and grapes marked the vegetables section. The cereals were still burning, giving off a faint smell of overcooked rice, and all around was an overwhelming odor of burnt plastic and the crackle of exploding Pepsi cans. Dozens of men, merchants and workers, were trying to rescue what they could. From the carnage appeared a militiaman wrapped in the Iraqi flag followed by two of his comrades. The trio were trying to stop looters digging into the incinerated merchandise."[9] Much of the fighting was in the Wadi al-Salaam cemetery. Muqtada's position looked more and more desperate as the marines closed in on the shrine and cut off Najaf from the outside world. In the other Shia cities, the Mehdi Army kept up pinprick attacks.

On August 13, Muqtada himself was wounded in three places by shrapnel from a bomb, according to his spokesman. This must have been when rumors of his death briefly circulated among the militiamen. They were swiftly quashed by his brief appearance among the militiamen. The following day he gave a press conference declaring that "Najaf has triumphed over imperialism and the imperial hubris." The press conference was run in full by al-Jazeera satellite television, and his words echoed around the Middle East. He added acidly that calling Iyad Allawi a "Shi'ite" was like calling Saddam Hussein a "Muslim."[10] Once again, as in April, the U.S. forces, though militarily dominant, hesitated to launch the final attack on the shrine. Its capture, particularly if it was damaged or destroyed in a last stand by the Mehdi Army, would do the Americans nothing but harm, unless they could also kill or capture Muqtada.

There is strong evidence that the U.S. military tried to do just that. All sides had a lot to lose if the assault on the shrine went ahead. The Shia Islamists in particular wanted to prevent an assault. Dr. Mowaffaq al-Rubai'e, the Iraqi national security adviser and an independent Shia Islamist, led a mediation effort supported by the Americans that at the time he thought was close to success. However, in retrospect, he is convinced that the Americans' willingness to negotiate was actually a cover for an attempt to lure Muqtada to a place where he could be killed or captured. "I believe that particular incident made Muqtada lose any confidence or trust in the [U.S.-led] coalition and made him really wild," says Dr. Rubai'e. As he recounts it, what happened was that he obtained the backing of Allawi, the U.S. embassy, and the U.S. military command, and then met with Muqtada, giving him a list of conditions to end the fighting. "He actually signed the agreement with his own handwriting," says

Dr. Rubai'e. "He wanted inner Najaf, the old city around the shrine, to be treated like the Vatican." Dr. Rubai'e returned to Baghdad to show the draft agreement to Allawi, who approved it, and then went back to Najaf for Muqtada to sign an agreement at a final meeting. This was to take place in Muqtada's father's old house in Najaf. As Dr. Rubai'e and the other mediators approached the house, the U.S. Marines targeted it with an intense bombardment. They then saw U.S. Special Forces racing to surround it. The marines were a few vital minutes too early and missed Muqtada, who had not yet arrived.

Both Muqtada and Dr. Rubai'e, who was considered to be very close to the Americans, believed they were victims of a setup. "When I came back to Baghdad I was really infuriated, I can tell you," said Dr. Rubai'e. "I went berserk with both [the U.S. commander General George] Casey and the ambassador [John Negroponte]." They denied they knew of a trap and said they would investigate, but he heard nothing more from them.

The impact of what he deemed to be a failed attempt to kill or arrest him under the guise of peace talks made Muqtada even more wary than he had been before. "I know him very well and I think his suspicion and distrust of the coalition and any foreigner is really deep-rooted," says Dr. Rubai'e. After it had happened Muqtada retreated to the Imam Ali shrine itself as the safest place for him to be in Najaf.[11] Back in Baghdad, Dr. Rubai'e found that the interim government, and the Western intelligence services, which seemed to direct many of its actions, had backed away from any idea of compromise. He found himself suspected of working for the Iranians— a permanent obsession on the part of the Allawi government when dealing with the Shia Islamists.

The Mehdi Army militiamen holding out in the Wadi al-Salaam suffered serious losses but did not stop fighting. Their morale, however, was beginning to wilt. Abbas Khoederi, a thirty-three-year-old militiaman, is frank about the difficulties they were in. "At the beginning of the battle, which went on for about a month, we had plenty of weapons and supplies," he says. "But with the passage of time and because of the blockade these had started to run out. Especially serious was when they cut off the supply of water to the Imam Ali shrine and the buildings nearby. Frankly, we went through very difficult times, but we remained steadfast and we were hearing Muqtada's orders, which encouraged and strengthened us. When there were periods of calm we would talk about what would happen at the end of the battle, and some of us were hesitant and fearful.

When somebody talked like that we would always shut him up before he had finished, in case what he said reached Muqtada. We began to feel that we were weak and the Americans were so strong."[12]

In the face of vastly superior U.S. military equipment, the pious and naïve young men fighting in Najaf believed they were receiving divine aid. "My brother returned from Najaf and told us there was a huge bird which cried out in a loud voice," said a teenager in Baghdad. "It appeared when the Americans began bombing Mehdi Army positions." The bird would brush falling bombs with its wings so they would not explode. "It's a sign from God—that he has soldiers of all kinds," he added. "That bird was a soldier of God." Other militiamen said they had seen mysterious shadows flitting around American tanks, which they believed were angels intervening to disable the guns or tracks of the tanks. "Those tanks could not move—something had fixed them to the ground," claimed one fighter, Sayf Adnan, a twenty-five-year-old fighting near the Imam Ali shrine with a group of Mehdi Army militiamen when it was heavily bombed. "It went on for half an hour," he said. "Bombs struck every metre, but eighty percent of them did not blow up. Not one of us was hurt. We knew we were under the protection of Imam Ali . . . and nothing would happen to us."[13]

In any event, it was Grand Ayatollah Ali al-Sistani, and not angels or other emissaries of divine assistance, who saved Muqtada and the Mehdi Army fighters. Sistani and the Marji'iyyah wanted the Sadrists out of Najaf but did not want to see them or the city destroyed, permanently dividing the Shia community. They were also very careful—as Iyad Allawi, the defense minister Hazem al-Shalaan, and Interior Minister Falah al-Naqib were not—to avoid being seen as American pawns. Sistani had not left Iraq through the U.S.-controlled Baghdad airport, but made the arduous journey by car through southern Iraq to get a plane from Kuwait. The United States and its favored ministers in the government behaved as if their propaganda about the Sadrists being "foreign fighters," Iranian puppets, or "anti-Iraq forces" (the latter term was dreamed up by an American PR company) were true. As late as August 25, Hazem al-Shalaan, speaking from the safety of a U.S. Army base outside Najaf, boasted: "This evening, Iraqi forces will reach the doors of the shrine and control it and I appeal to the Mehdi Army to throw down their weapons. If they do not, we will wipe them out."[14] He spoke as if Iraqi security forces were leading the assault, but most Iraqis were aware that they were only playing a cosmetic role in the fighting. Mainstream Shia clergy were often far more realistic about what was happening on the ground than Allawi or his American mentors. Ayatollah Mohammed Bahr al-Ulum, long an exiled opponent of Saddam Hussein, said bluntly: "The government has lost control of the Middle Euphrates region and the south, even if it manages to calm down these areas, temporarily, by using brute force."[15]

Muqtada was also looking for a compromise, despite all his predictions of his own imminent martyrdom. His abortive negotiations with Dr. Rubai'e in early August showed he was agreeable to a deal including leaving Najaf, but not to an admission of defeat. As in April, his men had stood up to the U.S. war machine and defied the U.S. occupation, which solidified his support among poor and young Shia. For youthful fighters in Sadr City his legitimacy exceeded that of the four grand ayatollahs in Najaf, all very old, three of whom were Iranians. "Sayyid Muqtada: Don't pay attention to the elderly clerics, they are spies," shouted an unemployed young man carrying a rocket-propelled grenade launcher in Sadr City as he celebrated an attack that had destroyed a U.S. Humvee. A Shia policeman added: "We will remain behind Muqtada. He is still a holy warrior even if he leaves the shrine and becomes less visible."[16]

But this support was by no means universal. Muqtada was feared and despised by the Shia shopkeepers, businessmen, and professionals just as the *sans-culottes* who manned the barricades during the French Revolution were regarded with visceral terror by the Paris bourgeois. The Sadrists were particularly unpopular in Najaf, where many blamed them and not the Americans for the destruction of part of their city. Dr. Ahmed, a firm supporter of Sistani in Najaf and an opponent of Muqtada, says: "In the center of Najaf, shopkeepers whose businesses had been devastated hated the followers of al-Sadr. People asked: 'Why did they have to choose Najaf for their battle? Why don't they fight in Kufa instead?' We hoped that American forces would eliminate all those who took part in the battle."[17] For Dr. Ahmed the Sadrists were an arm of the criminal classes.

Among the Shia leadership there was also a belief that Muqtada's confrontation with the United States was ill-advised. The broad strategy approved by the Shia political parties and the Marji'iyyah was to cooperate with the U.S. occupation in order to compel the holding of elections in 2005, which the Shia as the majority of the population would inevitably win. Armed resistance by the Mehdi Army and anti-American nationalism, however popular on the street, might have the disastrous effect of alienating the United States at the very moment when the Shia community in Iraq was within touching distance of winning the greatest victory in its history.

Until quite late in the day, the hawks in the Iraqi government and the Anglo-American intelligence agencies seemed to think they were winning. On August 19 Qassim Dawood, the minister of state for military affairs, demanded that Muqtada publicly announce that he would disband the Mehdi Army, hand over weapons in all provinces, leave the shrine in Najaf, and confirm in writing that he would not undertake any armed action in the future. But Muqtada categorically refused to disband the Mehdi Army.[18] Furthermore, on the same day Dawood was making his demands, Sistani left his hospital in London and his spokesman indicated that the Grand Ayatollah would accept the symbolic key to the shrine and control of the shrine complex. There was no mention of the Mehdi Army being disbanded. Sistani's action preempted the interim government's plan to storm the shrine in order to eliminate Muqtada. The government's first reaction was to indulge in fanciful wish fulfillment similar to that of the Mehdi Army militiamen who saw angels disabling American tanks. A government spokesman announced, wholly falsely, that Iraqi security forces had captured the shrine of Imam Ali without a fight, the Mehdi Army militamen had thrown down their arms, and Muqtada himself had escaped "under the cover of darkness." All this was fantasy, as journalists in the shrine swiftly reported. On August 25, Sistani returned to Basra and, after meeting the governor of the city, it was announced that he would lead a peace march to Najaf to save the shrine of Imam Ali. The Sadrist spokesmen accepted a cease-fire and said they would do whatever Sistani ordered. The Sadrists inside the shrine were particularly joyful. "The situation is getting worse day by day and only God's intervention can save us," Mohammed al-Battat was quoted as saying. "I think this march is a gift from God." Though the peace marchers were shot at by police and national guardsmen, Sistani's presence in Najaf checkmated the hawks, who could no longer storm the shrine. On August 26, the U.S. military declared a cease-fire and Muqtada visited Sistani. They agreed to a five-point peace plan under which Najaf and Kufa were to be demilitarized and the Mehdi Army would withdraw from them. The Iraqi police would take over control. There was a call for the withdrawal of foreign forces from both cities and for compensation for those whose property had been damaged. In the margin of the agreement Muqtada wrote the significant words: "These are not requests, but the instructions of the *Marji'iyya* and I am prepared to implement whatever is in them in response to the *Marji'iyya's* instructions."[19] A few days later he ordered the Mehdi Army to cease fighting in the rest of the country.

The main losers in the second battle of Najaf were Iyad Allawi and the interim government. They had intended to isolate Muqtada from the rest of the Shia political and religious leadership, and had ended up isolating themselves. Allawi was blind to the consequences of appearing as a U.S. proxy in Iraq and relying on U.S. military might. On December 4, 2005, while campaigning in the second of two parliamentary elections held in that year, Allawi unwisely visited the shrine of Imam Ali in Najaf. Worshippers reacted furiously at the sight of him, shouting abuse and hurling their shoes in his direction. One of the few television news reports to cause general amusement in Iraq in recent years was one showing the portly figure of Allawi running speedily through the gates of the shrine followed by a hail of shoes, a traditional method of showing contempt. He later claimed there had been an attempt to assassinate him by "about sixty people dressed in black carrying machetes and pistols," though nobody else saw them or heard shots.[20]

The United States had also lost because for the second time it had deployed its full might against Muqtada, only to see him and his movement live to fight another day. As so often happened to the United States in Iraq, its military strength failed to produce political gains. The outright winner of the August battle in Najaf was Grand Ayatollah Sistani, who showed his immense authority over the Iraqi Shia, which neither the interim government in Baghdad nor the U.S. administration in Washington dared confront. Sistani had broken Muqtada's grip on Najaf and shown that the Sadrists could not survive without heeding the wishes of the grand ayatollahs. Muqtada could not credibly go on denouncing and disregarding the "passive" Marji'iyyah that had just saved him from possible extinction. His militiamen had suffered dreadful losses but these could be replaced. He had survived, but he had come close enough to defeat to be wary of fighting the U.S. Army for a third time.

CHAPTER FOURTEEN

A Turn to Politics

Muqtada and his surviving militiamen were at first depressed by what they saw as a serious defeat in the second battle for Najaf. After losing many dead and injured they had been forced to withdraw from the city for which they had fought for so long. "At the end of the battle we felt a sense of disappointment and failure," says Abbas Khoederi, a Mehdi Army militiaman who had been fighting near the shrine. "We believed we had moved away from what the people wanted. Even Muqtada retired from daily life and issued no statement for a long time, while we avoided letting people know we were Sadrists."[1] It was not until May 16, 2005, over eight months later, that Muqtada was to reemerge in public. By then it was clear that his defeat at Najaf was more military than political.

This was not initially obvious to either the Sadrists or their enemies. "I knew we had beaten Muqtada when I saw him walking on his own in Najaf without anybody beside him," recalls Sabah Khadim, a senior official at the Iraqi Interior Ministry.[2] In agreeing to leave Najaf the Mehdi Army lost its grip on the religious capital of Iraqi Shi'ism. The immediate winners in the three-week war were all Muqtada's rivals or opponents: Grand Ayatollah Sistani, the hawza, the al-Hakim family, and the Supreme Council for Islamic Revolution in Iraq (SCIRI). "After having resolved the Najaf crisis," said a student close to the Sadrists, "Sistani directed that religious schools belonging to the Sadr family be placed under the hawza's control and the Sadr family headquarters be moved outside the old city. The al-Hakim family, which leads SCIRI, thus recovered control of the city with Sistani's blessing. It bought several plots of land and buildings and deployed its Badr militia to protect the holy shrines. While SCIRI offices mushroomed in Najaf, the Sadrist movement virtually disappeared from sight. Even Muqtada's pictures could not be found in Najaf's old city."[3] Against these setbacks could be weighed the achievement of Muqtada and the Mehdi Army in surviving the onslaught of the U.S. Marines and the interim government. They no longer spoke of arresting him for the murder of Sayyid Majid al-Khoei (two of his senior advisers, Mustafa al-Yaqubi and Riyadh al-Nuri, detained for involvement in the crime, were released in August 2005). There was a further change in Muqtada's status: he had stopped even purporting to act under the auspices of Ayatollah Khadim al-Ha'eri in Qom, whom Sadr II had nominated as his official successor. "Al-Ha'eri criticized Muqtada secretly during the first battle for Najaf and never supported him," says Sheikh Ali, the Sadrist leader. "During the second battle he attacked him publicly and Muqtada later blamed him in his sermons."[4]

Most important in ensuring the Sadrists' continued significance, however, was that the political tide in Iraq was still running strongly in their favor on two crucial issues. First, the unpopularity of the U.S. occupation increased by the year, with the percentage saying that armed resistance was acceptable rising from seventeen percent in 2004 to fifty-one percent in 2007.[5] Second, the state remained weak, unable to provide ordinary Iraqis with security against sectarian killers and criminals, and this favored the growth of self-defense forces. As suicide bombers slaughtered people while they shopped in their markets or formed long queues to join the police or army, Shia with no sympathy for the militias nonetheless welcomed the protection of themselves and their families by men with guns. This naturally made the Mehdi Army more acceptable as a defense force in Shia districts. "If you don't have a militia you're not in politics in Iraq," remarked a veteran Iraqi observer of the political scene.

Having lost control of the old city of Najaf, Muqtada could no longer live in his father's house near the Imam Ali shrine, where Sayyid Majid al-Khoei had been brought by a furious mob in April 2003 and denied refuge by Muqtada minutes before he was murdered. It had been a convenient house as a family headquarters because, although the entrance was small, it was otherwise spacious and, like many older Najaf houses, had cavernous cellars extending far underground. Used for storage and keeping cool in summer, the cellars made excellent bomb shelters and places of concealment. In the coming years Muqtada moved, for obvious security reasons, from house to house in Najaf outside the old city and in Kufa, though he lived mainly in a modern blue-painted house in the middle-class al-Ashtraki district of Najaf.[6] His disappearance after the battle of Najaf was prolonged, but scarcely out of character. Ever since 2003 he has intermittently vanished from view when his political fortunes had been at a low ebb. These absences excited controversy among the foreign media, which routinely speculated on whether he had fled the country. But they are not out of the ordinary in Iraq, where ayatollahs are frequently secluded in their houses for years and where the Imam al-Mehdi, the Messiah whose return is longed for by the faithful, disappeared in Samarra over a thousand years ago.

It was during this period of seclusion that Muqtada adopted a new political approach. He replaced military with political action, though his opposition to the U.S. occupation remained unchanged. He explained that his strategy had evolved through three stages: "The Sadrist movement first resorted to peaceful resistance, then to armed resistance, and finally to political resistance. This does not present any problem: every situation requires its own response."[7] He admitted that the military option had failed, but said he was right to try it.[8] His new strategy was intelligent and in keeping with the times. It recognized that Sistani's policy of conditional cooperation with the U.S. occupation had worked. The Grand Ayatollah had compelled Washington to agree to two elections and one referendum in 2005, all of which would inevitably be won by the Shia majority. Iraqis would vote for a transitional government on January 30, for or against a new constitution on October 15, and, finally, for a four-year parliament on December 15. Muqtada expressed doubts about the validity of polls that were taking place under the auspices of the occupation, but even so, they would mean a radical transfer of power to the Shia. The Shia parties agreed to form an electoral coalition called the United Iraqi Alliance (UIA) on December 16, 2004, which, since it was backed by Sistani and the Marji'iyyah, was to prove unbeatable at the polls. Once the Sadrists had publicly forsworn armed resistance to the occupation, the main difference between their approach and that of Sistani disappeared (though Muqtada has not seen Sistani since 2004). Inevitably they became part of the UIA, winning 32 out of 275 seats in the December election. Essentially, Muqtada intended to have his cake and eat it: he wanted to control service ministries in the government such as health and transport, both big employers, but he also sought to distance himself from the government's blunders, failures, and corruption. Iyad Allawi, high up in the Sadrists' demonology, was replaced as prime minister in May 2005 by Ibrahim al-Jaafari, the Dawa leader who had denounced the attack on Najaf. It was going to be very difficult in the future to form an Iraqi government without Muqtada's agreement.

Did Muqtada have any alternative to joining the Shia coalition? Could he ever have united with the Sunni insurgents to form a common front against the occupation? The Sadrists had always been antisectarian and Iraqi nationalist. Sadr II had called on Shia to go and pray in Sunni mosques. Muqtada enjoyed brief popularity among some Sunni up to the end of 2005 because of his vocal opposition to the United States. His first act on his reemergence in April 2005 had been to seek to arbitrate between Shia and Sunni. An important reason why the United States had been eager to bring the first battle for Najaf to an end in April 2004 was fear that the Shia and Sunni insurgencies might combine. I had watched outside the main blood bank in Baghdad as Shia as well as Sunni gave blood for the wounded of Fallujah when it was being shelled by the U.S. Marines. But six months later, after merciless suicide bombings over the summer, the Shia of Baghdad wanted the rebellion in Fallujah crushed as soon as possible. The followers of Abu Musab al-Zarqawi issued bloodcurdling denunciations of the Shia as heretics deserving death. The supposedly more nationalist insurgent groups were also increasingly *salafi* and *jihadi,* born-again Sunni fanatics waging holy war on the Shia as well as Americans. The romantic vision of a popular front of Shia and Sunni was never really feasible. Muqtada very reasonably demanded that Sunni constitutional politicians who wanted to cooperate with him on an anti-occupation platform must first unconditionally condemn the murderous bomb attacks on Shia civilians, but this they refused to do. Both communities frequently claimed to be Iraqi nationalists, but in reality their definition of Iraqi nationalism differed radically. Shia friends complained to me that foreign journalists such as myself always exaggerated the extent of Sunni-Shia divisions in Iraq. They would say they had Sunni friends and relatives married to Sunni, but then they would add all-important exclusion clauses to this supposed amity, such as saying that all former Baathists should be arrested. Sunni friends would likewise claim that sectarian strife was less than I supposed, but would then go on to dismiss Sistani, Muqtada, and the Shia religious parties as all pawns of Iran.

* * *

People in the Middle East are notoriously prone to believe in conspiracy theories, but the most poisonous myth in the region is surely the conviction that the Shia of Iraq are puppets manipulated by Iran. The long struggle of the Iraqi Shia against Saddam Hussein, in which Iran had played a minimal role, is ignored. The former regime had denounced Shia political activists and the insurgents of 1991 as Iranian proxies, and it had found willing, if not very well informed, listeners in Washington. Sunni leaders in the Arab world, notably in Saudi Arabia, Jordan, and Egypt, spoke nervously of the election victories of the Shia in Iraq in 2005 as presaging an Iranian drive to the west. Saudi envoys in Washington repeatedly denounced, to anyone who would listen, the Shia-dominated governments of Ibrahim al-Jaafari and Nouri al-Maliki. Much of the vituperation was ill-disguised sectarianism, but the White House progressively adopted a similar view by which the machinations of Iran were detected behind many of America's disasters in Iraq. The Bush administration had always been happiest with its "axis of evil" rhetoric demonizing Iran; obviously though, it was Saudi Arabia and the Sunni states that were the main support for the Sunni insurgents when it came to providing money and suicide bombers. "Shia extremists are just as hostile to America [as al-Qaeda]," said Bush in his State of the Union address on January 23, 2007, "and are also determined to dominate the Middle East." These were dangerous, absurdly exaggerated beliefs. The Shia Hezbollah movement in Lebanon and Muqtada's Mehdi Army in Iraq might be effective on their home territory but had no chance of making headway in Sunni states where Shia are usually a small and persecuted minority.

The Sadrist movement was historically anti-Iranian, as described above. But the U.S. accusations of Iranian complicity with Muqtada were to a degree self-fulfilling. "Iran can afford to compromise in Iraq, but it cannot afford for the U.S. to be victorious," a veteran Kurdish observer of Iraqi politics told me. "If the Americans threaten Iran, then the Iranians would prefer to fight the Americans in Baghdad than in Tehran." In many ways Iranian policy was simple and openly declared. In 2001 and 2003 the Iranian government had been overjoyed to see the overthrow by the United States of two of its inveterate enemies, the Taliban in Afghanistan and Saddam Hussein's regime in Iraq. It might have worried about the potential threat posed by the U.S. military forces in both countries, but these were soon tied down by Sunni insurgencies that had nothing to do with Iran. In Iraq, the only large Arab state with a Shia majority, fair elections inevitably meant a Shia-dominated government led by men with long links to Iran. The Iranian leaders wanted Iraq to stay together, but as a weak state under Shia leadership that would never threaten them again.

The United States had entirely played into Tehran's hands in 2003 and 2004. Despite frequent accusations of Iranian involvement there was little sign of it. But the Iranians could not always expect events in Iraq to develop in their favor. They wanted to have influence within every Iraqi Shia organization, religious or political. Tehran could also see the immense advantage to itself of having 160,000 American soldiers stuck in the Iraqi quagmire, who were therefore vulnerable to Iranian-backed forces if the Americans attacked Iranian nuclear facilities.

In the course of 2005, Iranian intelligence did start to increase its influence in the Sadrist movement and the Mehdi Army. According to a leading anti-Iranian Sadrist militant, whose nom de guerre is Hussein Ali, and who was proposing to flee Iraq in the fall of 2007, Muqtada strongly opposed this surge in Iranian material support and influence within his movement, but he was unable to oppose it effectively. "In 2005 the situation changed with the Sadrists," says Hussein Ali, "as the Iranians became more involved [in the Sadr movement] with the help of important advisers to Muqtada. Iranian policy was to offer aid in the shape of financial support, modern weapons, and a good communications system. Once lured into accepting them the recipient cannot do without them." The loose organization of the Sadrists made it easy for Iranian intelligence to penetrate it and bring certain of its units under their control, though they remained formally loyal to Muqtada. "They [Iranian intelligence] started giving $800 to anyone who would attack the Americans or assassinate some Iraqi figures," says Hussein Ali. "People were given lists of names of former Baathists, present-day political figures, or ordinary people to be killed because they were meant to be working against society. If they refuse to do what they are told then they face death." Two of Ali's fellow critics of Iranian influence within the Sadrist movement were mysteriously assassinated. In one case the killers took advantage of the surprise success of Iraq's soccer team over South Korea in the Asia Games in 2007 to murder their victim as Baghdad erupted with celebratory gunfire.

There was another reason why it was easy to infiltrate or suborn Mehdi Army units. Most of its men were not paid. "Iranian intelligence secretly recruited young people to train in Iran," continues Hussein Ali. "They give volunteers $300 to $400 a month, train them to use weapons and to fight the Americans. Of course this is an indirect way of controlling Iraq. It is easy enough for Iranian intelligence to persuade a man to join the groups it controls through money and good weapons if he is unemployed and the Mehdi Army pays no wages."⁹

The Mehdi Army was hardly the sole Shia organization to be penetrated and influenced by Iran. Muqtada's main rival in organizing the Shia, SCIRI, had carefully cultivated its connections with Washington, but there was never any real evidence that it had ever severed its traditional connection with Iran. Its leader, Abdul Aziz al-Hakim, now ailing with cancer, made visits to Tehran before announcing any fresh policy initiative. The Iranians had a particular reason for cultivating the Mehdi Army in that they had always found it frustratingly difficult to turn SCIRI's militia arm, the Badr Organization, into an effective military ally. They concluded that the Mehdi Army and the Sadrists had more grassroots support and would be easier to expand. The Iranian moves seem to have been precautionary because Iran did not want to overthrow the Iraqi government. Paradoxically, while abusing each other, Tehran and Washington both supported the Shia-Kurdish coalition government that ruled in Baghdad after 2005. But Iran also wanted to make sure that it had assets in Iraq that could help ignite an anti-American explosion in Iraq if the United States ever made good on its oft-repeated threats to attack Iran.

There were endless speculation and numerous newspaper articles published after Muqtada was first identified as a threat to the United States that discussed how far the Mehdi Army was trained and armed by the Revolutionary Guards in Iran. There was also some debate on the Mehdi Army's links to the Hezbollah movement in Lebanon. The focus on the supply of IEDs (improvised explosive devices) as a sign of Iran's secret involvement in Iraq was always misconceived. Roadside bombs have been common guerrilla weapons since the IRA was fighting the British army in Ireland in 1920–21. Lethal devices can be made out of weed killer. Shaped charges could be made in Iraqi workshops as well as Iran. Obtaining military equipment has never been a problem anywhere in Iraq so long as there is money to pay for it. As for training, which Iran and Hezbollah were supposedly providing, it is noticeable that all the Shia militias are notably badly trained. Muqtada may have aspired to lead a movement modeled on Hezbollah in Lebanon. His distant cousin Musa al-Sadr had been the inspirational leader of the Lebanese Shia until he disappeared in

Libya in 1978. But the Sadrists were never able to emulate the discipline and unity of the Lebanese guerrillas.

Many in the Mehdi Army were unhappy about Muqtada's turn toward constitutional politics in 2005. Hatred for the U.S. occupation ran deep among the militiamen, and there was a wholly justified disbelief that the new Iraqi administration was truly independent. "The American strategy was clever in drawing the Sadrists into the government," laments Abbas Fadhel, the battle-hardened militiaman who had fought in August amid the tombs in the Wadi al-Salaam cemetery in Najaf. "At the beginning, our movement was revolutionary because it was the only political trend for the poorest members of society. But this changed when we entered mainstream political life. Parliament didn't do anything for us. The Americans just wanted to make us believe that we were in power and at the same time to end our confrontation with them."[10] This explanation probably credits U.S. officials in Baghdad with more political imagination than they ever showed signs of possessing. It might have been in their interests to keep the Sadrists inside the government, but instead they regarded their presence there with deep suspicion and agitated to get rid of them.

Taking part in constitutional politics brought material benefits to the core areas of Sadrist support such as Sadr City, where unemployment had been around seventy percent. There was a desperate hunger for jobs of any kind. While Muqtada was confronting the government in 2003–4 he was, notes Sadrist veteran Sheikh Ali, "preventing anyone from joining the army and police, so many young people lost opportunities to get work." The government has always been the main source of employment in Iraq because it controlled the oil revenues that were the country's only wealth (Iraq's next biggest export used to be dates). For the first time the Shia underclass began to get a share of the cake. "There were no jobs immediately after the fall of Saddam Hussein, but things got better two years later in 2005," says Sheikh Ali. "Many of the jobs were for cleaning and garbage collection. If anything happens to Sadr City, Baghdad will sink into the dirt because the majority of the city's cleaning staff comes from Sadr City." (Given the prevailing filth in the rest of Baghdad it is not clear that Sadr City's garbage collection is as effective as he claims.) The provision of jobs at a more senior level became easier once the Sadrists had taken control of ministries in 2006. "Instead of writing to ministries asking them to give jobs, we appointed people wholesale as minor officials." Hospitals became Sadrist strongholds that Sunni were afraid to enter, and medical orderlies who did not have the correct Sadrist connections lost their jobs. "The economic situation in Sadr City became much better," says Sheikh Ali. "Before, people were using donkey carts, while now they have cars and good-quality televisions. The Ministry of Labor and Social Affairs provides loans of $10,000 for projects for which people apply with fake documents to get the money they later refuse to return. Many poor people who could only dream of an education under Saddam started doing intensive night study, even old people who want to catch up."[11] There were other practical benefits that people in Shia districts of Baghdad drew from Sadrist control: everybody else was frightened of them and with reason. Once, when electricity cuts were more than usually prolonged in Baghdad's al-Jadida district neighboring Sadr City, the Mehdi Army went to the house of the official responsible. "The Mehdi Army militiamen put him in the boot of their car and threatened to punish him," says Salim Shehab, a twenty-three-year-old student. "After that the electricity remained on permanently for many days, the streets were cleaned and fuel and gas were more available to people."[12]

Some of this sounds a little too good to be true, but the Shia poor of Baghdad were increasingly a power in the land. Despite murderous suicide bombing attacks, their districts were peaceful compared to Sunni neighborhoods. The Shia middle class in the center of the capital were often affected worse than the poor living in shantytowns in the east of the city. Immediately after the fall of Saddam, Sadrist militiamen had sold their mobile phones to buy weapons, but the movement now increasingly had access to money and jobs. Both were important in order to secure political allegiance and to compete with SCIRI, which controlled local government in most of southern Iraq. Many Mehdi Army members might not be paid directly, but they were given sinecure jobs in the government where the Sadrists were in control. Jobs, handouts, and political loyalty went together as in U.S. cities controlled by Irish American political machines a century ago. In each neighborhood in Sadr City there was a Sadrist office, with a social supervisor in charge of giving monthly salaries to the very poor. "I saw a family," says one visitor, "consisting of nine members, the father disabled because of a car accident and without a breadwinner. All their money came from Sadr's office, which even paid their rent. They love Muqtada because he keeps them alive."

The role of Mehdi Army gunmen is usually emphasized in explaining the strength of the Sadrists in Baghdad, but control of ministries was also very important. Manale Youssif, a thirty-two-year-old woman working in the Ministry of Health, gives a graphic description of what Sadrist control had meant at her ministry. "The main ministry building is close to Fadel, a Sunni district in central Baghdad, so all the security guards are from the Sadrist movement, although Muqtada gave orders from the beginning that jobs should not only go to his people. But what really happened was the precise opposite of his instructions. The head of the Sadr office in Sadr City would send to the ministry lists of names of people to be employed. There was no place for any Sunni." Manale says this is true of other ministries such as transport, where every Baathist employee was dismissed and the first jobs available went to a Shia who could claim a martyr in the family: "Good jobs go to those with education certificates and jobs as guards go to those without." All employees carry guns and when they are asked by the police if their weapons are licensed they simply reply: "It is on the orders of the Office of the Martyr [Sadr's office]."

Nobody is in doubt about who is in control from the moment they enter the Health Ministry building. "Before you reach the reception hall there is a room for searching women," says Manale. "All the women in this room wear the veil, a cloak, and gloves and their perfume is the same that you smell inside holy shrines. The women doing the searching treat people who are not from their [Shia] districts with a sort of arrogance, as if to have revenge for the lack of respect shown to them in past decades. The same thing happens to men."[13] Sunni doctors and medical staff are squeezed out. "I cannot go to the ministry," says Mahmoud Qassim, thirty-eight, a Sunni doctor. "All the Sunni doctors are now working in Sunni districts just as I do now, practicing in the Amariya district."[14] Many Sunni believe there is a room in the basement of the Health Ministry where Sunni are tortured; it is called the "cellar of the guillotine."

The Iraqi state never recovered from its collapse in 2003. Ministries became rackets for those who controlled them. What looked to Iraqi and U.S. embassy officials as much-needed reforms were often only a new form of corruption in disguise. When new vehicle number plates were introduced, the only way to obtain them was by bribery. The same was true of new passports, known as "G" passports, which were supposedly more secure than the old but could only be obtained by paying between $500 and $1,000 to a range of officials. Overall, the Sadrists were disappointed by their own ministers such as Dr. Ali al-Samari, Muqtada's personal doctor, who on becoming minister of health, stated: "Our work is professional and I do not want anybody who wears a turban interfering in my work." This did not go down well with the other Sadrists, who, in addition, complained that health services in Sadr City were no better than before. Salim al-Maliki, who was transport minister, attracted criticism of a different sort. He was seen as only "willing to help those who were close to him" and was much criticized for commandeering a whole plane to take his extended family on pilgrimage.[15]

The Sadrists' brand of Islamic puritanism spread rapidly on the fall of Saddam. "Before the fall, women in Sadr City were both veiled and unveiled," recalls one woman in Baghdad, "but on the second day after the fall all women started wearing the veil. I had a friend who was wearing the veil but not the black cloak until a threatening note was thrown into her house. Her brothers rushed out into the street screaming that whoever had written the note was a coward. Now she is forced to wear a cloak inside Sadr City, though she takes it off when she leaves."[16] All music and video shops in Sadr City were closed in 2003 and shop owners who insisted on reopening them had their premises burned. It used to be common to hear popular songs blaring from shops and houses in Sadr City, but today the only songs that can be heard are those praising Muqtada. Liquor stores were closed, though these had already been limited in number during Saddam Hussein's "Faith" campaign in the 1990s, and ownership was confined to Christians.

The Sadrists stood for the separation of men and women rather than the total subjection of women like the Taliban in Afghanistan. Most of the women students in al-Mustansariya University were from Sadr City. The Sadrists had their own courts up to 2005, when they were closed because of Muqtada's more conciliatory attitude to the government. While they operated, Manale Youssif reports, they "heard women's complaints and asserted their rights, particularly in matters of divorce and child custody." Muqtada's insistence on women wearing the veil was in keeping with the attitude of his father but did not make much difference in most of southern Iraq, where women traditionally wore the veil anyway. "The Sadrist current," says Manale, "gave women the freedom to work, but on one condition—that every woman who wants to work should not mix with men." Of three Shia religious parties—SCIRI, the Sadrists, and Fadhila—she thought SCIRI was the most bigoted against women and Fadhila, which controlled Basra, was the best because many of its leaders were well educated.[17]

It was not only state authority that collapsed after the fall of the old regime. In the universities the staff wholly lost authority over students and did not dare give them low marks or fail their exam papers. "The professors have no control over the students who openly cheat in front of them," says Mohammed Tariq, a twenty-five-year-old Sadrist student activist at Mustansariya University. When one female professor asked a student not to cheat on an exam, he replied chillingly: "Do you know that the price of a bullet is less than a dinar?" Mustansariya University is close to Sadr City, and Sunni students and teachers moved from there to Baghdad University. Mohammed Tariq says that the Sadrists tried to stop attacks on Sunni students, but they failed: "The students who were controlling the situation and the Mehdi Army in the university held religious celebrations like Ashura with black banners and black clothes and threatened to kill anybody who objected."[18]

The Sadrists had never been social revolutionaries, but their supporters were the millions of impoverished Iraqis whose lives had been destroyed by the disasters of war, insurrection, and sanctions that had shattered Iraqi society after 1980. This vast and dangerous underclass had little time for the Iraqi government or its American protectors, but Muqtada felt he had no choice after Najaf but to pursue a political rather than a military strategy. This essentially meant that he did not intend to confront the U.S. military again if he could help it, though the Mehdi Army did not disappear or even contract in size. Its checkpoints were still everywhere in Shia Baghdad and it was a potent weapon in intra-Shia feuding. One event in particular showed the Mehdi Army's continued strength. In August 2005 the Badr Organization in Najaf held a demonstration claiming that Muqtada's staff at one of the few offices he still maintained in the city were secret Baathists. None of the staff were armed, under the agreement of a year earlier, and they, along with other Sadrists praying near the shrine, were beaten up by Badr militiamen. Muqtada had a habit of either not retaliating at all to a provocation, because he considered the moment inopportune, or retaliating with far more vigor than expected. In this case he chose the latter option, and within hours some 350 SCIRI offices in Baghdad and across southern Iraq were ablaze. This ability of the Sadrists to mobilize thousands of militiamen was of great importance as Baghdad and central Iraq hurtled, with ever-increasing speed, toward a civil war between Shia and Sunni.

CHAPTER FIFTEEN

The Battle of Baghdad

I kept in touch with Bassim Abdul-Rahman, my driver, and Haider al-Safi, my translator and guide, who had nearly been killed with me by the Mehdi Army outside Kufa on April 19, 2004. Bassim continued driving for me occasionally, while Haider left Iraq for London to do a university course, though his family stayed in Baghdad. What happened to both men and the districts they came from vividly illustrates the differing fates of Shia and Sunni in Baghdad as the struggle for control of the city escalated. On February 22, 2006, men in police uniforms tied up the guards at the al-Askari Shia shrine in Samarra and blew it up. This turned the sectarian conflict in the capital into a raging civil war of extraordinary cruelty and bloodiness. I had always admired Bassim for his quiet competence and cool nerve, but after Samarra it had become too dangerous for him as a Sunni to drive in much of Baghdad. The Mehdi Army, by now the generic term used for all Shia militias, was winning the battle for the city. When Bassim picked me up at the airport in the summer of 2006, our journey back to the al-Hamra Hotel, where I was staying, took three times as long as usual because he had to take a serpentine route to avoid checkpoints that might be manned by police commandos doubling as Shia death squads. Sometimes it was too dangerous for Bassim and other Sunni working for my newspaper to go home, so they had to stay in the hotel overnight. When I went to visit Hussein al-Shahristani, the oil minister, in May 2007 in his towering ministry building, it was too deep in Shia-held territory in east Baghdad for a Sunni to go there, and I had to find Shia drivers and bodyguards.

For Bassim, as for many Sunni in Baghdad, life had turned into a nightmare. "I remember very well what happened to all of us when we were in Kufa in April 2004," recalled Bassim three and a half years later. "I thought we were dead men at the time and it is a terrible thing to think about." At the time he was living in a house in part of the al-Jihad district in southwest Baghdad that was largely Shia but with some Sunni. Though there was intense fighting in the rest of Baghdad, al-Jihad was relatively quiet until the Samarra bombing. Afterward the Mehdi Army began to attack Sunni mosques and houses and many people fled. "I was thinking of leaving," says Bassim, "but I did not have another house to stay in. Frankly, I was confused and decided to stay and I thought that the government would be able to control the situation very soon, but it could not. I decided to go for a short period to Syria with my family and we stayed there from the end of July until the middle of September 2006. When we returned I went to our district and found pictures of Muqtada pasted to the gate of our house. The people who put them there knew that I am a Sunni from al-Adhamiyah and they asked my neighbors if they knew my new address. I asked my Shia brother-in-law to go to my house in order to gather some stuff, like electrical goods and some important identity cards and other documents. He had only managed to pack up the television and some blankets when our neighbors came and warned him to be as quick as he could because if the [Shia] militia came they would stop him or even kill him."

The house in al-Jihad was locked and for a time remained empty. Bassim was forced to go to live in one small room in the house of his friend Mohammed, another driver, who lived in al-Khadra, a wholly Sunni district in southwest Baghdad from which Shia had fled. In this single cramped room Bassim lived with his wife, Maha, thirty-nine, and his children: Sarah, fourteen; Noor, nine; and Sama, four. "We used to have information about our house from time to time from my Shia neighbor, who told me on June 5, 2007, that it had been taken by the militia. They accused me of being a high-rank officer in the former intelligence service and because of that they got a permit [from al-Sadr's office] to take it over." Two Shia families moved into Bassim's house for two months and when they left they took all of his remaining belongings. They left the house unlocked and available for another Shia family to stay in. The permanent loss of his home, his only valuable possession, was a terrible blow to Bassim and Maha. "I have nothing else to lose aside from my house," he says, "and because of what happened I had a heart attack and so did my wife. I worked as a taxi driver for a few days, but I couldn't do it for any longer because of the dangerous situation, and I had no other way to make a living. Finally I sold my car and my wife's few gold things and I will try to go to Sweden, even if I have to go illegally. It has been a hard decision, but it is the best solution for a family who lost their home through threats."[1]

Losing his house and his ability to make a living as a driver, the twin disasters that devastated Bassim's life, were common enough occurrences in Baghdad by the fourth year of the war. Both communities were affected, but the Sunni were outnumbered and had more to lose. By the end of 2006 it was obvious that the Shia had won the battle for Baghdad. "The Mehdi Army dominates fifty percent of Baghdad and eighty percent of Shia regions in it," estimated Hussein Ali, the former commander.[2] At least ten neighborhoods that had been mixed a year earlier were entirely Shia, according to residents and Iraqi and American military commanders.[3] The push by the Mehdi Army continued during the so-called surge, and by the summer of 2007 the U.S. military estimated that the proportion of Baghdad's population that was Shia had risen from sixty-five to seventy-five percent.[4]

Haider had never much cared for the Sadrists or the Mehdi Army, even before our nerve-racking encounter with them in Kufa. At that time they had little influence in al-Khadamiyah, the predominantly Shia district centered on the shrine of Musa al-Khazim and his grandson Mohammed al-Jawad, the seventh and ninth imams, in northwest Baghdad where he and his family lived. "They only had one small *husseiniya* and nobody took them seriously at the beginning," says Haider. In the first year of the occupation the most influential person in Khadamiyah was a cleric, Hussain al-Sadr, a distant cousin of Muqtada and a beneficiary of the al-Sadr name, but in every other way the opposite of his revolutionary relatives. Claiming to be only interested in religion and not in politics, he had echoed the regime's pronouncements under Saddam Hussein, but "he spoke in such a way that implied he was speaking under compulsion. There was also a desperate need for religious leadership in al-Khadamiyah at the time." Al-Sadr's influence was strong enough to prevent looting in the district during the anarchy when Saddam Hussein fell, but afterward he made a mistake. "Like most of the political parties, he thought the best way to gain political power was to be close to the Americans," says Haider. "His house was fully protected by his followers and he received many of his new

American friends there. Like many others, he was cultivating the American ruler Paul Bremer and invited him to his home. What really broke the back of his credibility was that he was shown on television stamping his hot kisses on Bremer's cheeks and handing Bremer a holy Koran." Al-Sadr's influence waned and was replaced by that of the followers of his cousin Muqtada and the Mehdi Army. The other two religious parties, SCIRI and Dawa, had never been very strong in al-Khadamiyah. SCIRI tried to take over the shrine and the area around it but failed. Dawa, though it once had many followers in the area during Sadr I, was always a small party of the highly religious and well-educated elite.

Al-Khadamiyah was not natural Sadrist territory, even though Muqtada's family came from there. It is surprising but instructive to see how the Mehdi Army was able to take over in the following years. More prosperous than Sadr City, it had never been the home of the impoverished underclass, which was the main constituency of the Sadrists. Its people were generally well educated and famous for their solidarity against outsiders. "But during the high point of Hussain al-Sadr's power," recalls Haider, "the Sadrists succeeded in attracting young guys by opposing the occupation. Their influence increased day by day and they started to control al-Khadamiyah with checkpoints everywhere and militants in black clothes searching people's cars. The Mehdi Army started opening Sadrist offices . . . using the houses of Baath party members or just empty houses all over al-Khadamiyah. They made patrols everywhere and recruited unemployed guys. In order to finance the huge number of people they had on their payroll they started to collect fees for protection from every house, particularly from those with the better houses." Many local people were dubious about the presence of the Mehdi Army, and many of those coming into al-Khadamiyah were from two neighboring strongholds of the Sadrists in the districts of Shua'ala and Hurriya. As savage sectarian warfare spread through Baghdad, people in al-Khadamiyah felt that "if they had to choose between the *salafi* [Sunni fanatics who regarded the Shia as heretics who could be killed] and the Mehdi Army, then they would choose the Mehdi Army."

When the U.S. "surge" started in February 2007 it was partly directed at breaking the grip of the Mehdi Army over much of Baghdad. What happened in al-Khadamiyah is an example of why it did not entirely succeed. Muqtada, as we have seen, was particularly good at dodging a punch and, ever since the second battle of Najaf, was determined to avoid an outright military confrontation with the U.S. Army. The Mehdi Army, far larger, better trained, and better equipped than in 2004, was stood down and its commanders sent out of Baghdad. Militants blended back into the civilian population. Haider described the events that followed: "After the 'surge' began, most of the Sadrist militants left al-Khadamiyah and took down signs outside the Sadrist offices, but the Americans started raiding these houses anyway and arresting anybody there. They checked every single house in our area and gave my mother a phone number to call if she had any information about the Mehdi Army. Essentially al-Khadamiyah remained under the control of the Mehdi militia, but Hussain al-Sadr still had some influence there. [By another account he did a deal whereby the Mehdi Army came in as a protection force on condition they did not harm local Sunni.] He has his own protection force, which is a battalion from the Iraqi army. The Sadrists kept a very low profile during the whole period of the 'surge' and didn't resist the Americans. The Mehdi Army seemed determined to avoid any confrontation with them."[5]

Haider believed that the retreat of the Sadrists was temporary and deceptive, and beneath the surface they were still in command. One sign of this came in August 2007, when there were serious clashes in Kerbala during the Sha'aban pilgrimage, when the Mehdi Army fought SCIRI (now renamed the Supreme Islamic Iraqi Council, or SIIC). "What happened showed the power of the Sadrists, not only in the government but also in controlling the streets. When the fighting started in Kerbala they immediately burned three offices of SCIRI in al-Khadamiyah. Carloads of militants came from different directions, took over the offices, and arrested everybody who was there."

President George W. Bush was later to speak as if Sunni-Shia warfare started with the bombing of the Samarra shrine in 2006. In reality, suicide bombings clearly targeting Shia had begun at least as early as March 2004, when 270 Shia pilgrims were killed during religious celebrations in al-Khadamiyah and Kerbala. Grand Ayatollah Ali al-Sistani counseled against retaliation as a matter of principle and the Shia leaders saw the suicide bombings as an attempt to torpedo their plan to take power legally through elections in 2005. When organized Shia retaliation did occur it came after the first Shia government was formed in May 2005, and was carried out by the Shia-dominated police and police commandos. They dragged former Baathists from their houses in broad daylight and left their tortured corpses beside the road a few days later. Seldom have death squads operated so openly. The relentless suicide bombings and assassinations carried out by al-Qaeda in Iraq progressively infuriated the Shia community as a whole. Mixed districts in Baghdad were becoming less mixed. Excluded from power, the Sunni felt they had no choice but to fight. The Shia, for their part, believed they had been patient for far too long against a merciless assault on their community. By February 2006 all that was needed was a particularly spectacular bombing or assassination against a Shia target to trigger massive and bloody retaliation.

Many people expected an explosion of Shia, and when it came, in the hours after the attack on the shrine in Samarra, it was shocking. Mehdi Army commanders say they tried and failed to calm their people down. "As news spread of the Samarra bombing there was an explosion of rage among the people," says Sheikh Ali, the militia leader. "I was in the market at the time and I saw one young man who was so angry that he began to smash things inside his own shop. A group of youths ran toward a *husseiniya*, which opened its doors and began to distribute light weapons so they could march on Samarra to fight. But a group of older men came, closed the *husseiniya*'s doors and screamed at the youths to go away and not to act individually. One of them shouted at the angry crowd: 'Wait for orders from Muqtada.' Al-Sadr was in Saudi Arabia en route from Lebanon and had to cut short his visit to come back to Baghdad. We were under orders to stay calm, but we couldn't control the angry crowds of young men who went to the *husseiniyas* shouting 'Do something! We want to go to Samarra! Give us guns!' Even women were marching and screaming. Youth started advancing on Sunni mosques and killing people just because they were Sunni. They were dragging people out of cars in Palestine Street and slaughtering them." Sheikh Ali says that the Mehdi Army did not have the kind of organization that could restore order. "We could not control the situation because we are a popular movement without a salaried staff. When people went to the Sadrist leader in a district and he did not agree with an attack on Sunni mosques, they would leave him, saying he was a coward and feeling let down."[6]

Some thirteen hundred people, mostly Sunni, were killed in the next few days, and this was only the beginning of the butchery that was to increase every month up to December. "Armed men of the Mehdi Army took over the al-Neda'a mosque in al-Adhamiyah near Palestine Street, but it was empty because the imam and [Sunni] worshippers had fled," says one commander. "They gave orders to burn cars and take away Sunnis in cars to the Sada region on the edge of Sadr City, where they were killed and their bodies thrown into the street. Muqtada gave orders for this to stop but nobody listened."[7] All communities in Baghdad and central Iraq began to organize themselves for self-defense, which was not difficult in a city where everybody is armed. In the mixed al-Hamraa district in west Baghdad, Sunni families prepared themselves for an assault from the Shia Hay al-Ameel district, and the call to arms came from the mosques at eleven p.m. as Shia militiamen began to enter the area in their cars. "People shot from the roofs of the houses for ten minutes. The police arrived, saying they were there to protect al-Hamraa and asking for a cease-fire, but nobody obeyed them because they believed the police were cooperating with the Mehdi Army. The shooting went on until the mosques said the militiamen had retreated. Soon afterward Sunni gunmen attacked a big Shia *husseiniya* in al-Hamraa but were driven off by its armed guards." One of the attackers accidentally dropped his mobile phone, which was later found by the Mehdi Army. "The phone rang and one of their men answered it," says an eyewitness. "The caller was the attacker's wife who was asking for him and mentioned his name, which was that of a former army officer and a Sunni living in the neighboring Yarmouk district. Several days later we heard that the Mehdi Army killed him."[8]

Each community saw itself as a victim, its own acts of violence understandable retaliation for atrocities committed against it. There was little pity for the other side, and Shia as well as Sunni saw themselves as fighting for survival. Salim Shehab, a twenty-three-year-old Shia student from the al-Jadida district in east Baghdad, had a Sunni woman friend named Bida'a who was compelled to flee her house in the Hurriya district after the Samarra bombing. "She was forced to leave her home but she was allowed to take her furniture," he says. "The Sunni were expelling Shia from their homes without letting them take anything with them." He believes that Sunni families had often left their homes before they were threatened and later falsely claimed "We have been expelled from our houses." Of course, there were many people who sensibly ran away before they were threatened or killed without any prior warning. A pervasive sense of terror settled over Baghdad and central Iraq as people who had lived together for decades began to kill one another or identify targets for the death squads.

The Mehdi Army and all other militias, including the Sunni insur-

gents, were strengthened because everybody wanted security and the state
could not provide it. Baghdad broke up into dozens of warring townships
that began to exchange mortar and rocket fire. People in flight often
looked to the militias for help and protection. Given that by the summer
of 2007 there were some 2.2 million Iraqis internally displaced within the
country, the growth of this refugee population helped the militias expand
their authority. People became deeply suspicious of any strange face or car
in their district. For instance, Salim Shehab describes a Shia man, who,
after being shot at in the street by two Sunni gunmen, fled with his wife
and four children to the Shia part of Hai al-Jihad (from which Bassim had
been intimidated out). Having rented a house from an expelled Sunni
family, he contacted one of the leaders of the Mehdi Army in his district,
Abu Aya. He told him he was a Shia, described what had happened to him,
and asked for permission to stay in al-Jihad. Abu Aya listened and told
him reassuringly: "If anybody asks what you are doing here just say you
know Abu Aya." Several days later some Mehdi Army militiamen picked
up the man's fourteen-year-old son, Alaa, in the street. He was dark-
skinned enough to be from the south and therefore a Shia, but they were
suspicious of him because they did not know him and beat him up. He
mentioned that he knew Abu Aya, but the beating continued until they
finally decided he was telling the truth and released him. When he
returned home his father complained to Abu Aya, who sent the young
militiamen to a local building called the House of Happiness. "Inside this
house," reports Shehab with grim approval, "Abu Aya punishes Mehdi
Army young men who do not obey his orders. You could hear screams of
pain from it because they were tortured. For more serious offenses he
would sometimes send them to Najaf."[9]

Each community had isolated enclaves that were too small to be
defended. The Shia majority controlled the police, the police commandos, and part of the army. The majority of the dreadful harvest of bodies
found dumped in the streets every morning in Baghdad were Sunni, often
people picked up at police or Mehdi Army checkpoints. The main form of
Sunni retaliation was vehicle-borne suicide bombs exploded in crowded
Shia markets or in places where laborers would gather early in the morning to look for work. On the outskirts of Baghdad it was usually the Sunni
who were in the ascendancy because their gunmen controlled all the roads
radiating out of Baghdad. Shia workers on their way to work in the capital were regularly slaughtered there.

* * *

How far did the Mehdi Army foster the Shia death squads? Muqtada decried sectarian killings and declared that the priority was to end the U.S. occupation of Iraq, but did he covertly allow his movement to take the lead in sectarian cleansing as all Sunni were convinced he did? Iraq had become such an extraordinarily dangerous place for any reporter that it was impossible to get a clear picture. While Bush and Blair were absurdly denying that a civil war was taking place, hundreds of local civil skirmishes were erupting in central Iraq, turning every village, town, and city district into a battlefield. These bloody conflicts were difficult to follow because of the paucity of information and the complexity of Iraq's sectarian mosaic. I was in touch by e-mail and phone with Shia leaders in the isolated town of Balad north of Baghdad, which was one of the few Shia outposts in this predominantly Sunni region. My informants sent me highly detailed accounts of what was happening, which, though sometimes difficult to follow because they assumed encyclopedic knowledge on my part of the local sectarian and tribal geography, conveyed the flavor of this time of atrocity and counteratrocity.

The killings in this area had started with Shia laborers from Balad who were working in the Sunni town of Dhulu'iya a few miles away on the other side of the Tigris River. Elsewhere, in the nearby towns of Taji and Sabaa al-Bour, individual Shia were also being picked up, their heads cut off, and their bodies thrown into the Tigris River. "After the beheadings," said my informant, who was a tribal leader in Balad, "a local militia was formed to counter the increasing attacks. The people involved were mostly those families whose members had been killed." The nearest large Shia community that might aid those besieged in Balad was in al-Khadamiyah. The leaders in Balad "contacted Sayid Hazem and Ba'haa al-Arrajy in al-Khadamiyah, both clerics linked to [Muqtada] al-Sadr's movement. The clerics had expressed sympathy for armed groups but had declined to join the Mehdi Army or give any support for reprisals against innocent Sunni civilians. This was part of an agreement with Ayatollah Hussain al-Sadr in al-Khadamiyah, whereby the Mehdi Army was allowed to guard the shrine area on the condition that no innocent person was targeted."[10]

Between the besieged town of Balad and north Baghdad was the Taji area, which was mostly Sunni but had some Shia who had set up their own militia. "The militiamen were known to be the sons of locals with no connection to the Mehdi Army. One day they stopped a minivan full of Sunni civilians and slaughtered them. As an act of reprisal, the Sunni decided to attack Balad, despite the fact that those who had killed the Sunni were from Taji. The Sunni put Balad under siege, sabotaging the water, sewage, and electricity systems and stopping food getting in." The Shia in the town were by now becoming hysterical with fear, and my contact in Balad was worried that the systematic sabotage of the utilities in his town and the overall sophistication of the Sunni strategy meant that "we may witness the first sectarian cleansing of a town as big as Balad." He accused the Americans in their enormous airbase at Balad of doing nothing. "When the Mehdi Army and local volunteers tried to break the siege by attacking north from al-Khadamiyah and Taji, they were bombed by U.S. helicopter gunships, which inflicted heavy losses on them in the outskirts of northern Baghdad." The Shia fled to northern Baghdad, where they were given food and water. Then in October 2006 the refugees learned they could go home because the Mehdi Army had now taken over Sabaa al-Bour.[11] Anger at American attacks on what the Shia saw as purely defensive measures by their local militiamen reveals a fear on the Shia side—this was long before the Sunni tribes in Anbar started allying themselves with American forces to fight al-Qaeda in Iraq in 2007—that the Americans were changing sides and starting to back the Sunni against them.[12]

The Sunni population of Iraq almost universally blamed Muqtada and the Mehdi Army for any sectarian attack on them. Yet many of the militiamen who formally acknowledged Muqtada's leadership had no intention of accepting his orders. The Mehdi Army had always had a loose structure and its fighters were largely unpaid. Units often had their origin in locally raised vigilante groups that were never amenable to discipline from the center. And as the sectarian war got bloodier, local commanders became more independent and more powerful. Muqtada himself stoutly denied that the Mehdi Army, as he conceived it, was involved in sectarian killings and asserted that his name was being misused to give the killers an alibi. He complained that "death squads that say they kill on behalf of the Mehdi Army are trying to destroy us and divide us and prevent us from raising arms against the forces of occupation. Criminals are using my name as cover for their actions." He added that the Mehdi Army had been dragged into sectarian fighting when trying to defend Shia pilgrims from Sunni gunmen on the road between Baghdad and Kerbala. "They were killing anyone called Haider or Hussein or Karrar, [in fact] anyone with a Shia name," he said. "The Mehdi Army wanted to defend these innocent people."[13]

A convincing account of the relationship between the death squads, the Mehdi Army, Muqtada, and the Sadrist movement as a whole was given by a Mehdi Army member and self-confessed death squad leader named Abu Kamael in Jordan at the end of 2006. A lawyer by training, he said he had fled to Amman earlier in the year after being threatened by other death squad members because he had objected to one proposed killing. On the overall objective of the campaign, he admits: "It was very simple, we were ethnically cleansing. Anyone Sunni was guilty. If you were called Omar, Uthman, Zayed, Sufian, or something like that, then you would be killed. These are Sunni names and you are killed according to identity." Sometimes the killings were in retaliation to Sunni attacks and sometimes they were in implementation of a death sentence by a Sadrist religious court. "The Mehdi Army is supposed to kill only Baathists, Takfiris [Sunni fanatics who do not regard Shia as Muslims], those who cooperate with the occupation and the occupation troops," says Abu Kamael. "It does not always happen like that though, and it can turn into a mafia gang." As with the confiscation of the house of Bassim Abdul-Rahman, my former driver, it was easy enough to label a Sunni whose property somebody else wanted as a Baathist official and take it. At the time, Abu Kamael estimated that the Mehdi Army was killing 30 Sunni a day. In September 2006 alone, 3,539 Iraqi security forces and civilians were killed.[14]

Abu Kamael did not believe that Muqtada personally agreed with the murder campaign being carried out in his name. "Sadr was sometimes surprised by the actions of his soldiers. He has banned the killing of any Baathist or Iraqi unless there was evidence that they had blood on their hands. There are hundreds of thousands of fighters and office workers, how can he possibly know what they are doing all day? Sadr is trying to impose control, he is trying to imbue religious values in the soldiers, make them learn the Quran and the Hadiths. Only God knows if this will be successful. In my opinion, the political wing of the Sadr line is being weakened by the worsening security situation. Those who refused the political way are saying 'we were right.' The arrests of Sadr figures and the [U.S. military] missions against Sadr City are seen as evidence that politics are failing."[15]

Other Mehdi Army leaders of death squads had no qualms about what they were doing. Abu Rusil, previously a taxi driver in the Hai al-Salaam district, which was formerly mixed, would leave a note on the bodies of dead Sunni saying "best regards." "There is no innocent Sunni," he said, claiming that his brother had been shot dead at a Sunni checkpoint. Abu Rusil's victims are found with drill holes in their bodies, their bones smashed by being pounded with gas canisters, and their hands and feet pierced by nails. Once a poor man, the death squad leader preyed on his victims, confiscating their goods. He now has a house and three sport-utility vehicles, and consequently an incentive for the killing to go on. It would only end, Abu Rusil said, when every Sunni had left the country and Muqtada al-Sadr was the ruler of Iraq. "The Mehdi Army will lead the revolution in Iraq as Imam Khomeini did in Iran," he predicted. He candidly admitted going to Iran eight times for training, and said all the Mehdi Army's weapons aside from their AK-47s were supplied by the Iranians. Other arms, he said, such as rocket-propelled grenade launchers and improvised explosive devices, came from the Iraqi security forces. On occasion his men wore army and police uniforms. Overall, Abu Rusil was typical of the district warlords thrown up by the sectarian warfare after Samarra. Pledging loyalty to the distant figure of Muqtada, his gunmen were wholly controlled by himself and killed any Shia who criticized his actions.[16] The revolution he had in mind would be a purely sectarian one. Iraq was breaking up. Sunni, Shia, and Kurds could no longer live on the same street.

CHAPTER SIXTEEN

The Surge

Muqtada was feeling as if he were under attack from all sides. "I am being described as Azrael, the angel of death, as if I was the cause of all the killing in Iraq," he complained to a group of supporters who visited him.[1] To other Iraqis and the outside world he might have looked like the king-maker of Iraq with a powerful militia at his command. But Muqtada saw himself as surrounded by enemies. "I have transferred my family to a safe place," he told an interviewer in January 2007. "I have even made my will, and I move around constantly, acting in such a way that only a very few people know exactly where I am." Others might see the Mehdi Army as infiltrating the Iraqi police and army and thereby knowing every move of the U.S. Army before it was made, but Muqtada took a far gloomier view. "The exact opposite is true," he said. "It is our militia group that is crawling with spies. Of course, it does not take much to infiltrate a grassroots army." He said there were no less than four armies ready to move against his movement: the U.S. Army; the Kurdish Peshmerga; the private army of Iyad Allawi, the former Iraqi prime minister; and a "shadow army," Iraqi troops trained by the U.S. military in the Jordanian desert. The reference to Allawi, who had no militia, is mysterious, but if by the "shadow army" Muqtada meant Iraqi army units wholly under the control of the United States, these certainly existed. The United States criticized Iraqi prime minister Nouri al-Maliki for not acting firmly enough against the Sadrists because his majority in parliament depended on them, but Muqtada suspected treachery from his ally. "Between myself and [Maliki] there has never been much sympathy," he admitted frankly. "I have always suspected that he was being manipulated, and I have never trusted him. We have met only on a couple of occasions. At our last meeting he told me: 'You are the country's backbone,' and then he confessed that he was 'obliged' to fight us. Obliged! Can you believe it?" The crackdown had already begun: "They arrested over 400 of my people last night. We will not put up any resistance for the time being." He repeated vigorously that there was just one long-term solution to the crisis in Iraq: "An immediate American withdrawal."[2]

Muqtada's outrage at Maliki's two-faced attitude to his movement was understandable. It was the Sadrists who had, in effect, made him prime minister in May 2006 after the Americans had turned decisively against his predecessor Ibrahim al-Jaafari, the leader of the Dawa party. While outwardly treating the Iraqi administration as sovereign, Washington was brutal in asserting its authority in private. It threw its weight against Jaafari, partly because of his good relationship with the Sadrists, and in favor of Adel Abdul Mehdi, the chosen candidate of SCIRI. The U.S. ambassador Zalmay Khalilzad was told to inform SCIRI's leader Abdul Aziz al-Hakim that Bush "doesn't want, doesn't support, and doesn't accept" that Jaafari should lead the next government.[3] It was Muqtada's influence that had kept Abdul Mehdi out of the prime minister's office and led the Shia coalition, the United Iraqi Alliance, to select Maliki, for many years Dawa's representative in Damascus, as a compromise candidate. At the time Maliki was chosen, he was so obscure that the U.S. embassy was not even sure of his real name (like many opponents of Saddam Hussein he had operated under a pseudonym). But from the moment he was appointed, he was under constant pressure from Washington to clamp down on Muqtada and his movement. This was justified by the pretense that all militias in Iraq were to be dissolved, though this was not going to affect the powerful armed wings of the Kurdish parties and SCIRI, friendly to the United States, which operated under the guise of being part of the Iraqi security services.

Maliki was squeezed between the United States and the Sadrists, and though he had responsibility, he had limited real power. The Iraqi government was far less independent than it looked, and its authority over security was seriously curtailed. Its intelligence service, the Iraqi National Intelligence Service (INIS) under General Mohammed al-Shahwani, was still openly funded and controlled by the CIA ("What! Are all our secret agents volunteers?" exclaimed an Iraqi member of parliament on discovering that funding for INIS does not appear in the Iraqi budget).[4] Al-Maliki declared ruefully that he could not move a company of troops without American permission. One Iraqi army commander who obeyed an order from the prime minister, without getting approval from the Americans first, was promptly dismissed and imprisoned by the U.S. military.[5] Ultimately dependent on the United States, Maliki was always likely to come out against Muqtada, though he tried to avoid making a choice between them for as long as possible.

Washington never deviated from its deep hostility to Muqtada, though the battles for Najaf in April and August 2004 made the United States wary of confronting him again. But on January 10, 2007, President Bush surprised the world by announcing that he was going to escalate American involvement in Iraq by sending over twenty thousand U.S. soldiers as reinforcements. Spelling out the new direction of U.S. policy in his State of the Union Address on January 23, Bush gave priority to regaining control of Baghdad. It was a move which was bound to affect the Mehdi Army, which was now emerging as the winner in the battle for the city. Ominously for the Sadrists, Bush spoke of "an escalating danger from Shia extremists," who he claimed were just as hostile to the United States as Osama bin Laden. He also targeted Iran, which was "funding and arming terrorists," and asserted that "Shia and Sunni extremists are different faces of the same totalitarian threat."[6] The Sadrists were evidently going to be one of the targets of the "surge," though the U.S. military in Iraq was more chary than the White House of taking on a new enemy in Iraq. Muqtada thought the United States was trying to provoke him into armed confrontation. Predictably, he announced that his militiamen would not resist U.S. forces, and he even supported negotiations aimed at easing U.S. deployment in Sadrist strongholds.

Muqtada's followers admit that they came under intense pressure. They might control most of the Baghdad police, but there were also Iraqi military units that obeyed the U.S. military and were known in Sadr City as "the dirty squad." "Many arrests have occurred as a result of the dirty squad," says Hussein Ali, the Mehdi Army leader who was planning to leave the country because he believed he was in danger of assassination by a pro-Iranian faction of the militia. "It consists of Iraqi army soldiers supervised and under the orders of the Americans. They understand Iraqi society and know how to deal with people. They come to Sadr City, or any other Shia district, moving from house to house, sometimes shooting innocent people and supported by U.S. helicopters." When the Mehdi Army returned fire it was in response to raids and arrests by U.S. forces. "Most young people do not stay in their homes at night because if the Americans arrest one of us they will never release him."

Mehdi Army commanders were ordered to go deep undercover or leave Baghdad. Media attention was focused on their departure, but in reality Muqtada was most interested in preserving his political lieutenants, the militant clerics often referred to collectively as the "sheikhs," who were the cadres for his movement. These were usually clerics of his own age, some of whom had worked with his father, who were influential in different parts of Iraq. Their importance often determined the extent to which the Sadrists controlled the local Shia community. "Muqtada had sent an order to the sheikhs to 'save themselves' because he greatly depended on them and did not want to lose them," says Hussein Ali. This happened not only in Baghdad but also in Shia cities such as Diwaniyah in the south. The most important sheikhs acting on his behalf at this period were Saheb Ismail Hwade, Baquer al-Moubarqa, Ali Smaisin, Ahmed al-Sheibani, and Abdel Hadi al-Daraji. Daraji was arrested on January 19 and accused of being involved in death squad activity, as was Ali Smaisin, though both men were released later in the year. "These sheikhs are very important because they were the main operational leaders of the movement and sometimes took Muqtada's place in issuing instructions," says Hussein Ali.[7] He often moved them around, but they were central to ensuring that the movement would be able to regenerate itself however many of its militants were arrested or killed.

Muqtada believed that the U.S. government wanted to eliminate him if it could do so without provoking a political explosion from the Shia. His suspicions are scarcely surprising given that most of his close family had been killed by Saddam Hussein and his conviction that the Americans had deliberately set him up to be killed or arrested in Najaf in August 2004. Just as he did after the second battle of Najaf, Muqtada now disappeared from view and was not seen again in public until four months later.

Exactly where he was concealed during this period became a topic of rancorous dispute. American sources swiftly claimed he had fled to Iran, a story that fit with Washington's scenario that the Sadrists were creatures of Tehran. The aim was to puncture Muqtada's credibility as an Iraqi nationalist. Obvious though the propaganda was behind these allegations, this does not necessarily mean they were untrue. But his closest lieutenants, including some who later left the movement, say they are certain that Muqtada stayed in his house in Najaf all this time. "He did not go anywhere," says Hussein Ali. "But the Americans spread the rumor he had left the country because they feared a big reaction from Sadr's offices after there were so many arrests. Their aim was to reduce his authority so people would not obey his instructions, though in fact he was in Najaf all the time."[8] On the street, supporters of Muqtada stridently denied he was in Iran and sang songs about how he was still in Iraq. At the entrance to the Valley of Peace cemetery in Najaf, where so many Mehdi Army volunteers had fought and died in 2004, small kiosks had been set up selling cassette tapes of religious songs. One of the most popular of these, which was widely played during the months of his disappearance, spoke of how he would never leave Iraq.

There was a further reason why Muqtada may have wanted to go underground at this time. After vastly expanding in the previous two years, the Mehdi Army was riven by factions; its name had become the label attached to every Shia vigilante or criminal gang or units controlled by Iran. "Muqtada did not disappear," says Hussein Ali, "but since his orders weren't implemented by his followers who began to cooperate with Iran, he stayed in his house and did not meet anyone. Muqtada gave Prime Minister Nouri al-Maliki a list of 450 names to arrest because they were criminals."[9] If Muqtada was allowing the Iraqi government forces, backed by the United States, to purge the Mehdi Army of gangsters and sectarian killers, this alone would be a reason for him to hide. There were those who believed that differences between Muqtada and Maliki were publicly exaggerated by the former to conceal from the Americans the extent of their covert cooperation. Maliki himself, after all, belonged to the Damascus wing of Dawa, which had been founded by Muqtada's father-in-law, Mohammed Baqir al-Sadr. One of Maliki's senior government officials in Baghdad said Maliki "emulated Mohammed [Baqir] al-Sadr as a father figure and he is loyal to the movement and his memory." He added that three months earlier, on February 14, 2007, when the Americans began to implement their "Baghdad Security Plan," "the prime minister urged Muqtada to make sure that his ten most vulnerable security people could not be found" or arrested. The official was contemptuous of reports that Muqtada had left Iraq. "We heard these reports on CNN and Fox News that Muqtada had 'fled' to Tehran and we laughed. They are gullible, for they have received this from the White House. Muqtada going to Iran! He would do no such thing. Do you believe we are afraid of the Americans? Are they worse than Saddam? If Muqtada went into exile it would be a repudiation of his family. This he would not do." The official said that the Americans did not understand the Iraqi prime minister's loyalties or political background. "We are continuously asked 'do we support Muqtada al-Sadr?'" said the official. "It is as if the Americans had never looked at our website. His [father-in-law and cousin Mohammed Baqir al-Sadr's] picture is right there. His sermons are right there. Do you think that we would forget this part of our glorious history?"[10]

The question was rhetorical, but many Sadrists were, indeed, convinced that Maliki and his supporters had forgotten their Iraqi roots and were now puppets of the Americans. This was why, in December 2006, Muqtada had "frozen" his ministers' participation in the government, giving as his reason that Maliki had met President Bush in Jordan without demanding an American withdrawal. It was a pattern that was to continue through 2007, with the Sadrists pulling out of government, announcing their return, withdrawing from the United Iraqi Alliance Shia coalition, but somehow not voting the government out of office in parliament. Even to the most cynical Iraqi political observers it was never clear who was two-timing whom. Contradictory allegiances were the outcome not just of the byzantine and treacherous nature of Iraqi politics but of the muddled and contradictory nature of American policy in Iraq. Washington was trying to create a strong Iraqi government to replace Saddam, but was also trying to marginalize the Sadrists, who provided the government with its popular base insofar as it had one. A so-called moderate Iraqi government shorn of its Sadrist wing, consisting of the Kurds, SCIRI, Dawa, the Sunni Iraqi Islamic Party, and Iyad Allawi, a scenario that was the dream of some U.S. officials, would have had even less legitimacy in the eyes of Iraqi Arabs than its predecessors.

There was a second contradictory element in U.S. policy to which Iraqi politicians had to accommodate themselves. In the course of 2007, the United States became increasingly confrontational with Iran and edged toward air strikes against Iranian nuclear facilities. Iran was demonized, as Saddam Hussein had once been, as the dark and secret force behind every act of hostility toward the United States. This was a more peculiar policy than the American public ever realized. Paradoxically, Iran—in contrast to Saudi Arabia, Egypt, Jordan, and the Sunni Arab states—supported the Shia-Kurdish government in Baghdad. "This government is as good as it is going to get for them," Hoshyar Zebari, the Iraqi foreign minister, told me.[11] The U.S. confrontation with Iran and accusations that it was funding and arming anti-American insurgents was self-fulfilling. The more Tehran feared an American attack, the more it had an incentive to prepare a potential counterstrike in Iraq. On a visit to Washington in October 2007, Mowaffaq al-Rubai'e, the Iraqi national security adviser, pleaded with his audience not to attack Iran, saying there should be "absolutely no—big fat no, N-O—bombing of Iran. They will react against us. They will not come to New York. They will not come to Washington. They will come to us, I can tell you that, and we will be in big, big trouble." He said that there were already signs in late 2007, as U.S.-Iranian relations became even frostier, that more modern weapons—such as upgraded grenade launchers and roadside bombs—were being supplied by Iran to Shia militiamen.[12]

Muqtada had a further important reason for keeping his distance from the Iraqi government while at the same time not severing his links to it. Isolated in the Green Zone in Baghdad, the Iraqi administration was almost universally loathed by Iraqis because of its failure to provide security or the basics of life—rations, electricity, and clean water. American politicians and the foreign media focused too exclusively on war and the number killed as the sole indicators of what was wrong in Iraq. Too little attention was paid to other failures, such as the collapse of the food-rationing system, which reduced the millions of Iraqis to a life of malnutrition and near starvation. By the end of 2007 food rations were half what they had been under Saddam Hussein four years earlier. Some five million Iraqis depended on the state-subsidized ration to survive, but two million of these people were no longer being fed because they had been forced to flee their homes. "It is rare to find items such as baby formula among rationed food," said Mohammed Ala'a Jabber, director of the west Baghdad office responsible for the delivery of food rations. "This never happened under Saddam Hussein's regime, when it was common to see an abundance of baby formula. The rice which is available is of bad quality and the beans might require hours to cook. The quantity of flour and tea given to each family has decreased and at least 20 per cent of families in search of food rations return home empty-handed." Iraq was filled with more and more utterly desperate people. "I've had a delay in my food ration for more than two months," said Abu Akram, a father of four in Baghdad. "My children are sick, suffering from malnutrition, and I'm unemployed. I don't know where to go to get money to feed them."[13]

Outside the fortifications of the Green Zone, Iraqi society was dissolving. Three-quarters of doctors, pharmacists, and nurses had left their jobs, and half had fled abroad. It was becoming impossible to find even simple medicines in Baghdad. A cholera epidemic had started in Sulaimaniyah and was spreading to the rest of the country. The misery of people living in central Iraq—and the 4.2 million people who had fled within Iraq, or to Syria and Jordan, mostly came from this area—began to equal that of sub-Saharan Africa. The difference was that Iraq was still a rich country in terms of oil revenue, much of which was unspent. (This was why foreign aid donors were unwilling to fund programs in Iraq; they did not see why the Iraqi finance ministry should not provide the money.) Not surprisingly, the political class that had flourished in the post-Saddam era was regarded with general hatred. One of the most spirited denunciations of this governing elite came from Ayatollah Sheikh Mohammed al-Yaqubi, the lieutenant of Sadr II who had refused to follow Muqtada in 2003 and had set up the Fadhila party, which was the main authority in Basra and had fifteen members of parliament. Given his reputation for moderation, Yaqubi's scathing attack on the failings of the returned exiles who had taken power in Iraq was particularly telling. It is worth quoting because it shows Iraqis' true attitude to politicians who were treated with respect by presidents and prime ministers abroad during their frequent foreign trips. Speaking from Najaf, Yaqubi said the returned exiles "set out to plunder and greedily fill their pockets and [bank] accounts and those of their followers with no efforts to serve people and rebuild the country; they have cocooned themselves inside the Green Zone and have not mingled with the people or experienced their hardships."[14]

Muqtada reappeared on May 25, 2007, traveling in a long motorcade from Najaf to Kufa to deliver his Friday sermon to six thousand worshippers. He began with an elaboration on his father's traditional chant: "No, no to Satan! No, no to America! No, no to the occupation! No, no to Israel!" He repeated his demand for the United States to leave Iraq. "We demand the withdrawal of the occupation forces, or the creation of a timetable for such a withdrawal," he said. "I call upon the Iraqi government not to extend the occupation by even a single day." He also denounced sectarianism, saying he was ready to cooperate with Sunni Arabs "on all issues," adding, "It is prohibited to spill the blood of Sunnis and Christians. They are our brothers, either in religion or in the homeland."[15]

There were signs during the summer of 2007 that Muqtada was regaining control over the Mehdi Army. It had largely, but not entirely, obeyed his instructions not to put up armed resistance to the "surge." There were other signs of a centralized authority in command. When, on June 13, 2007, two minarets that remained standing after the earlier attack by Sunni on the al-Askari shrine in Samarra were toppled by twin bomb blasts, Baghdad braced itself for a furious reaction from the Mehdi Army. Muqtada called for restraint and ordered that there must be no attacks on Sunni mosques. This time he was obeyed. "Muqtada's full control of the Mehdi Army was shown after the second bombing of Samarra in June," claims a Sadrist militant. "First, he called for a peaceful march on Samarra and all his followers prepared to go. But when the Sadrist offices called it off, everybody followed his order. No one went and nobody even discussed the change in our instructions."[16] His followers may exaggerate the degree of his success in asserting control over his militiamen, but it was certainly greater than a year earlier. "Muqtada al-Sadr's recent move to control and centralize his Mahdi Army appears to be working," wrote Babak Rahimi, an academic specialist on the Iraqi Shia, "and his immediate call for restraint after the second attack indicates the extent to which he has successfully gained control over his militia since his reappearance in May—or perhaps earlier this spring."[17] The split in the Sunni insurgency between al-Qaeda in Iraq and the Sunni tribes, along with other more nationalist anti-American groups, encouraged Muqtada to stress his nationalist program. Shia hatred of the Sunni was no longer being reinforced every few days in Baghdad by car bombs in the middle of crowds. "The enemy of all Islam has become the Takfir," Muqtada told Iraqi television. "Before they were killing Shiites with their car bombs. Now they are killing Sunni with their car bombs. They have become a common enemy." He rejected any negotiations with the Americans, as had been proposed by Lieutenant General Raymond Odierno, the number-two American commander in Iraq. "I refuse any sitdown with the occupation, whether in Iraq or outside."[18] His aides said Muqtada wanted a nationalist front of Sunni and Shia against all "foreign elements" in Iraq, with al-Qaeda being considered equally as enemies.[19]

At the beginning of the year Muqtada had spoken of four armies preparing to attack him: the Americans, the Kurds, Iyad Allawi's forces, and a "shadow army" of Iraqis under U.S. control. Strangely, he did not mention a fifth army that posed far more of a threat to him than any of the others. This was the Badr Organization, the military wing of SIIC, previously

SCIRI, the party that was the traditional rival of the Sadrists as the political voice of the Shia of Iraq. There had been clashes between the two
movements since 2004, and by 2007 the conflict was turning into all-out
war. SIIC had many political and military assets: it was a dominant force
in the Interior Ministry in Baghdad and controlled most of the provincial
councils in southern Iraq, and its supporters made up much of the police
forces in the south. Ever since the second battle of Najaf in 2004, the Badr-
led forces had held Najaf and Kerbala, the Shia Vatican, though not nearby
Kufa, where Muqtada was in control. Politically, SIIC was very powerful
as the mainstay of Prime Minister Maliki's government and the preferred
party of Grand Ayatollah Ali al-Sistani and the Marji'iyyah. Remarkably,
SIIC even had good relations with the United States, though many Iraqis
believed the party was still effectively controlled from Tehran. It had the
resources to buy political and military support. For instance, when the
Mehdi Army, far stronger in Baghdad than Badr, started burning SIIC
offices in August 2007, Badr responded by hiring a thousand tough tribal
mercenaries from Amara province and busing them to Baghdad.[20]

There were intra-Shia clashes all over southern Iraq between Badr-
controlled government forces and the Mehdi Army. These were essentially
turf battles over control of political and economic resources and had
nothing to do with the U.S. occupation or the Shia-Sunni conflict. American forces generally supported SIIC and Badr, claiming, hypocritically,
that they were simply backing the Iraqi government, while knowing full
well that the police and army were effectively militiamen in uniform. In
Basra, from which the British were withdrawing, there was a complex
three-cornered fight between SIIC, Fadhila, and the Sadrists. Muqtada had
no illusions about what the battle in Basra, which sits atop some of the
largest oil reserves in the world, was really about. When two of his commanders from Basra came to see him, he reputedly sniffed sourly and said:
"I smell gasoline." But in Basra, unlike Baghdad, he was prepared to claim
credit for armed resistance to the occupying force, which in this case was
the British Army. His different attitude is probably explained by the fact
that in Basra he knew the British were going. "The British have given up
and they know they will be leaving Iraq soon," Muqtada said. "They are
retreating because of the resistance they have faced. Without that, they
would have stayed much longer. . . . The Mehdi Army has played an important role."[21]

Muqtada's strategy toward the United States was shaped by his assessment that, sooner or later, they would follow the British by drawing down their forces. It therefore made sense to avoid a military confrontation with them whatever the short-term provocations or losses through U.S. raids. But SIIC, Badr, and the al-Hakim family were not going to leave Iraq. The battle with them, which had started twenty-five years earlier, was for the future of Iraq and would have to be fought to the finish. The Mehdi Army might lie low during U.S. operations, but against the Badr militiamen they had to come out and fight. There were bloody clashes in Nassariya, Diwaniyah, Kut, Najaf, and many other Shia cities and towns. Senior officials from all groups and parties were mysteriously and very professionally assassinated. They included two SIIC-affiliated governors of Diwaniyah and Muthanna, Sadrist officials in Hilla, and several senior aides of Sistani in Najaf.

The Sadrist-SIIC violence culminated at the end of August during the Shabaniyah festival in Kerbala marking the birth of Mohammed al-Mehdi, the twelfth and last Shia imam. Up to one million pilgrims were in the city, many of them Mehdi Army from Baghdad, who were highly identifiable since they were wearing their white martyr's shrouds over their black shirts. Some were carrying weapons to protect themselves from attack in Sunni towns along the road. Since the police and shrine guards in Kerbala were drawn from SIIC and Badr, the situation was tailor-made for the clashes that predictably broke out around the shrines of Hussein and Abbas on August 28. By the time the fighting ended fifty-one people had been killed and hundreds injured. A government committee later accused the Mehdi Army of starting the violence, but the claim relied on dubious evidence from the SIIC-controlled Kerbala police and a confession extracted by them from a single Sadrist prisoner.[22] The account of one Mehdi Army pilgrim from Baghdad may better explain the origins of the violence and chaos of that day. "We left our cars in the outskirts of Kerbala and then walked," he said. "We asked the policemen what was going on and they said nothing. We entered the city in groups, all of us from the Mehdi Army, and we were clapping and singing religious songs or chants, though we had been forbidden from holding the 'Tajeel prayer,' which would have identified us as Sadrists. [The al-Tajeel prayer is only used by Sadrists. It begins with the words: "I ask Allah to send Imam Mehdi to us soon and spread peace upon all mankind."] The shrine guards came and asked us to stop our celebration and there was a quarrel with them, which led to a nine-year-old child being killed. Things escalated very fast after that. We were near the Imam al-Abbas shrine and we saw bullets being fired at us from the Imam al-Hussein shrine [four hundred yards away]. I was unexpectedly hit in my back and fell on the ground, but my friends pulled me away. I saw many people killed and wounded. The shrine guards opened heavy fire and others retaliated against them until they fled inside the shrine and closed the gates."[23]

Muqtada responded to the violence by freezing on August 29 all actions of the Mehdi Army for six months. All Sadrist offices were closed. He said he felt that the Mehdi Army's proclivity for violence was discrediting his movement and took further measures to assert central control by ordering that all Friday sermons should be centrally vetted to prevent calls for retaliation or vengeance. If Muqtada was to confront the United States, the Iraqi government, or his Shia rivals for power, he intended the battle to come at a moment of his own choosing.

CHAPTER SEVENTEEN

The Disintegration of Iraq

Muqtada al-Sadr is the most important and surprising figure to emerge in Iraq since the U.S. invasion. He is the Messianic leader of the religious and political movement of the impoverished Shia underclass whose lives were ruined by a quarter of a century of war, repression, and sanctions. From the moment he unexpectedly appeared in the dying days of Saddam Hussein's regime, U.S. emissaries and Iraqi politicians underestimated him. So far from being the "firebrand cleric" as the Western media often described him, he often proved astute and cautious in leading his followers. During the battle for Najaf with U.S. Marines in 2004, the U.S. "surge" of 2007, and the escalating war with the Supreme Islamic Iraqi Council, he generally sought compromise rather than confrontation. So far from being the inexperienced young man whom his critics portrayed—when he first appeared they denigrated him as a *zatut* (an "ignorant child," in Iraqi dialect)—he was a highly experienced political operator who had worked in his father's office in Najaf since he was a teenager. He also had around him activist clerics, of his own age or younger, who had hands-on experience under Saddam of street politics within the Shia community. His grasp of what ordinary Iraqis felt was to prove far surer than that of the politicians isolated in the Green Zone in Baghdad.

Mass movements led by Messianic leaders have a history of flaring up unexpectedly and then subsiding into insignificance. This could have happened to Muqtada and the Sadrists but did not, because their political and religious platform had a continuous appeal for the Shia masses. From the moment Saddam was overthrown, Muqtada rarely deviated from his open opposition to the U.S. occupation, even when a majority of the Shia community was prepared to cooperate with the occupiers. As the years passed, however, disillusion with the occupation grew among the Shia until, by September 2007, an opinion poll showed that seventy-three percent of Shia thought that the presence of U.S. forces in Iraq made the security situation worse, and fifty-five percent believed their departure would make a Shia-Sunni civil war less likely.[1] The U.S. government, Iraqi politicians, and the Western media habitually failed to recognize the extent to which hostility to the occupation drove Iraqi politics and, in the eyes of Iraqis, delegitimized the leaders associated with it.

All governments in Baghdad failed after 2003. Almost no Iraqis supported Saddam Hussein as U.S. troops advanced on Baghdad. Even his supposedly loyal Special Republican Guard units dissolved and went home. Iraqis were deeply conscious that their country sat on some of the world's largest oil reserves, but Saddam Hussein's Inspector Clouseau–like ability to make catastrophic errors in peace and war had reduced the people to a state in which their children were stunted because they did not get enough to eat. The primal rage of the dispossessed in Iraq against the powers-that-be exploded in the looting of Baghdad when the old regime fell, and the same fury possessed Muqtada's early supporters. Had life become easier in Shia Iraq in the coming years, this might have undermined the Sadrist movement. Instead, people saw their living standards plummet as provision of food rations, clean water, and electricity faltered. Saddam's officials were corrupt enough, but the new government cowering in the Green Zone rapidly turned into a kleptocracy comparable to Nigeria or the Congo. Muqtada sensed the loathing with which the government was regarded, and dodged in and out of government, enjoying some of the fruits of power while denouncing those who held it.

Muqtada's political intelligence is undoubted, but the personality of this highly secretive man is difficult to pin down. While his father and elder brothers lived he was in their shadow; after they were assassinated in 1999 he had every reason to stress his lack of ability or ambition in order to give the *mukhabarat* less reason to kill him. As the son and son-in-law of two of Saddam Hussein's most dangerous opponents, he was a prime suspect and his every move was watched. When Saddam fell, Muqtada stepped forward to claim his forbears' political inheritance and consciously associated himself with them on every possible occasion. Posters showed Muqtada alongside Sadr I and Sadr II against a background of the Iraqi flag. There was more here than a leader exploiting his connection to a revered or respected parent. Muqtada persistently emphasized the Sadrist ideological legacy: puritanical Shia Islam mixed with anti-imperialism and populism.

The first time I thought seriously about Muqtada was a grim day in April 2003 when I heard that he was being accused of killing a friend of mine, Sayyid Majid al-Khoei, that intelligent and able man with whom I had often discussed the future of Iraq. Whatever the involvement of Muqtada himself, which, as we saw earlier, is a matter of dispute, the involvement of the Sadrist supporters in the lynching is proven and was the start of a pattern that was to repeat itself over the years. Muqtada was always a man riding a tiger, sometimes presiding over, sometimes controlling the mass movement he nominally led. His words and actions were often far apart. He appealed for Shia unity with the Sunni against the occupation, yet after the bombing of the Shia shrine in Samarra in February 2006, he was seen as an ogre by the Sunni, orchestrating the pogroms against them and failing to restrain the death squads of the Mehdi Army. The excuse that it was "rogue elements" among his militiamen who were carrying out this slaughter is not convincing, because the butchery was too extensive and too well organized to be the work of only marginal elements. But the Sadrists and the Shia in general could argue that it was not they who had originally taken the offensive against the Sunni, and the Shia community endured massacres at the hands of al-Qaeda for several years before their patience ran out. Muqtada had repeatedly demanded that Sunni political and religious leaders unequivocally condemn al-Qaeda in Iraq's horrific attacks on Shia civilians if he was to cooperate with them against the occupation. They did not do so, and this was a shortsighted failure on their part, since the Shia, who outnumbered the Sunni Arabs three to one in Iraq, controlled the police and much of the army. Their retaliation, when it came, was bound to be devastating. Muqtada was criticized for not doing more, but neither he nor anybody else could have stopped the killing at the height of the battle for Baghdad in 2006. The Sunni and Shia communities were both terrified, and each mercilessly retaliated for the latest atrocity against their community. "We try to punish those who carry out evil deeds in the name of the Mehdi Army," says Hussein Ali, the former Mehdi Army leader. "But there are a lot of Shia regions that are not easy to control and we ourselves, speaking frankly, are sometimes frightened by these great masses of people."

American officials and journalists seldom showed much understanding of Muqtada, even after Paul Bremer's disastrous attempt to crush him. There were persistent attempts to marginalize him or keep him out of government instead of trying to expand the Iraqi government's narrow support base to include the Sadrists. The first two elected Shia prime ministers, Ibrahim al-Jaafari and Nouri al-Maliki, came under intense pressure from Washington to sever or limit their connection with Muqtada. But government officials were not alone in being perplexed by the young cleric. In a lengthy article on him published in its December 4, 2006, issue, *Newsweek* admitted that "Muqtada al-Sadr may end up deciding America's fate in Iraq." But the best the magazine could do to assist its readers in understanding Muqtada was to suggest that they should "think of him as a young Mafia don."[2] Of course, Muqtada was the complete opposite to the type of Iraqi leader who proponents of the war in Washington had suggested would take over from Saddam Hussein. Instead of the smooth, dark-suited, English-speaking exiles who the White House had hoped would turn Iraq into a compliant U.S. ally, Muqtada looked too much like a younger version of Ayatollah Khomeini.

Muqtada epitomized the central dilemma of the United States in Iraq, which it has never resolved. The problem was that the overthrow of Saddam Hussein and his Sunni regime was bound to be followed by elections that would produce a government dominated by the Shia allied to the Kurds. It soon became evident that the Shia parties that were going to triumph in any election would be Islamic parties, and some would have close links to Iran. The Arab Sunni states were aghast at the sight of Iran's defeat in the Iran-Iraq war being reversed, and spoke of a menacing "Shia axis" developing in Iran, Iraq, and Lebanon. Much of this was ignorance and paranoia on the part of the Arab leaders. Had the Iranians been tempted to make Iraq a client state they would have found the country as prickly a place for Iranians as it was to be for Americans. It was the U.S. attempt to create an anti-Iranian Iraq that was to play into Iranian hands and produce the very situation that Washington was trying to avoid. The more Washington threatened air strikes on Iran because of its nuclear program, the more the Iranians sought to make sure that it had the potential to strike back at American forces in Iraq. Before he was executed, Sadr I believed that he had been let down by Iran; Sadr II had bad relations with Tehran; and at first Muqtada denounced his Shia opponents in SCIRI and the Marji'iyyah as being Iranian stooges. But American pressure meant that the Sadrists had to look to Iran for help, and in a military confrontation the Mehdi Army saw Iran as an essential source of weapons and military expertise.

On reappearing after his four-month disappearance in May 2007, Muqtada called for a united front of Sunni and Shia and identified the U.S. occupation and al-Qaeda in Iraq as the enemies of both communities. The call was probably sincere, but it was also too late. Baghdad was now largely a Shia city, and people were too frightened to go back to their old homes. The U.S. "surge" had contributed to the sharp drop in sectarian killings, but it was also true that the Shia had won and there were few mixed areas left. The U.S. commander General David Petraeus claimed that security was improving, but only a trickle of Iraqis who had fled their homes were returning. Muqtada was the one Shia leader capable of uniting with the Sunni on a nationalist platform, but the Sunni Arabs of Iraq had never accepted that their rule had ended. If Sunni and Shia could not live on the same street, they could hardly share a common identity.

The political and military landscape of Iraq changed in 2007 as the Sunni population turned on al-Qaeda. This started before the "surge," but it was still an important development. Al-Qaeda's massive suicide bombs targeting civilians had been the main fuel for Shia-Sunni sectarian warfare since 2003. The Sunni Arabs and many of the insurgent groups had turned against al-Qaeda after it tried to monopolize power within the Sunni community at the end of 2006 by declaring the Islamic State of Iraq. Crucial in the change was al-Qaeda's attempt to draft one son from every Sunni family into its ranks. Sunni with lowly jobs with the government such as garbage collectors were killed. By the fall of 2007 the U.S. military command in Baghdad was trumpeting successes over al-Qaeda, saying it had been largely eliminated in Anbar, Baghdad, and Diyala. But the Sunni Arab fighters, by now armed and paid for by the United States, did not owe their prime loyalty to the Iraqi government. Muqtada might speak of new opportunities for pan-Iraqi opposition to the U.S. occupation, but many anti-al-Qaeda Sunni fighters had quite different ideas. They wanted to reverse the Shia victory in the 2006 battle of Baghdad. A new breed of American-supported Sunni warlords was emerging. One of them, Abu Abed, is a former member of the insurgent Islamic Army. He operates in the Amariya district of west Baghdad, where he is a commander of the U.S.-backed Amariya Knights, whom the U.S. calls Concerned Citizens. His stated objectives show that the rise of the new Sunni militias may mark only a new stage in a sectarian civil war. "Amariya is just the beginning," says Abu Abed. "After we finish with al-Qaida here, we will turn towards our main enemy, the Shia militias. I will liberate Jihad [the mixed Sunni-Shia area near Amariya taken over by the Mehdi Army], then Saadiya and the whole of west Baghdad."[3]

The al-Sadr family has an extraordinary record of resistance to Saddam Hussein, for which they paid a heavy price. One of the gravest errors in Iraq by the United States was to try to marginalize Muqtada and his movement. Had he been part of the political process from the beginning, the chances of creating a peaceful, prosperous Iraq would have been greater. In any real accommodation between Shia and Sunni, the Sadrists must play a central role. Muqtada probably represented his constituency of millions of poor Shia better than anybody else could have done. But he never wholly controlled his own movement, and never created as well-disciplined a force as Hezbollah in Lebanon. None of his ambitions for reconciliation with the Sunni could take wing unless the Mehdi Army ceased to be identified with death squads and sectarian cleansing. The war in Iraq has gone on longer than World War I and, while violence diminished in the second half of 2007, nothing has been resolved. The differences between Shia and Sunni, the disputes within the respective communities, and the antagonism against the U.S. occupation are all as great as ever. The only way the Sadrists and the Mehdi Army could create confidence among the Sunni that Muqtada meant what he said when he called for unity, would be for them to be taken back voluntarily into the areas in Baghdad and elsewhere from which they have been driven. But there is no sign of this happening. The disintegration of Iraq has probably gone too far for the country to exist as anything more than a loose federation.

Afterword

At five a.m. on March 25, 2008, units of the Iraqi army started moving into Basra, targeting the Mehdi Army. It was the biggest military confrontation between Muqtada's militiamen and the Iraqi government since the battles for Najaf in 2004. The government deployed some fifteen thousand soldiers and police. Prime Minister Nouri al-Maliki belligerently announced that gunmen had seventy-two hours to lay down their weapons and turn themselves in or they would "face the most severe penalties."[1] But the black-clad militiamen showed no sign of surrendering and swarmed into the streets of Basra, carrying rocket-propelled grenade launchers and setting up mortar positions. Plumes of black smoke rose over the city as Iraqi army vehicles on the main roads were hit by fighters shooting from the alleyways on either side. The fighting immediately spread to Baghdad and the Shia cities of southern Iraq. Iraqi army units backed by American armor sealed off Sadr City as the Mehdi Army militiamen set up hundreds of checkpoints. Mortar bombs and rockets began to explode in the Green Zone, seriously wounding three American civilians. Sadrist fighters took over seven districts in Kut and large parts of Nassariya. In Najaf, protestors chanted: "Oh Nouri, you coward, you spy of the Americans" and "The army is with America."[2] At this stage the United States was eager to emphasize that the assault on Basra was an all-Iraqi affair. "These are Iraqi decisions," said the U.S. spokesman Major-General Kevin Bergner. "These are Iraqi government forces and these are Iraqi leaders implementing and directing these decisions."[3]

But it soon became clear that the army offensive was in deep trouble. Soldiers were not able to enter the narrow streets of Sadrist bastions such as al-Hayaniyah in Basra. Some abandoned their armored vehicles, which militia fighters spray-painted with Islamic slogans. There were many desertions from two special police commando units, each 300 strong, sent from Baghdad. "We did not expect the fighting to be this intense," said an officer, describing how he and his men were pinned down by mortars and sniper fire in Basra's Tamimiyah district, another Sadrist stronghold. Four of his men were killed and 15 wounded. "Some of the men told me they did not want to go back to the fight until they have better support and more protection."[4] Three days into the offensive, government health and security officials said 189 people had been killed and 300 wounded, though this was probably an underestimate since many of the dead could not be brought to hospitals and their bodies were kept in the mosques. The government suffered fresh and very public humiliations: instead of Mehdi Army militiamen surrendering their arms, Iraqi television viewers saw pictures of dozens of policemen in Sadr City ceremoniously handing over their weapons to the local Sadrist office. "We can't fight our brothers in the Mehdi Army, so we came here to give up our weapons," said an anonymous policeman. A group of a dozen policemen handed over their guns and ammunition to Sheikh Salman al-Feraiji, Muqtada's chief representative in Sadr City, and received an olive branch and a copy of the Koran in return.[5]

The Sadrists began to take the offensive. In Baghdad the government spokesman for the Baghdad security plan was Tahsin al-Sheikli, who frequently appeared on television to tell people in the capital that Iraq was becoming a safer place, more electricity would soon be available, and reconstruction was on target. But from the afternoon of March 27, Sheikli was in no position to make any more reassuring statements because he had been kidnapped. By his own account forty masked men from the Mehdi Army came to his house and fought a gun battle with his five bodyguards for forty-five minutes, at the end of which, his house ablaze, Sheikli surrendered (local people give a slightly different story and say the attackers wore police uniforms and arrived in police vehicles). Sheikli was worried that his captors were not masked, which he took to be a sign that they intended to kill him so they did not care if he could identify them. He successfully asked them to allow him to contact the media by telephone "and let me ask the prime minister to withdraw from Basra and solve this whole thing peacefully. . . . I said to [the prime minister, through a television sound recording], 'These people [the Mehdi Army] are not your target:

They are the social base of society."[6] His public defense of the Mehdi Army was good propaganda for the Sadrists, but also made it obvious who had abducted him. Four days after he was taken from his house his captors released him unharmed.

These humiliations were in sharp and damaging contrast to Maliki's confident statements a few days earlier about humbling the militiamen. After a couple of days' fighting in Basra some Iraqi army units began to go hungry because their logistics were too poor to deliver food. But Maliki still had a powerful card to play that made these failings irrelevant. Whatever setbacks were inflicted on the Iraqi army and police by the Mehdi Army, the most important armed force in Iraq by far was the U.S. military. The militiamen, for all the allegations of special training by Iranian Revolutionary Guards and Lebanese Hezbollah, were no more capable of fighting the American army than they had been four years earlier in Najaf. The Americans had been caught by surprise by Maliki's offensive, which they had imagined was going to be a much more limited operation aimed at eliminating some 150 militants working for Iran but not the Mehdi Army as a whole.[7] "Nothing was in place on our side," said the U.S. ambassador Ryan C. Crocker. "It all had to be put together."[8] But as Maliki's offensive stalled, it swiftly became apparent to the Americans that they could not afford to let him fail. Iraqi governments since 2004 had been slow to grasp the fact that, while they might be militarily reliant on the United States, the United States was more politically dependent on them than they imagined. This was all the more true in 2008, when there was a presidential election in which the White House and the Republican Party were claiming that it was making progress toward victory in Iraq.

The United States reacted swiftly to redress the military balance in Basra and southern Iraq as a whole. Claims that the Iraqi armed forces were acting on their own were forgotten. Two senior American officers were sent to Basra to coordinate Iraqi planning. Combat advisers were attached to Iraqi units, air controllers were positioned to call in air strikes, and U.S. planes ferried in supplies and five hundred extra troops.[9] On March 27, U.S. planes made their first strikes on Basra and U.S. helicopters destroyed buildings in Sadr City. American Stryker armored vehicles advanced into Sadr City while American helicopters and drones roared overhead. "We've engaged the enemy with artillery, we've engaged the enemy with aircraft, we've engaged the enemy with direct fire," said Major Mark Cheadle, spokesman for the U.S. forces in Baghdad.[10] In Basra, air strikes intensified, hitting trucks carrying gunmen in al-Hayaniyah, and in one case destroying a mosque. AC-130 gunships were used alongside fixed-wing aircraft and helicopters. To this firepower the Mehdi Army had no answer.

It was a crisis Muqtada had long tried to avoid. He had sought to prevent a confrontation either directly with the U.S. Army or with his Shia rivals when supported by American firepower. This was one reason why he had called a cease-fire on August 29, 2007, after the fighting in Kerbala, and renewed it six months later, on February 22, 2008, against the advice of many of his younger lieutenants. As the fighting spread from Basra to Baghdad and across southern Iraq during the last week of March, Sadrist spokesmen were insisting, against all the evidence, that there was still a truce. There was a further reason why Muqtada did not want to get back to war. Provincial elections were due at the end of the year and the Sadrists were expected to do well. One study by U.S. military intelligence at this time estimated that the Sadrists would win sixty percent of the vote in southern Iraq.[11] The movement's reputation among the Shia has benefited from the long cease-fire during which the Mehdi Army had been effectively purged and brought more fully under Muqtada's control. In Shia areas, particularly in Baghdad, it was losing its reputation as an umbrella for every local warlord and racketeer. A motive for the decision by Maliki, whose core support is his wing of the Dawa party and the Supreme Islamic Iraqi Council, to make such a fierce and unexpected attack on the Sadrists in Basra was probably to weaken them before the election.

Muqtada was in the Iranian holy city of Qom when the fighting started in Iraq and had made no public appearance since May 2007. During the following ten months he appears to have made only occasional forays to Najaf, explaining his long silence by saying that he was studying to be a *mujtahid*. "Who among you doesn't want to be a *mujtahid*?" he asked an interviewer from al-Jazeera, broadcast during the fighting in Basra but recorded before it began. "I have given my community five years [of my life], now I want a few years to study."[12] The need to spend more time at their studies has always been a convenient excuse for Shia clerics who do not want to say anything, but Muqtada was genuinely receiving religious instruction from Ayatollah Mahmoud Hashemi Shahroudi, according to several of his senior aides. Shahroudi is an interesting choice of mentor. A politically powerful cleric from Najaf, he was one of the two most highly regarded disciples of Mohammed Baqir al-Sadr, Muqtada's martyred father-in-law. The head of the Iranian judicial system since 1999, Shahroudi has a moderate reputation, having spoken out against torture and having placed a moratorium on stoning. Muqtada was at the third level of study, known as external research, and was expected to qualify as a *mujtahid* in 2008.[13]

Although Muqtada may not want his militiamen to fight the American army, his central political theme since early 2007 has been to end the occupation. In his interview with al-Jazeera he said his militia's "strategic objective" was "the liberation of Iraq from the occupier," meaning the Americans. Speaking of the overthrow of Saddam Hussein, he repeated his old mantra: "A small Satan has gone and a bigger one replaced him." He reiterated in a slightly different form the old Sadrist formula of revivalist Islam, populism, and Iraqi nationalism. He said his objective was to rid Iraq of sectarian politics, prevent the breakup of the country, and create an Islamic society. Muqtada asserted that he remained in almost complete control of the Mehdi Army. The government of Maliki was as "distant" from the people as Saddam's and was "looking after its own interests and not those of the people." Probably in an effort to burnish his nationalistic credentials, and rebut allegations that he was becoming a puppet of the Iranians, he said he had recently told Iran's supreme leader, Ayatollah Ali Khamenei, that he did not approve of the "political and military interests" that Iran was pursuing in Iraq. "Iran and others must adopt different agendas in Iraq,"[14] he said.

Nevertheless, it was Muqtada and the Iranians who, each for different reasons, now wanted to bring the crisis in Basra to an end. On the sixth day of the fighting, though his militiamen were more than holding their own, Muqtada issued a nine-point statement calling on them to stop carrying arms against the government. To preserve the "unity" of Iraq, he demanded an end to "armed manifestations in Basra and in all provinces."[15] His aides in Iraq said that a deal had been arranged with the government under which the authorities would end roundups of Sadrists, cease detaining Mehdi Army members, and implement an amnesty. Caught by surprise, his followers suspected—and their suspicions turned out to be well-grounded—that the government was not going to keep to these terms and they were averse to giving up the fight. "We respect the orders of Muqtada al-Sadr, but at the same time the government should also accept his statement," said Abu Mudhil al-Tamimi, a Mehdi Army group leader in the Tamimiyah district of Basra. "We will not lay down arms until government forces stop chasing and arresting Mehdi Army fighters. We have been fighting for six days and some of our fighters lost their lives along with innocent civilians. We are not ready to stay home waiting to be arrested by the army."[16] Militiamen in Sadr City had similar doubts. "We don't have a choice," lamented Abu Aqeel, a low-level commander there. "We should respect the order of Muqtada al-Sadr. But we will respect it with unease. There are worries because this order will allow the American forces to capture and kill us one by one."[17] If nothing else, the speed with which the Mehdi Army retreated from the streets on Muqtada's orders showed that he was very much in control of his military organization.

How far was Muqtada acting under pressure from Iran? If he was to confront militarily the United States and the Iraqi government he would need Iranian support. But in this crisis the Iranians had their own agenda: they did not want Muqtada to be crushed, but they equally did not want Maliki to be humiliated or weakened. For them, his government in Baghdad, dominated as it was by their Shia coreligionists, was as good as it was going to get. They maintained close relations with SIIC, whose leaders and bodyguards in Najaf often spoke Farsi among themselves and kept their families in Iran. Public events staged by SIIC were invariably covered sympathetically by Iranian television. Iran's main policy-maker, when it came to furthering Iran's influence within Iraq, was Brigadier Qasim Suleimani, commander of the Quds force of the Iranian Revolutionary Guards. Though named in U.S. and UN Security watch lists for alleged involvement in terrorism and the proliferation of nuclear and missile technology, he had long been meeting, both inside and outside Iraq, with Iraqi leaders, including President Talabani. What was different about Iranian mediation between the Sadrists and the government in 2008 was that it was very public, geared to demonstrating that Iran could arrange a cease-fire and the United States could not. Tehran clearly wanted to show that if the United States and the Iraqi government wanted peace in Iraq, then they could not exclude Iran. Any doubts about where Iran stood over the confrontation in Iraq was removed when the Iranian ambassador to Iraq, Hassan Kazemi Qumi, praised the Iraqi government's move into Basra. "The idea of the government in Basra was to fight outlaws," he said. "This was the right of the government and the responsibility of the government. And in my opinion the government will be able to achieve a positive result in Basra."[18]

The crisis in Najaf at the end of March was the first in a series of con-

frontations between the Iraqi government and Muqtada's followers during the first half of 2008. Initially, the Sadrists appeared to be the winners.
They had demonstrated their military strength in Basra and in the first
days of fighting in Sadr City. Muqtada had also shown moderation by
agreeing to a cease-fire. But this could also be interpreted as a sign of
weakness. Muqtada himself was far away in Qom and not visiting his
fighters in the alleyways of Basra as he had done four years earlier in
Najaf. His alternate calls for his men to fight and to go home were con-
fusing. It also rapidly became evident that the militiamen's suspicion that
the government would not stick to the terms of the cease-fire in Basra
was correct. Soon Iraqi army troops were moving peacefully into al-
Hayaniyah in Basra. Maliki stepped up his political as well as military
offensive against the Sadrists, saying they would be banned from taking
part in elections unless their militia was disbanded. "A decision was
taken," he said, that the Sadrists "no longer have a right to participate in
the political process or take part in the upcoming elections unless they
end the Mehdi Army. We have opened the door for confrontation, a real
confrontation with these gangs, and we will not stop until we are in full
control of these areas."[19]

Maliki was as good as his word. The focus of the confrontation moved
from Basra to Sadr City, this time with U.S. forces openly taking the lead.
By April 18 the United States had started to wall off the southern end
of Sadr City to prevent the Mehdi Army firing mortars and rockets into
the Green Zone. Although the U.S. intermittently claimed to be fighting
Iranian-backed "Special Groups" or criminals, it was the Mehdi Army as
a whole that was under attack. Muqtada threatened "war until liberation"
unless American and Iraqi troops stopped their assault. "I'm giving the
final warning to the Iraqi government," he said in a statement, "to desist
and take the path of peace and denounce violence against its people . . . or
we will announce open war until liberation."[20] But a week later he back-
tracked from this, saying his men should fight only American occupiers
and not shoot at "Iraqi brothers."[21] In reality he was following his old policy of avoiding an all-out military confrontation. He was politically isolated. The Iranians, whose support he would have needed for an all-out
war, were clearly chary of letting their proxy war with the United States
escalate past the point where Washington might start a real war. When
Muqtada was besieged in Najaf in 2004 it was the Grand Ayatollah Ali al-
Sistani who had come to his rescue in the name of Shia solidarity, but Shia

throughout the world noticed that this time there was no condemnation by Sistani of the American and Iraqi government assault on Shia neighborhoods, despite the heavy loss of life. The Interior Ministry recorded that 2,012 Iraqi civilians, soldiers, police, and other security forces had died in March.[22] "The Iraqi prime minister is waging a political war," said Sadrist member of parliament Falah Shanshal. "But he is committing a big mistake because the Sadr movement enjoys the support of a large portion of the Iraqi public."[23] This might be true, but the Sadrists also had a lot of enemies within the Shia as well as among the other Iraqi communities. There is no doubt that Muqtada was right in thinking this was a bad moment for a fight to the finish. He had always had a good sense of timing. "He is not the kind of man," said his lieutenant Salah al-Obaidi, "who plucks the fruit before it is ripe."[24]

The battle for Sadr City ended with an agreement, once again brokered by the Iranians, under which the Iraqi army, but not the Americans, entered the Sadrist bastion for the first time since the fall of Saddam Hussein five years earlier. On May 20, after seven weeks of fighting, armored columns from the Iraqi forces rumbled down the main avenues and the militiamen, still undefeated, went home. The following month the Sadrists did not fight at all when the army moved into Amara province, from which so many people in Sadr City originally came. The government in Baghdad was becoming more confident, though its leaders still did not believe they would survive without American support. The Iraqi state machine was reconstituting itself. It had almost half a million men in the army, police, and other security forces. The high price of oil meant that its income in 2008 was likely to reach $70 billion. The era of dual power between the government and the militias was ending. But at the same time, the American occupation was continuing and the Status of Forces Agreement, which President Bush was determined to sign before he left office, laid out future military relations between the United States and Iraq that would make the American occupation of Iraq permanent. The United States would keep an army in Iraq and that army would do what it wanted. By the summer of 2008 this was creating a nationalist reaction among Iraqis, and the Sadrists were holding large demonstrations every Friday against the signing of the agreement. Iraqi politics was changing. The sectarian slaughter from 2005 to 2007 ensured that Shia and Sunni in Iraq hated and feared each other more than they hated and feared the Americans. Paradoxically, the fall in sectarian killings and the growing strength of the Iraqi state meant that many Iraqis began to talk once more in national terms. For all its much-vaunted successes against the Mehdi Army, the Iraqi government was still short on self-confidence. "They lack faith in themselves," said the veteran Kurdish leader and member of parliament Dr. Mahmoud Othman. "The people outside the Green Zone would like the Americans to go; the people inside, including the government, want them to stay."[25] This was an oversimplification, since the Kurds themselves wanted the Americans to remain in Iraq, but as a summary of Iraqi opinion on the occupation it was generally true. Muqtada was wise to emphasize his nationalist credentials so frequently. "Religiously, I am a Shiite, but politically I am closer to the Sunnis," he had said at the start of the year.[26] Once again he had survived. Iraqi politicians, who have a keen sense of where power lies, noted that the Mehdi Army had not been defeated, but had disappeared into the shadows. They had not gone very far. In Shia districts a spray-painted slogan began to appear on the walls saying, in imitation of a phrase used by Iraqi television stations: "Sorry for the interruption, but we will be back." Once again the Sadrists, who had successfully defied Saddam Hussein and Paul Bremer, had managed to survive as one of the arbiters of the fate of Iraq.

Acknowledgments

When Colin Robinson of Scribner first asked me to write a book about Muqtada al-Sadr and the Shia of Iraq, I regretfully turned him down. I believed the topic he had in mind was extraordinarily interesting, but I feared it would be far too dangerous to carry out research. I wanted to rely wholly on Iraqi eyewitnesses, but I knew that many of them lived in districts of Baghdad or provincial cities that I dared not visit. It was entirely due to Colin's persistence that I came back to the project, after deciding that I could get the information I needed if I proceeded very carefully and relied on Iraqi intermediaries to contact people I wanted to talk to and to carry out many of the interviews. I first went to Iraq in 1977, and over the following thirty years I witnessed a large number of the crises and battles described. In other cases, I have relied on Iraqis to ask questions, and without their assistance this book could not have been written. I am very grateful to these anonymous helpers whose identities must be concealed for reasons of personal safety.

Thanks are also due to my agents, David Miller of Rogers, Coleridge and White and Melanie Jackson in New York. I am also grateful for the assistance of Simon Blundell, the librarian of the Reform Club in London, who has a magical ability to make obscure publications and books appear moments after I asked for them.

Notes

1. THE ROAD TO KUFA

1. Wilferd Madelung, *The Succession to Muhammad: A Study of the Early Caliphate* (Cambridge: Cambridge University Press, 1997), p. 308.
2. Associated Press, January 2, 2007.
3. I asked Haider al-Safi and Bassim Abdul-Rahman in February 2007 to write separately their own accounts of what happened to us to cross-check my own recollections.
4. UNHCR press briefing by Jennifer Pagonis, Palais des Nations, Geneva, June 5, 2007.

2. THE SHIA OF IRAQ

1. Interview with Sheikh Ali, a veteran Sadrist leader, Baghdad, August 2007.
2. Barnaby Rogerson, *The Heirs of the Prophet Muhammad and the Roots of the Sunni-Shia Schism* (London: Abacus, 2006), pp. 339–45.
3. Edward Mortimer, *Faith and Power: The Politics of Islam* (London: Faber and Faber, 1982), pp. 39–55.
4. www.Sistani.org, June 3, 2007. There are four different questions asking if it is permitted to play chess, all of which receive the same negative answer.
5. Faleh A. Jabar, *The Shi'ite Movement in Iraq* (London: Saqi Books, 2003), pp. 185–98.
6. Gavin Young, *Iraq: Land of Two Rivers* (London: Collins, 1980), pp. 123–24.
7. Jabar, *The Shi'ite Movement in Iraq*, p. 191.
8. Yizhak Nakash, *The Shi'is of Iraq* (Princeton, N.J.: Princeton University Press, 2003), pp. 3–9.
9. Ibid., p. 14.
10. Jabar, *The Shi'ite Movement in Iraq*, p. 55.

3. THE FIRST MARTYR

1. *Iraq's Muqtada al-Sadr: Spoiler or Stabiliser?* International Crisis Group report, no. 55, July 11, 2006.
2. Anonymous interview in Baghdad, May 2007.
3. Faleh A. Jabar, *The Shi'ite Movement in Iraq* (London: Saqi Books, 2003), pp. 226–34.

4. Answer to written questions submitted to Jafar al-Sadr, son of Mohammed Baqir, Baghdad, August 2007.

5. Hanna Batatu, *The Old Social Classes and the Revolutionary Movements of Iraq* (Princeton, N.J.: Princeton University Press, 1978), p. 1141.

6. Interview in Najaf, June 6, 2007.

7. Interview with Ghanim Jawad, London, June 11, 2007.

8. Interview with Hussein al-Shami, Najaf, June 2007.

9. Fuad Matar, *Saddam Hussein: The Man, the Cause and the Future* (London: Third World Center, 1981), p. 70.

10. Interview with Kamran Karadaghi, Iraqi journalist, June 1997.

11. Interview with Hussein al-Shami, Najaf, June 5, 2007.

12. Ibid.

13. Transcript of videotaped meeting shown on WGBH, *Frontline,* June 26, 1991.

14. Jabar, *The Shi'ite Movement in Iraq,* pp. 206–7.

15. Interview with a student of Baqir's, Najaf, June 2007.

16. Interview with Hussein al-Shami, June 5, 2007.

17. Jabar, *The Shi'ite Movement in Iraq,* pp. 208–15.

18. Interview with International Crisis Group, Baghdad, December 2005; *Iraq's Muqtada al-Sadr: Spoiler or Stabiliser?*

19. Jabar, *The Shi'ite Movement in Iraq,* pp. 280–93.

20. Ibid., pp. 227–32.

21. Jafar al-Sadr, son of Mohammed Baqir, Baghdad, August 2007.

22. Interview with Al-Sheikh, Najaf, June 2007; account of Mohammed Reda al-Noumani, who was with Baqir in his final days.

23. Matar, *Saddam Hussein,* pp. 130–35.

24. Andrew Cockburn, "Iraq's Oppressed Minority," *Smithsonian,* December 2003.

25. Interview with an Iraqi intelligence officer, May 2007.

26. Interview with Najem al-Sadi, June 2007.

4. AN EIGHT-YEAR WHIRLWIND

1. DIA report obtained under Freedom of Information Act; *The Independent,* London, December 12, 1992.

2. Fuad Matar, *Saddam Hussein: The Man, the Cause and the Future* (London: Third World Center, 1981), p. 134.

3. Faleh A. Jabar, *The Shi'ite Movement in Iraq* (London: Saqi Books, 2003), p. 346.

4. Robert Fisk, *The Great War for Civilisation: The Conquest of the Middle East* (London: Fourth Estate, 2005), p. 217.

5. Matar, *Saddam Hussein,* pp. 131–48.

6. Interview with Russian diplomat in Baghdad, December 1990.

7. Interview with Jafar Ali, Baghdad, June 2007.

8. Interview with Mohammed Yassin, Baghdad, June 2007.

9. Fisk, *The Great War for Civilisation,* p. 222.

10. Interview with Jafar Ali, Baghdad, June, 2007.

11. Interview with officer, Baghdad, June 2007.

12. Interview with Rasheed Abdul Gafoor, Baghdad, June 2007.

13. Interview with former Iraqi soldier in Najaf, May 2007.

14. Amatzia Baram and Barry Rubin, eds., *Iraq's Road to War* (New York: St. Martin's Press, 1993), p. 52.

15. Interview with Ghanim Jawad, London, June 2007.

16. Interview with cleric close to Mohammed Baqir al-Sadr, Najaf, June 2007.
17. Interview with Ghanim Jawad, June 25, 2007.
18. Edward Mortimer, *Faith and Power: The Politics of Islam* (London: Faber and Faber, 1982), pp. 370–71.
19. Dilip Hiro, *Dictionary of the Middle East* (London: MacMillan, 1995), p. 164.
20. Interview with Ghanim Jawad, June 2007.
21. "The Endless Torment: The 1991 Uprising and Its Aftermath," Human Rights Watch, June 1992, p. 28.
22. Interview with Sayyid Mohammed al-Musawi, Najaf, June 1, 2007.
23. Interview with a professor at Najaf University, June 2007.
24. Interview with survivor from Najaf, April 2007.
25. Interview with Ghanim Jawad, London, June 24, 2007.

5. THE SHIA RISE UP

1. Interview with Grand Ayatollah al-Khoei, Kufa, April 1991.
2. "The Endless Torment: The 1991 Uprising and Its Aftermath," Human Rights Watch, June 1992, p. 49.
3. Interview with Sayyid Majid al-Khoei, London, June 2, 1998.
4. Interview with General Wafiq al-Samarrai, head of Iraqi Military Intelligence, London, October 3, 1998.
5. Interview with Sanaa Mohammed, Baghdad, June 2007.
6. Interview with Hussein al-Shahristani by Andrew Cockburn, Tehran, March 10, 1998.
7. Interview with Colonel Othman, former army officer, Baghdad, June 28, 2007.
8. Interview with Brigadier Ali, London, March 13, 1998.
9. Interview with Captain Azad Shirwan, Salahudin, June 1991.
10. Faleh al-Jabber, *Why the Intifada Failed,* edited by Fran Hazelton (London: Zed Books, 1993), p. 107.
11. "The Endless Torment," p. 42.
12. Interviews with eyewitnesses in Basra, April 22, 1991.
13. "The Endless Torment," p. 42.
14. Interview with General Wafiq al-Samarrai, London, October 3, 1998.
15. Kanan Makiya, *Cruelty and Silence* (New York: W. W. Norton, 1993), p. 61.
16. Interview with Brigadier Ali, London, March 13, 1998.
17. Makiya, *Cruelty and Silence,* p. 68.
18. Interview with Sanaa Mohammed, Baghdad, June 27, 2007.
19. Makiya, *Cruelty and Silence,* p. 74.
20. Interview with Ali Mohammed, Kut, June 30, 2007.
21. Interview with Sayyid Majid al-Khoei, London, June 2, 1998.
22. Interview with Brigadier Ali, London, March 13, 1998.
23. Michael R. Gordon and General Bernard E. Trainor, *The Generals' War* (Boston: Little, Brown and Company, 1994), pp. 518–19.
24. The proportion of Shia to Sunni in Baghdad is a vexing question. Sunni often claim that they are equal in numbers to the Shia, but the referendum on the constitution in October 2005 and the general election two months later indicated that Shia made up at least seventy percent of the capital's population, and possibly more.
25. Gordon and Trainor, *The Generals' War,* President Bush writing on June 13, 1994, p. 517.
26. Ibid., p. 516.
27. "The Endless Torment," p. 37.

28. Ibid.
29. Interview with Sayyid Majid al-Khoei, London, June 2, 1998.
30. Interview with Saad Jabr, London, March 12, 1998.
31. al-Jabber, *Why the Intifada Failed,* pp. 108–9.
32. Interview with Sanaa Mohammed, Baghdad, June 27, 2007.
33. Interview with Colonel Othman, Baghdad, June 28, 2007.
34. Interview with Hussein, Baghdad, July 3, 2007.

6. SADDAM'S REVENGE

1. Interview with Sanaa Mohammed, Baghdad, June 2007.
2. "The Endless Torment: The 1991 Uprising and Its Aftermath," Human Rights Watch, June 1992, p. 51.
3. Interview with Colonel Othman, Baghdad, June 2007.
4. *The Mass Graves of al-Mahawil: The Truth Uncovered* (New York: Human Rights Watch, May 2003), pp. 10–11.
5. Ibid., pp. 11–12.
6. Ibid., p.13.
7. "The Endless Torment," p. 44.
8. Interview with Dr. al-Rawi, Basra, April 1991.
9. "The Endless Torment," p. 44.
10. Interview with friend of Jassem, Basra, July 2007.

7. THE WHITE LION

1. Ali Allawi, *The Occupation of Iraq: Winning the War, Losing the Peace* (New Haven, Conn.: Yale University Press, 2007), p. 54.
2. Interview with Ali Hussein Khidr, Baghdad, July 2007.
3. Interview with Sheikh Yassin al-Assadi, June 2007.
4. Interview with Mohammed Hassan Ibrahim, July 2007.
5. Mohammed Sadiq al-Sadr CD, 1998.
6. Allawi, *The Occupation of Iraq,* p. 57.
7. Answer to written questions submitted to Jafar al-Sadr, Baghdad, September 2007.
8. Andrew Cockburn and Patrick Cockburn, *Out of the Ashes: The Resurrection of Saddam Hussein* (New York: HarperCollins, 1999), pp. 132–33. The Baghdad study of children is in the *Lancet,* 346, December 2, 1995.
9. Cockburn and Cockburn, *Out of the Ashes,* p. 290.
10. Allawi, *The Occupation of Iraq,* p. 57.
11. Dan Murphy, "Sadr the Agitator: Like Father, Like Son," *Christian Science Monitor,* April 27, 2004.
12. Interview with Sheikh Yassin al-Assadi, June 2007.
13. Conversation with Haider al-Safi, August 2007.
14. Conversation with Ghaith Abdul-Ahad, June 2007.
15. Answer to written questions submitted to Jafar al-Sadr, Baghdad, September 2007.
16. Interview with Mohammed Hassan Ibrahim, July 2007.
17. Interview with Ali Hussein Khidr, July 2007.
18. *Iraq's Muqtada al-Sadr: Spoiler or Stabiliser?* International Crisis Group report, July 11, 2006, p. 5, footnote 29.
19. Interview with Yassin Sajad, Sadr City, July 2007.

20. *Iraq's Muqtada al-Sadr: Spoiler or Stabiliser?* p. 5.
21. Interview with Sheikh Yassin al-Assadi, June 2007.

8. A SECOND ASSASSINATION

1. Interview with Sheikh Akram al-Assadi, former hawza student, July 5, 2007.
2. Ibid.
3. Interview with Mohammed Salem, July 2007.
4. Faleh A. Jabar and Hosham Dawod, eds., *Tribes and Power: Nationalism and Ethnicity in the Middle East* (London: Saqi Books, 2003), pp. 90–96.
5. Ibid., p. 95.
6. Mahan Abedin, "The Sadrist Movement," *Middle East Intelligence Bulletin* 5, no. 7 (July 2003).
7. Interview with Ali Hussein Khidr, 2007.
8. Tape recording made by Mohammed Sadiq al-Sadr in 1998.
9. Interview with Mohammed Hassan Ibrahim, July 2007.
10. Abedin, "The Sadrist Movement," p. 3.
11. Interview with Mohammed Hassan Ibrahim, July 2007.
12. Interview with Ali Hussein Khidr, July 2007.
13. *Iraq's Muqtada al-Sadr: Spoiler or Stabiliser?* International Crisis Group report, July 11, 2006, p. 4, footnote 24.
14. "World Report 1999," Human Rights Watch, p. 2.
15. Interview with Sheikh Yassin al-Assadi, July 2007.
16. Interview with Dr. Hassan Mustafa, Najaf, August 2007.
17. Interview with Ali Hussein Khidr, July 2007.
18. Interview with Mustafa al-Khadimi, London, July 8, 2007.
19. *The Times*, February 28, 1999.
20. Interview with Sajad Ali, Baghdad, July 2007.
21. "Ali Hassan al-Majid and the Basra Massacre of 1999," Human Rights Watch, February 2005, pp. 9–10.
22. Interview with Jassem, Basra, July 2007.
23. Interview with Tariq Mahmud, Baghdad, July 2007, relating what he was told by an eye-witness in Qom at the time.
24. *Iraq's Muqtada al-Sadr: Spoiler or Stabiliser?* p. 6, footnote 17.

9. MUQTADA SURVIVES

1. Nimrod Raphaeli, "Understanding Muqtada al-Sadr," *Middle East Quarterly,* Fall 2004, p. 2.
2. "World Report 1999," Human Rights Watch, p. 2.
3. Interview with Dr. Hassan Mustafa, Najaf, July 2007.
4. Interview with Sheikh Ali, Baghdad, August 2007.
5. Raphaeli, "Understanding Muqtada al-Sadr," p. 2 .
6. *Iraq's Muqtada al-Sadr: Spoiler or Stabiliser?* International Crisis Group report, July 11, 2006, p. 6.
7. Interview with Sheikh Ali, Baghdad, August 2007.
8. Answer to written questions submitted to Jafar al-Sadr, Baghdad, September 2007.
9. Interview with Sheikh Ali, Baghdad, August 2007.
10. ICG interview, Najaf, June 26, 2007.

11. Muqtada al-Sadr interviewed on al-Jazeera, February 18, 2006. Translated with a commentary by Juan Cole in "Informed Comment" on February 19, 2006.
12. Interview with Sadrist militant, Baghdad, August 2007.
13. Interview with Haidar Abdul Hussein and Abdul Hassan Ali, Baghdad, March 2007.
14. Interview with Abu Hatem, Amara, June 2003.
15. *Iraqi Shi'ites under Occupation,* International Crisis Group report, September 9, 2003, pp. 15–20.
16. Interview with Abbas, Baghdad, August 2007.

10. MURDER IN THE SHRINE

1. Interview with Ma'ad Fayadh, London, May 2003.
2. Ibid., London, August 2007.
3. *Sunday Telegraph,* London, April 14, 2003.
4. Interview with Abdul Mohsin al-Khafaji, London, May 2003.
5. Interview with Radwan Hussein al-Rufaie, London, May 2003.
6. Interview with Sheikh Salah Bilal, London, May 2003.
7. Interview with Sheikh Ali, Baghdad, August 2007.

11. SEIZING THE MOMENT

1. Interview with Abbas, Baghdad, August 2007.
2. Interview with Sadrist militant, Baghdad, August 2007.
3. Interview with Abbas, Baghdad, August 2007.
4. Interview with Sadrist militant, Baghdad, August 2007.
5. Interview with Dr. Ahmed, Najaf, August 2007.
6. Andrew Cockburn, "Iraq's Oppressed Minority," *Smithsonian,* December 2003.
7. Juan Cole, "Informed Consent," April 17, 2003.
8. Mahan Abedin, "The Sadrist Movement," *Middle East Intelligence Bulletin* 5, no. 7 (July 2003).
9. Interview with Haidar al-Safi, London, August 2007.
10. Abedin, "The Sadrist Movement."
11. *Iraq's Shi'ites Under Occupation,* International Crisis Group report, September 9, 2003, citing interview with Mohammed al-Fartousi, May 21, 2003.
12. Interview with Sheikh Ali, Baghdad, August 2007.
13. Abedin, "The Sadrist Movement."
14. Agence France-Presse, cited by "Informed Comment" by Juan Cole, April 15, 2003.
15. Nimrod Raphaeli, "Understanding Muqtada al-Sadr," *Middle East Quarterly,* Fall 2004.
16. Abedin, "The Sadrist Movement."
17. Interview with Sheikh Ali, Baghdad, August 2007.
18. Loretta Napoleoni, *Insurgent Iraq: Al Zarqawi and the New Generation* (London: Constable, 2005), p. 157.
19. Raphaeli, "Understanding Muqtada al-Sadr."

12. THE SIEGE OF NAJAF

1. L. Paul Bremer III with Malcolm McConnell, *My Year in Iraq: The Struggle to Build a Future of Hope* (New York: Simon & Schuster, 2006), p. 317.

2. Ibid., pp. 121–22.
3. Ali A. Allawi, *The Occupation of Iraq: Winning the War, Losing the Peace* (New Haven, Conn.: Yale University Press, 2007), p. 211.
4. Bremer, *My Year in Iraq,* pp. 191–92.
5. Allawi, *Occupation of Iraq,* pp. 267–68.
6. *Iraq Shi'ites Under Occupation,* International Crisis Group report, September 9, 2003, p. 17.
7. Interview with Professor Fadhel Mohammed, Baghdad, September 2007.
8. Interview with Munawar Mashelah, Baghdad, August 2007.
9. Institute of War and Peace Reporting, Kerbala, www.iwpr.org, March 4, 2004.
10. Juan Cole, "Informed Comment," April 3, 2004.
11. Bremer, *My Year in Iraq,* p. 318.
12. Rory Stewart, *Occupational Hazards: My Time Governing Iraq* (London: Picador, 2006), pp. 341–42.
13. Juan Cole, "Informed Comment," April 4–7, 2004.
14. Interview with Ali Ahmed, Baghdad, August 2007.
15. Juan Cole, "Informed Comment," April 9, 2004.
16. Interview with Ali Ahmed, Baghdad, August 2007.

13. THE FALL OF NAJAF

1. Interview with Abbas Fadhel, Baghdad, August 2007.
2. Interview with Ali Ahmed, Baghdad, August 2007.
3. Institute of War and Peace Reporting, www.iwpr.org, July 13, 2004.
4. Interview with Abbas Fadhel, Baghdad, August 2007.
5. Nimrod Raphaeli, "Understanding Muqtada al-Sadr," *Middle East Quarterly,* Fall 2004.
6. Interview with Abbas Fadhel, Baghdad, August 2007.
7. Associated Press, August 6, 2007.
8. BBC, August 7, 2007.
9. *The Guardian,* August 9, 2004.
10. Juan Cole, "Informed Comment," August 14, 2004.
11. Interview with Mowaffaq al-Rubai'e, national security adviser, Baghdad, May 2007. The story was first mentioned in Ali A. Allawi, *The Occupation of Iraq: Winning the War, Losing the Peace* (New Haven, Conn.: Yale University Press, 2007), pp. 324–25.
12. Interview with Abbas Khoederi, Baghdad, August 2007.
13. Institute of War and Peace Reporting, www.iwpr.org, September 6, 2004.
14. Juan Cole, "Informed Comment," August 25, 2004.
15. Ibid., August 15, 2004.
16. Reuters, August 21, 2004.
17. Interview with Dr. Ahmed, Najaf, July 2007.
18. Allawi, *The Occupation of Iraq,* p. 328.
19. Ibid., p. 330.
20. CNN, December 4, 2005.

14. A TURN TO POLITICS

1. Interview with Abbas Khoederi, Baghdad, August 2007.
2. Interview with Sabah Khadim, London, September 2007.
3. *Iraq's Muqtada al-Sadr: Spoiler or Stabiliser?* International Crisis Group report, July 11, 2007.

4. Interview with Sheikh Ali, Baghdad, August 2007.
5. Ibid.
6. Interview with Abbas Khoederi, Baghdad, August 2007.
7. Interview with Muqtada al-Sadr, al-Arabiya, January 13, 2006.
8. Interview with Muqtada al-Sadr, al-Jazeera, February 18, 2006.
9. Interview with Hussein Ali, Baghdad, September 2007.
10. Interview with Abbas Fadhel, Baghdad, August 2007.
11. Interview with Sheikh Ali, Baghdad, August 2007.
12. Interview with Salim Shehab, Baghdad, September 2007.
13. Interview with Manale Youssif, Baghdad, September 2007.
14. Inteview with Dr. Mahmoud Qassim, Baghdad, September 2007.
15. Interview with Abbas Fadhel, Baghdad, August 2007.
16. Interview with Shia woman, Baghdad, September 2007.
17. Interview with Manale Youssif, Baghdad, September 2007.
18. Interview with Mohammed Tariq, September 2007.

15. THE BATTLE OF BAGHDAD

1. Letter from Bassim Abdul-Rahman, September 2007.
2. Interview with Hussein Ali, Baghdad, September 2007.
3. *New York Times,* December 22, 2006.
4. Leila Fadel, "Security in Iraq Still Elusive," *McClatchy,* September 7, 2007.
5. Account by Haider al-Safi, London, September 2007.
6. Interview with Sheikh Ali, Baghdad, August 2007.
7. Interview with Hussein Ali, former Mehdi Army commander, September 2007.
8. Interview with resident in al-Hamraa district, Baghdad, September 2007.
9. Interview with Salim Shehab, Baghdad, October 2007.
10. E-mail from sheikh in Balad, August 2006.
11. *New York Times,* December 22, 2006.
12. E-mail from sheikh in Balad, August 2006.
13. Phil Sands, "Inside the Mehdi Army Death Squads," *Jane's Terrorism and Security Monitor,* February 14, 2007.
14. Iraqi Body Count citing news reports, iCasualties.org, October 2, 2007.
15. Sands, "Inside the Mehdi Army Death Squads."
16. Leila Fadel, "Chilling Stories from the Mehdi Army," *McClatchy,* June 22, 2007.

16. THE SURGE

1. Interview with Hussein Ali, October 2007.
2. Interview with Muqtada al-Sadr in *La Repubblica,* January 19, 2007.
3. Ali A. Allawi, *The Occupation of Iraq: Winning the War, Losing the Peace* (New Haven, Conn.: Yale University Press, 2007), p. 443, citing *New York Times,* March 28, 2006.
4. Interview with Ahmed Chalabi, Baghdad, May 2007.
5. Allawi, *The Occupation of Iraq,* p. 450.
6. State of the Union address, President George W. Bush, January 23, 2007.
7. Interview with Hussein Ali, September 2007.
8. Ibid.
9. Ibid.
10. *Financial Times,* May 17, 2007.

11. Interview with Hoshyar Zebari, Baghdad, May 2007.
12. Iraqslogger, October 5, 2007.
13. "Iraq: Food rationing system failing as Ramadan approaches," IRIN, UN Office for Coordination of Humanitarian Affairs, September 2007.
14. Zeyad Kasim, "Fadhila Leader Slams Iraqi Politicians," Iraqslogger, May 25, 2007.
15. Reuters, Kufa, May 25, 2007; *New York Times,* July 18, 2007.
16. Interview with Mehdi Army militant, Baghdad, October 2007.
17. Babak Rahimi, "Askariya Bombing Strengthens Sadr's Hand," Jamestown Foundation, June 2007.
18. Leila Fadel, "Al-Sadr Radio Interview Decries U.S. Presence in Iraq," *McClatchy,* August 28, 2007.
19. Interview with Muqtada al-Sadr, Kufa, in *The Independent,* August 20, 2007.
20. "Hired Tribesmen Save SIIC in Sadr Stronghold," Iraqslogger, August 31, 2007.
21. Interview with Muqtada al-Sadr, Kufa, in *The Independent,* August 20, 2007.
22. *Washington Post,* October 7, 2007.
23. Interview with Mehdi Army member, Baghdad, October 2007.

17. THE DISINTEGRATION OF IRAQ

1. ABC/BBC/NTV poll, September 2007.
2. "The Most Dangerous Man in Iraq: The Shi'ite Cleric Moqtada al-Sadr," *Newsweek,* December 4, 2006.
3. Ghaith Abdul-Ahad, "Meet Abu Abed: The US's New Ally Against al-Qaida," *The Guardian,* November 10, 2007.

AFTERWORD

1. "Iraq's Maliki Orders Militants to Surrender," Reuters, March 26, 2008.
2. "Battles Wrack Basra, Threatening Success of U.S. Surge," *McClatchy,* March 25, 2008.
3. "Battle Rages in Basra as Government Cracks Down," Reuters, March 26, 2008.
4. "Shiite Showdown Pushes Iraqi Prime Minister Towards Critical Movement," AP, March 28, 2008.
5. AP, March 29, 2008.
6. "A Kidnapped Maliki Aide Tells His Tale," *Time,* April 1, 2008.
7. Interview with senior U.S. official, London, June 25, 2008.
8. Michael R. Gordon, Eric Schmidt, and Stephen Farrell, "The U.S. Cites Planning Gaps in Iraqi Assault on Basra," *New York Times,* April 3, 2008.
9. Ibid.
10. "U.S. Forces Drawn Deeper into Iraqi Crackdown," Reuters, March 28, 2008.
11. Private information from consultant working with U.S. military.
12. "Al-Sadr Says He Remains in Control of the Mehdi Army, Attacks Government, Americans," Reuters, March 29, 2008.
13. Amit R. Paley, "Sadr Pursues Image to Match His Power," *Washington Post,* May 27, 2008.
14. "Al-Sadr says he remains in control of the Mehdi Army," Reuters.
15. "Iranian General Played Key Role in Brokering Iraq Cease-fire," *McClatchy,* March 30, 2008.
16. "Sadr Followers Caught Off Guard by Truce," Reuters, March 30, 2008.
17. Ibid.
18. James Glanz and Alissa J. Rubin, "The Iraqi Army Takes Last Basra Areas from Sadr Force," *New York Times,* April 20, 2008.

19. Peter Graff, "Iraq's Maliki Threatens to Bar Sadr from Vote," Reuters, April 7, 2008.
20. Raviya H. Ismail, "Sadr Threatens Unending 'War' in Iraq If Attacks Don't End," *McClatchy,* April 19, 2008.
21. Alissa J. Rubin, "Sadr Tells Forces Not to Attack Iraqis," *New York Times,* April 24, 2008.
22. James Glanz, "Iraqi Deaths Are on the Rise Again During Clashes with the Militias," *New York Times,* April 2, 2008.
23. "Iraqi Prime Minister Gets Political Show of Support but Sadrists Excluded," AP, April 11, 2008.
24. "Sadr Pursues Image to Match His Power," *Washington Post.*
25. Anonymous interview in Baghdad, June 4, 2008.
26. Hamza Hendawi, "Maverick Cleric Trumps al-Maliki's Government in Southern Showdown," AP, April 1, 2008.

Index

Abbas:
    martyrdom of, 9, 13, 17, 20–21, 23, 144
    shrine of, 19, 50, 70, 136, 197
Abbas, Sayyid, 5–7, 144
Abbasid dynasty, 24–25
Abdul-Ahad, Ghaith, 90, 156
Abdul-Rahman, Bassim, 1–3, 5, 10, 147, 175–77, 182, 185
Abed, Abu, 203–4
Abu Bakr, Caliph, 25
Abu Ghraib prison, 2, 58, 103
Adhwa, 34–35
Afghanistan, 87, 131, 133, 167, 173
Ahmed, Ali, 147, 148, 149, 153
Akram, Abu, 193
al-Askari shrine, 175, 195
al Hawza, 138, 139, 144, 146
al-Huda, 93, 112
Ali, Hussein, 168–69, 177, 189–90, 191, 201
Ali, Imam, 25, 50, 123
    assassination of, 7, 9, 17, 20
    green flags as symbol of, 16, 18
    mosque of, 4, 5
    relationship to Mohammed of, 5, 7, 20, 22
    shrine of, 2, 3, 7, 8, 9, 10, 62, 65, 71, 82, 119, 123, 142, 150, 151, 152, 158, 161, 162
    sons of, see Abbas, Imam; Hussein, Imam
    turba and, 118
Ali, Jafar, 47, 48
Ali, Sajad, 106

Ali, Samir Nuri, 42
Ali, Sheikh, 111, 112, 125, 126, 130, 135, 170–71, 180
al-Jazeera, 135, 208, 209
al-Jumhuriyah, 110
Allawi, Ali, 139, 142
Allawi, Iyad, 153, 157, 158, 159, 160, 162, 166, 187, 192
al-Qaeda in Iraq, 166, 180, 184, 195, 203
"al-Sadr intifada," 107–8, 109
al-Thawra (Baath newspaper), 79
Aqeel, Abu, 210
Arabic language, 49
    Iraqi dialect of, 102, 199
Arabs, 19–20, 30, 33, 45, 64, 78
Arafat, Yasser, 41
Araqi, Sayyid Hazim al-, 145
Arba'in pilgrimage, 16–19, 23, 36, 37–38, 128
Arbil, 128
Ardebili, Ahmed Mustafa, 110
Army, U.S., 12, 14, 16–17, 146, 153, 187
Asharq Al-Awsat, 122, 154
Ashura rituals, 23–24, 36, 143, 174
Assadi, Sheikh Akram al-, 95, 97
Assadi, Sheikh Yassin al-, 88, 100, 104
"axis of evil," 167
Aya, Abu, 182
ayatollahs, 30, 36, 112, 165
Aziz, Abdul Khaliq Abdul, 70–71
Aziz, Tariq, 42, 44

Baath Party, 8, 9, 16, 23, 39, 128, 145, 166, 172, 174, 179, 185

Baath Party *(cont.)*
  de-Baathification and, 28
  Mohammed Sadiq al-Sadr and, 89–90,
    96–100, 108–9, 112, 132
  newspaper of, 79, 110
  in 1963 and 1968 coups, 33–34, 81
  security and intelligence services of,
    33, 34, 35, 36, 37, 38, 40, 41–43, 44,
    45, 51, 55, 56, 57, 60, 62, 65, 74, 79,
    82, 88, 95–96, 97, 100, 105, 108,
    110, 111, 113, 115, 127
  Shia members of, 32, 33
  Shia opposition to and repression by,
    8, 9, 13, 19, 23, 24, 27–28, 35–43,
    44, 50–53, 55–69, 70–77, 78,
    79, 85–86, 88, 93–94, 98,
    99–100
Babylon, 19, 26
Badr Organization, 53, 67–68, 107–8, 132,
    141, 164, 169, 174, 195
Baghdad, 8, 16, 18, 20, 27–28, 29, 31, 36,
    40, 45, 53, 57, 65, 66, 72, 85, 86,
    116, 128, 138
  as center of Muslim world, 24
  Green Zone of, 139, 141, 145, 193, 194,
    199, 205, 211, 213
  Iraqi army offensive in, 205, 206
  Khadamiyah district of, 1, 18, 28, 29,
    144, 177–78, 179
  looting of, 128–30
  Mongol invasion of, 12, 26
  Rusafa district of, 128
  sectarian violence in, 11, 12, 175–86
  Shia districts of, 1, 50, 176; *see also*
    Sadr City
  Shia population of, 177
  U.S. bombing of, 103
  U.S. "surge" and, 178–79
Baghdad University, 174
Bakr, Ahmad Hassan al-, 34, 37, 38
Barak, Fadhil al-, 37, 40
Basra, 21, 23, 36, 47, 56, 59, 60, 61, 66,
    68–69, 75, 92–93, 107, 108, 118,
    132, 135, 142, 150, 161, 173,
    205–11
Beirut, 41, 156
Bejat clan, 34
Bergner, Kevin, 205
Bilal, Sheikh Salah, 124, 125
bin Laden, Osama, 189
Blackwater security, 145
Blair, Tony, 6, 183
blood money, 91, 98

Bremer, Paul, 11, 12, 139–40, 141, 142,
    143, 144, 145, 147, 148, 153, 178,
    202, 213
British troops, 6, 108, 139, 197
Burujurdi, Ayatollah, 103
Bush, George H. W., 58, 66, 76
Bush, George W., 6, 22, 96, 132, 134, 167,
    179, 183, 188, 189, 192, 212
Bush (George W. Bush) administration, 167

caliphate, 20
"cellar of the guillotine," 172
Central Intelligence Agency (CIA), 54,
    117, 121, 123, 139, 153, 188
Chalabi, Ahmed, 105
Cheadle, Mark, 207–8
chess, 22
Christians, 9, 17, 21, 23, 24, 30, 50, 72, 81, 93
  in Iraq, 8, 173, 194
church and state separation, 23, 25–26, 140
clans, 26
clergy, Shia, 9, 23, 29, 34–35, 45, 68, 89–90
  activist vs. quietist factions in, 28, 35,
    37, 39, 50–51, 82, 92, 99, 113, 131,
    140–41
  Arab vs. Iranian, 30, 36
  church-state separation and, 25–26
  donations made to, 9, 30
  Mohammed Sadiq al-Sadr made head
    of, 78–79
  Muqtada al-Sadr's opponents in, 141
  structure of, 25
  see also Marji'iyyah; *mujtahids*
Clinton, Bill, 103
Coalition Provisional Authority (CPA),
    19, 139, 140, 141, 142, 144–49, 153
Cockburn, Andrew, 116
Commerce Ministry (Iraqi), 45
Communist Party, 31, 32, 33
Crocker, Ryan C., 207

Damascus, 17, 20, 21, 52, 96, 188, 191
Dawa, al- (the Call) Party, 34, 35, 36, 37,
    39–40, 52, 58, 68, 81, 89, 96, 105,
    109, 134, 141, 142, 156, 166, 178,
    188, 191, 192, 208
  Baath repression of, 36, 38, 41, 43, 44,
    45, 50–51
  formation of, 31
  IGC and, 140
  legacy of, 32
  Muqtada al-Sadr as enemy of, 133
Dawood, Qassim, 161

Defense Intelligence Agency (DIA) (U.S.), 44, 45, 65
democracy, 14, 18
Dra'am, Karim, 151

Egypt, 31, 33, 167, 192
Europe:
    Eastern, 53
    Western, 46, 54

Fadhel, Abbas, 150–52, 154, 170
Fadhila Party, 173, 194
Faili (Shia) Kurds, 36
Fallujah, 2, 145, 149, 153, 166
Falsafatuna (Our Philosophy) (Mohammed Baqir al-Sadr), 34
Faqih, Wilayat al-, 103
Farsi language, 39
Fartousi, Sheikh Mohammed al-, 127–28, 131–32
Fatah movement, 41
Fatima, 20
Fatimid dynasty, 25
Fayadh, Ayatollah Mohammed al-, 131
Fayadh, Ma'ad, 122–24
Fedayeen Saddam, 105, 122
Feraiji, Shaikh Salman al-, 206
Fiqh al-Asha'ir (Tribal Jurisprudence) (Mohammed Sadiq al-Sadr), 99
First Popular Islamic Conference (1983), 51
Fisk, Robert, 47–48
flags:
    Iraqi, 88
    symbolism of, 16, 18, 24, 118
Foreign Office (British), 120
France, 40, 140
French troops, 67

Gafoor, Rasheed Abdul, 49
Gharawi, Ayatollah al-, 103
Ghazali, Sheikh Qais al-, 2, 3, 4, 10–11
Great Britain, 40, 58, 86, 121, 155
    Iraqi monarchy established by, 26
    1920 uprising against, 29, 49, 81, 120
    see also British troops
Great Depression, 84–85
Gulf War, 8, 19, 23, 54, 58, 62, 63, 66, 88, 114, 116, 121
gypsies, 92, 143

Habubi family, 62
Haeri, Ayatollah Khadim al-, 113, 117, 128, 130, 133–34, 164

hajj, 133
Hajman, Sheikh Ali Qazim, 110
Hakim, Abdul Aziz al-, 169, 188
Hakim, Grand Ayatollah Muhsin al-, 30, 31, 32, 36, 52
Hakim, Mahdi al-, 36
Hakim, Mohammed Baqir al-, 38, 68–69, 82, 96, 99, 108, 114, 120
    assassination of, 136, 140, 144
    return from exile of, 132
    SCIRI formed by, 31, 52
    U.S. and, 133
Hakim family, 30, 52, 57, 62, 81, 99, 163–64
Halliday, Denis, 87, 93
haram (forbidden), 5, 22, 112
Hashemite monarchy, 31
Hashimi, Sayyid Mahmoud al-, 40
Hassnawi, Sheikh Mithal al-, 155
hawza (Shia seminary), 30, 31, 34, 35, 36, 40, 51, 79, 80, 95–96, 97, 113, 130, 131, 154, 163
Health Ministry (Iraqi), 11, 172, 173
Hezbollah:
    in Iraq, 107
    in Lebanon, 24, 107, 155, 167, 169, 204, 207
Higher Security Court, 33
Hizb al-Fadhila, 118
honor killings, 145
House of Happiness, 182
Huda, al-, 93, 112
Huda, Amina Sadr Bint al-, 27–28, 42, 45
Hussein, Haidar Abdul, 116–17
Hussein, Imam, 23, 118, 123
    martyrdom of, 9, 13, 17, 20–22, 23, 24, 99, 143–44
    relationship of Mohammed and Ali to, 17, 20
    shrine of, 19, 70, 72, 136, 197
Hussein, Jassem, 77
Hussein, Uday, 93
Husseini, Nasir Khadir Hazim al-, 73–74
husseiniyas (Shia places of worship), 68, 90, 117, 135, 179, 180, 181

Ibn Muljam, 7
Ibrahim, Mohammed Hassan, 80, 90, 93, 100–101
identity papers, 11
IGC (Iraqi Governing Council), 134–35, 139
Imam Ali mosque, 4, 5

imams, 22–23, 25, 29, 177
  political power not sought by, 23
  as true heirs of Mohammed, 22
  Twelfth Imam, 22, 93, 100, 103, 165, 197
improvised explosive devices (IEDs), 169, 186
Information Ministry (Iraqi), 8, 9, 47, 54, 55, 85, 116
INIS (Iraqi National Intelligence Service), 153, 188–89
Interior Ministry (Iraqi), 133, 163, 196, 212
International Crisis Group, 92
Iqtisaduna (Our Economics) (Mohammed Baqir al-Sadr), 34
Iran, 29, 58, 67, 68, 71, 76, 114, 127, 202
  conversion to Shi'ism of, 25, 49
  holy city of, *see* Qom
  Iraqi Shias and, 15, 36, 121, 132, 153–55, 159, 166–70, 186, 203, 207, 211
  Mohammed Sadiq al-Sadr resented in, 103, 108–9
  SCIRI and, 133
  Shi'ism as state religion in, 38
  "Twelver" branch of Shia in, 22
  U.S. criticism of, 155, 167, 192, 202
Iranian revolution, 24, 27, 28, 35, 37, 38–40, 49, 51
Iran-Iraq war, 8, 38–39, 44–54, 60, 78, 86, 132
  casualty figures in, 23, 48
  description of, 45–48, 52, 53–54
Iraq:
  atmosphere of fear in, 11–12
  as birthplace of urban civilization, 19, 26
  breakup of, 66, 186, 204
  civilian casualty figures in, 11
  civil war in, 174, 175–86
  as collapsed state, 172–73, 200
  constitution of, 140–41, 165
  currency of, 83, 90
  economy of, 23, 33, 34, 83–87, 91, 114, 121, 170–71, 193, 205
  elections held in, 133, 135, 140–41, 142, 160–61, 165, 167, 179, 202, 208
  flag of, 14
  internal displacement in, 12, 182, 194, 203
  Iranian nationals in, 36, 37, 45, 89, 97
  marsh area of, 23, 48, 60, 61, 76, 90
  monarchy in, 26, 31
  1919 and 1947 census in, 26
  1958 coup in, 31, 32
  1963 coup in, 33
  1968 coup in, 33–34, 81
  no-fly zone enforced over, 76
  opposition to U.S. occupation of, 6, 13, 19, 134–35, 160, 164, 170, 200, 204, 205
  parliament of, 123, 126, 142, 165, 170, 188, 192, 194
  police of, 205–7
  population of, 18
  post-Saddam governments in, 134–35, 139, 153
  referendum held in, 102, 165
  refugees from, 12, 53, 68, 76, 108, 194
  senate of, 29
  UN sanctions enforced against, 23, 83–87, 114, 121
  U.S. invasion of, 116
  U.S. officials' misunderstanding of, 10, 11
  WMD and, 103
Iraqi army, 6, 19, 108
  in Gulf War, 8, 54, 55, 58–59, 63, 66, 114, 128
  in Iran-Iraq War, 44–54
  in offensive against Medhi Army, 205–7, 210, 211, 212
  1991 Shia uprising and, 58–62, 65–67, 70–77
  Shia in, 37, 46–49, 51, 53, 54, 55, 58–59, 116–17, 201
  Sunni domination of, 33
  U.S.-trained "shadow army" units of, 187
  in war against Kurds, 37
Iraqi Civil Defense Corps (ICDC), 19
Iraqi exiles, 10, 115, 121–22, 127, 132, 141, 202
Iraqi Governing Council (IGC), 134–35, 139
Iraqi National Intelligence Service (INIS), 153, 188, 189
Iraq News Agency, 110
Ireland, 17, 50, 169
Islamic Action Organization, 41–42
Islamic Arab army, 19–20
IIsma'il, Shah, 25
Ismail, Sheikh Abdel Karim, 104, 107
Israel, 5, 24
Italian troops, 155

Jaafari, Ibrahim al-, 25, 156, 166, 167, 188, 202

Jabar, Faleh, 24
Jabber, Mohammed Ala'a, 193
Jabr, Saad, 67–68
Jarad, Yassin, 136
Jawad, Ghanim, 30, 51
Jawad, Imam Mohammed Jawad, 29
Jerusalem, 9, 17
Jesus, 100
Jews, 72
Jizani, Sheikh Saleh al-, 92, 107
Jordan, 55, 72, 167, 185, 192, 194

Ka'abi, Sheikh Ali al-, 106, 113
Kabul, 133
Kalal, Abu al-, 43
Kamael, Abu, 185
Kamel, Hussein, 71–72
Kassem, Ali, 92–93
Kerbala, 9, 26, 29, 36, 41, 43, 47, 50, 57,
    179, 196
  author in, 19
  bombings in, 18, 144
  Hussein and Abbas's martyrdoms on
    site of, 13, 17, 20–22, 23, 24, 143–44
  1991 Shia uprising and, 63–64, 65, 68,
    70, 72
  pilgrimages to, 16–18, 31, 37–38,
    100–101, 103–4, 128, 141, 143–44,
    179
  shrines to Hussein and Abbas in, 19,
    38, 70, 72, 136, 197
Khadim, Sabah, 163
Khafaji, Abdul Hassan al- "Abu Tariq," 62,
    63, 65, 67, 122–24
Khalilzad, Zalmay, 120–21, 188
Khamenei, Ayatollah Ali, 103, 109, 134, 209
Khazim, Imam Musa al-, 29
Khidr, Ali Hussein, 79, 90–91, 93, 101–2,
    104–5
Khoederi, Abbas, 153, 158–59
Khoei, Grand Ayatollah Abu al Qasim al-,
    9, 40, 49, 52, 54, 61, 81, 91, 104, 119
  death of, 78
  Mohammed Baqir al-Sadr and, 30
  1991 uprising and, 55–57, 67
  quietist stance of, 36, 37, 39, 50–51, 56,
    92, 100
Khoei, Sayyid Majid al-, 64–65, 67, 96, 99,
    114, 119–20, 127, 153
  assassination of, 9, 119, 122–26, 130,
    139, 140, 164, 201
  return from exile of, 121–23
Khoei Foundation, al-, 51, 99, 120, 122, 123

Khomeini, Ayatollah Ruholla, 28, 32, 37,
    38–40, 42, 45, 46, 49, 50, 52, 54, 58,
    81, 103, 202
Killidar, Haidar al-Rufaie al-, 123, 126
Kufa, 2, 3, 7, 9, 10, 12, 14, 17, 19, 20–21,
    36, 55, 72, 88, 105, 132, 135, 154,
    156, 165, 175, 176, 196
  demilitarization of, 161–62
  Imam Ali mosque in, 4, 5
  Mohammed Sadiq al-Sadr's Friday
    prayers and sermons in, 79–80,
    100, 101–2, 104, 112
  Muqtada al-Sadr's Friday prayers and
    sermons in, 16, 128, 146
  Muqtada al-Sadr trapped in, 22, 146–47
Kufi, Sheikh Abd al-Hassan Abbas al-,
    110
Kurdish Peshmerga, 187
Kurdistan, 6, 57, 58, 65, 76, 87, 116
Kurdistan Democratic Party, 116, 120
Kurds, 18, 25, 26, 33, 36, 37, 41, 45, 49, 58,
    64, 65, 66, 76, 78, 86, 103, 120, 121,
    128, 169, 186, 188, 192, 195, 202
Kut, 205
Kuwait, 8, 19, 23, 54, 55, 58, 62, 63, 66, 78,
    83, 86, 88, 114, 121, 128, 159

Labor and Social Affairs Ministry (Iraqi),
    171
Labor Ministry (Iraqi), 84, 140
Lebanon, 2, 24, 25, 29, 40, 41, 155, 167,
    180, 202, 204
Libya, 92
London, 9, 51, 61, 99, 109, 114, 119, 133,
    155, 161, 175
looting, 17, 26, 64, 73, 118, 128–30

Mahmoud, Karim, 107
Majid, Ali Hassan al- "Chemical Ali,"
    76–77, 108
Maliki, Nouri al-, 23, 96, 187–88, 189, 191,
    192, 196, 202, 205, 207, 208, 209,
    210, 211
Maliki, Salim al-, 173
Marine Corps, U.S., 150–51, 155, 156,
    158, 164, 166, 199
Marji' al-Taqlid, 25, 30
Marji'iyyah, 30, 32, 34, 35, 40, 64, 82, 91,
    102–3, 111, 114, 140, 149, 165, 196,
    202
  function and description of, 25, 30, 36
Mecca, 133
Medina, 20, 21

Mehdi, Adel Abdul, 188
Mehdi Army, 10, 12, 18, 96, 111, 122, 125, 130, 132, 167, 171–72, 178–79, 201
    author's encounter with, 1–7, 11, 147, 175
    in battles in Najaf, 141, 142, 144–49, 150–62, 163
    checkpoints controlled by, 1–4, 11, 126, 147
    continued strength of, 174
    formation of, 133–34, 135
    as generic term for Shia militias, 175, 191
    growth of, 154–55
    Iran and, 168–69, 203
    Iraq army offensive against, 205–7, 208, 210, 211, 212
    Najaf opposition to, 136–37
    recruits of, 4, 135, 147
    in sectarian violence, 176, 177, 180–86
    self-image of members of, 6
    U.S. denunciations of, 134, 139
    U.S "surge" and, 178–79, 189–97
    weaponry of, 2
    see also Sadrist movement
Mehdi, Imam al-, 22, 93, 100, 103, 165, 197
"minders," 85
mines, 87
Mohammed, Fadhel, 143
Mohammed, Prophet, 4, 17, 24
    Ali's relationship to, 5, 7, 20, 22
    birthday of, 2
    descendants of, 3, 29
    imams as true heirs of, 22
Mohammed, Sanaa, 57, 63–64, 68, 71–72
Mongols, 12, 26, 29
Muawiya, Caliph, 20
Mubarqaa, Sayyid Qassim al-, 43
mujtahids, 29, 30, 39, 49, 82, 114
    Sharia law interpreted by, 25, 81
Musawi, Sayid Mohammed al-, 52
Musawi, Sheikh Mohammed Fadhil al-, 154
Mustafa, Hassan, 105–6, 110–11
Mustansariya University, al-, 138, 173

Najaf, 2, 3, 5, 6, 11, 14, 19, 26, 29, 30, 32, 34, 36, 37, 39, 40, 42, 43, 50, 51, 53, 54, 75, 79, 81, 89, 95, 99, 105, 110, 112, 113, 122, 128, 130, 132, 146, 154, 170, 191, 210, 211

Ali's shrine in, 2, 3, 7, 8, 9, 10, 62, 65, 71, 82, 119, 123, 142, 150, 151, 152, 158, 161, 162
    author in, 8, 10–11
    battles in, 1, 14, 141, 142, 144–49, 150–62, 163, 189, 196, 199, 205, 210–11
    description of, 7
    founded on site of Ali's death, 7
    under Hakim family control, 163–64
    Mehdi Army opposed in, 136–37
    Mohammed Sadiq al-Sadr assassinated in, 4, 96, 122–26
    1991 Shia uprising and, 55–57, 61–63, 65, 71, 72
    pilgrimages to, 2, 31, 100
Naqib, Falah al-, 153, 159
Nassariya, 205
Nasser, Gamal Abdul, 31
nationalism, 19–20, 24, 30, 31, 33, 49–50, 54, 79, 89, 109, 127, 134, 166, 203
nationalization, 33, 41
Natural History Museum, 129
Nuri, Riyadh al-, 124, 164

Office of the Martyr (Sayyid al-Shahid), 138, 172
oil, 5, 28, 41, 83, 84, 196, 200
    Iran-Iraq war and, 47, 54
    Iraq's revenues from, 86, 170, 194
    oil-for-food program, 86
    price of, 34, 45, 212
Omar, Caliph, 25
Operation Desert Fox, 103
Organization for Islamic Action, 52
orphanages, 142
Othman, Caliph, 25
Othman, Colonel, 58, 68, 72, 75
Othman, Mahmoud, 213
Ottoman Empire, 25, 26, 29
Out of the Ashes (Cockburn and Cockburn), 116

Pahlevi, Muhammad Reza, Shah of Iran, 27, 30, 39, 45, 49, 51
Palestinians, 41
Paris, 39
Persians, 20, 29
Petraeus, David, 203
pilgrimages, Shia, 6, 7, 29, 31, 71, 100–101, 141, 179, 197
    Arba'in, 16–19, 23, 36, 37–38, 128

descriptions of, 2, 10, 16, 143–44
Saddam's repression of, 2, 100, 103–4, 128
Poland, 50, 72, 146

Qadassiya, al-, battle of, 20
Qassim, Abdel Karim, 31, 32–33
Qom, 30, 108–9, 113, 130, 164, 208, 211
Quds Brigade, 134, 154, 210
Qumi, Hassan Kazemi, 210

Rawawi, Sayyid Ali al-, 117
Rawi, Walid al-, 59–60, 75
Republican Guard, 19, 54, 59, 63, 65, 71, 74–75, 77, 104, 105, 150
Republican Party, U.S., 207
Revolutionary Guards (Iranian), 68, 71, 134, 154, 169, 200, 207, 210
Revolution Command Council, 34, 40, 41
Roman Catholics, 17, 30, 50
Roman Empire, 26, 100
Rouhani, Ayatollah Mohammed, 30
Rubai'e, Mowaffaq al-, 157–58, 160, 193
Rufaie, Haidar al-, 124–25
Rufaie, Radwan Hussein al-, 123
Rusil, Abu, 185–86

Sabri, Adnan, 8
Saddam City, 4, 16, 18, 33
see also Sadr City
Saddam Hussein, 1, 10, 12, 14–15, 16, 22, 26, 32, 38, 55, 82, 85, 86, 87, 88, 97, 98, 131, 141, 150, 153, 155, 167, 177, 188, 190, 192, 199, 204, 213
attempted assassinations of, 18, 41
clan and tribe of, 34
downfall of, 115–18, 121, 127, 133, 209, 212
execution of, 8, 18, 25
Faith campaign of, 89, 173
"final battle" claim of, 130
general amnesty declared by, 115
Gulf War and, 8, 19, 116
Iran-Iraq war and, 8, 38–39, 44–54, 78
militia force established by, 105, 122
Mohammed Baqir al-Sadr executed by, 9, 27, 42–43
Mohammed Sadiq al-Sadr ordered assassinated by, 4, 27, 105–6, 109, 110–11
mythic historical self-identification of, 19–20
in 1966 coup plot, 33

1991 Shia uprising and, 56–57, 61, 62, 65–66, 69, 70–77, 78
referendum held on leadership of, 102
rise of, 34, 35, 38, 40
Sadrists and, 103–4
Shia pilgrimages limited or banned by, 2
weaknesses of, 46, 78
see also Baath Party
Sadr, Ayatollah Mohammed Baqir al- (Sadr I), 27–43, 50, 79, 80, 81, 83, 103, 105, 112, 114, 118, 131, 191, 202, 208–9
arrests of, 36, 40–41, 42, 81
birth and family background of, 28–29
covert political activism of, 35, 36–37, 39–40
Dawa and, 31–32, 35
education of, 29–30
execution of, 9, 27, 42–43, 44, 45, 51, 200
Khomeini and, 38–39
Muqtada al-Sadr's relationship to, 9, 14
Sadrist movement and, 27
writings of, 34–35
Sadr, Hussain al-, 177, 178, 179, 183
Sadr, Jafar al-, 29, 41, 83, 90, 105, 108–9, 113
Sadr, Mohammed Sadiq al- (Sadr II), 16, 42, 49, 78–94, 95–109, 118, 128, 131, 142, 164, 166, 190, 194, 202
arrests of, 81–82, 88, 97
assassination of, 4, 9, 14, 27, 96, 97, 105–9, 110–11, 117, 128, 200
Baath regime and, 89–90, 96–100, 108–9, 112, 132
background of, 80–81
commemorative prayers for, 113
Friday prayers led by, 79, 89–91, 97, 100–101, 103–4
as head of Shia clergy, 78–79, 87–91, 109
personality of, 82, 91, 97, 102
political activism of, 80, 82–83, 85–86, 87–94, 101–4
religious views of, 82
Sadr City named after, 4, 91
semi-divinity of, 96, 106
U.S. as enemy of, 132, 133, 187–98
Sadr, Muammal al-, 80, 83, 90, 96, 102, 105, 110–11

Sadr, Muqtada al-:
   after Mohammed Sadiq al-Sadr's
      assassination, 110–12
   al-Huda edited by, 93, 112
   author's attempt to see, 1–4, 12
   Baghdad newspaper of, 138, 139, 144
   in battles in Najaf, 14, 144–49, 152–62
   birth of, 14, 112
   cease-fire called by, 208, 211
   coalition forces called "guests" by, 137
   early career of, 112–13
   enemies of, 133, 141, 163, 187, 195–96
   Friday sermons of, 16, 128, 194, 198
   IGC denounced by, 134–35
   location kept secret by, 12, 148, 149,
      153, 164–65, 191
   looting fatwa issued by, 130
   marriage of, 83, 112
   media portrayals of, 13, 111, 115, 199
   militia founded by, *see* Mehdi Army
   nine-point statement of, 209–210
   personality of, 12–13, 14, 115
   political ambitions of, 165–66, 170,
      174
   political skills of, 13, 110–11, 114, 125,
      133, 137, 141–42, 200
   popular support for, 154, 160
   religious studies of, 113–14, 208–9
   rift between Sistani and, 131
   rise of, 9, 13–14, 27, 86, 109, 113,
      117–18, 127–28, 199
   Sayyid Majid al-Khoei's assassination
      and, 9, 119, 122–26, 139, 164, 201
   sectarian killings decried by, 183, 184,
      204
   semi-divinity of, 115
   September 11, 2001 attacks praised by,
      139
   Shia political movement and, *see*
      Sadrist movement
   in studies to be *mujtahid,* 208
   U.S. occupation opposed by, 5, 13, 15,
      134, 137, 160, 165, 166, 183, 200,
      209
Sadr, Murtada al-, 80, 111
Sadr, Musa al-, 169–70
Sadr, Mustafa al-, 80, 83, 96, 97, 102, 105,
   110–11, 112
Sadr City, 11, 16, 34, 43, 100, 105, 106, 112,
   117, 136, 146, 150, 154, 155, 173
   Iraq army offensive in, 205, 206, 207,
      211
   location of, 4

   Muhsin mosque in, 128
   population of, 4, 32, 91, 142
   previous names of, 4, 33
   thieves' markets of, 129
   underclass of, 4, 91, 98–99, 170, 178
   U.S.-installed council in, 137
Sadr family, 13, 27, 28–29, 79, 83, 100, 122
Sadrist movement, 9, 12, 13, 37, 39, 49, 88,
   113, 124, 125, 138, 177, 201
   Baath infiltration of, 95–96
   courts established by, 131, 173
   hospitals controlled by, 170–71
   Iran and, 167–70, 211
   Islamic puritanism of, 173
   looting and, 128–30
   magazine published by, 93
   middle class distrust of, 132, 133, 154,
      160
   ministries controlled by, 172
   Mohammed Baqir al-Sadr as
      progenitor of, 27
   Muqtada al-Sadr's description of, 114
   political prisoners' release demanded
      by, 115–16
   as political resistance group, 165–66
   popularity and influence of, 138–40,
      142–43, 174
   popular support for, 115
   religious and political ideology of,
      91–92
   renewal of, 127–28
   Saddam and, 103–4
   sectarian violence and, 185
   start of, 90–91
   underclass at core of, 4, 90, 91–92,
      98–99, 139–40, 154, 174
   youth appeal of, 93, 101, 117, 143
   see also Mehdi Army
Safavid dynasty, 25, 29, 49
Safi, Haider al-, 1, 3–5, 10, 11, 147, 175,
   177–78, 179
Sajad, Yassin, 91–92
Salem, Mohammed, 97
Samari, Ali al-, 172–73
Samarra, 22, 29, 165, 175, 176, 179, 180,
   186, 195
Samarrai, Wafiq al-, 60–61, 69
Saudi Arabia, 61, 86, 133, 167, 180, 192
Sayyid al-Shahid (Office of the Martyr),
   138, 172
sayyids, 3, 4, 24
SCIRI, *see* Supreme Council for Islamic
   Revolution in Iraq

secularism, 30–31
September 11, 2001, attacks, 139
Shahristani, Hussein al-, 58, 67, 131, 175
Shahroudi, Mahmoud Hashemi, 208–9
Shahwani, Mohammed al-, 153, 188
Shalaan, Hazem al-, 122, 153, 159–60
Shami, Hussein al-, 30, 34
Shanshal, Falah, 212
Sharia law, 25, 99, 131
Shehab, Salim, 171, 181, 182
sheikhs:
    definition of, 4
    "flying" and "Taiwan," 98
Sheikli, Tahsin al-, 206
Shia:
    armed resistance by, 104–5, 205
    Ashura ritual of, 23–24, 36, 143, 174
    "axis" of, 202
    church-state separation and, 23, 25–26
    clergy of, *see* clergy, Shia
    conversion of Iran and southern Iraqi tribes to, 25, 26, 49
    cooperation between Sunni fighters and, 149
    divisions among, 119–21, 130, 132–33, 141–42, 174, 196
    enduring oppression as ideology of, 22–23, 24, 82, 99
    folk art of, 23
    Friday prayers introduced to, 79, 89–91
    global population of, 55
    history and description of, 7, 16–26
    Iranian compared with Iraqi, 38, 49
    Iranian control of, 15, 36, 121, 132, 154–55, 159, 166–70, 186, 203
    Iranian revolution and, 24, 27, 28, 35, 37, 38–40
    in Iraqi army, 37, 46–49, 51, 53, 54, 55, 58–59, 116–17, 201
    as key to understanding Iraq, 13
    Kurds, 36
    as majority in Baghdad, 177, 201, 203
    as majority in Iraq, 15, 18, 26, 32, 38, 103, 135, 161, 165, 168
    martyrs of, 9, 10, 13, 17, 19–22, 99; *see also* Sadr, Ayatollah Mohammed Baqir al-; Sadr, Mohammed Sadiq al-
    middle class, 23, 31, 132, 133, 154, 160
    1920 uprising by, 29, 49, 81, 120
    1991 uprising by, 8, 9, 13, 19, 23, 24, 52, 55–69, 70–77, 78, 79, 88, 97, 99, 103, 104, 114, 115–16, 117, 121, 122, 128, 132
    pilgrimages by, *see* pilgrimages, Shia
    political power of, 15, 18, 23, 24, 25, 118, 133, 140–41, 161, 165, 202
    and reaction to Mohammed Sadiq al-Sadr's assassination, 106–8, 111
    Saddam's persecution of, 23
    sectarian violence between Sunnis and, 11, 18, 32, 33, 53, 57–58, 60, 63–64, 70–77, 85, 136, 143, 144, 164, 174, 175–86, 203, 212
    seminaries of, *see* hawza
    shrine cities of, *see* Kerbala; Najaf; Samarra
    skin color of, 105
    traditional signs of identity of, 118
    "Twelver" branch of, 22, 25
Shia Amal militia, 41
SIIC (Supreme Islamic Iraqi Council), 179, 197, 199, 208, 210
    see also Supreme Council for Islamic Revolution in Iraq
Sistani, Grand Ayatollah Ali al-, 22, 50, 81, 90, 91, 92, 93, 96, 99, 136, 142, 148, 154, 155, 160, 164, 165, 166, 179, 196, 211–12
    political power of, 10
    quietist stance of, 100, 113, 127, 140–41
    rift between Muqtada al-Sadr and, 131
    and second battle at Najaf, 159, 161, 162, 163
socialists, 28, 30–31, 33, 37
Soviet Union, 46
Spanish troops, 1, 10, 12, 141, 146, 147
Special Forces, U.S., 158
State Department, U.S., 66, 120, 121
Status of Forces Agreement, 212
Stewart, Rory, 146
suicide bombings, 12, 136, 137, 164, 166, 167, 171, 179–80, 182, 203
Sunni Iraqi Islamic Party, 192
Sunnis, 1, 8, 23, 74, 89, 102, 119, 203–4
    church and state not separated by, 25–26
    common given names of, 11
    cooperation between Shia fighters and, 149
    insurgency by, 11, 18, 136, 141, 153, 155, 166, 167, 181, 195

Index

Sunnis *(cont.)*
  Iraqi army dominated by, 33
  1991 Shia uprising and, 65–66
  Ottoman Empire ruled by, 25
  political power of, 26, 32, 33, 39,
      120
  salafi ultra-orthodoxy of, 136, 166
  sectarian violence between Shia and,
      11, 18, 32, 33, 53, 57–58, 60, 63–64,
      70–77, 85, 136, 143, 144, 164, 174,
      175–86, 203, 212
  skin color of, 105
  victory and power as ideology of, 22
Supreme Council for Islamic Revolution
    in Iraq (SCIRI), 68, 96, 97, 108,
    114, 120, 132, 134, 142, 171, 173,
    174, 178, 188, 192, 197, 202
  armed wing of, *see* Badr Organization
  formation of, 31, 52
  IGC and, 140
  Iran and, 133, 169
  Najaf under control of, 163–64
  name change of, 179
  U.S. and, 132–33, 141
Supreme Islamic Iraqi Council (SIIC),
    179, 197, 199
Suwaidan, Ali Ahmed, 85
Syria, 37–38, 46, 52, 92, 116, 194

Talabani, Jalal, 210
Taliban, 87, 133, 167, 173
Tamimi, Mudhil al-, 209
Taqqiyya, 50, 82, 93
Tariq, Mohammed, 174
Tehran, 28, 39, 40, 52, 96, 97, 120, 133, 134
Thawra, al-, 4, 33, 128
  see also Sadr City
Tikrit, 25, 34
Tikriti, Rokan Ghafour al-, 97, 98
Timimi, Hamid al-, 125
tribalism, 26, 34, 98–99, 142
Tulfah, Khairallah, 38
turba (clay tablets), 118
turbans:
  black, 4, 121, 142
  white, 4
  winding of, 95
Turkey, 76, 86
Twaireej, 23–24
"Twelvers," 22, 25

Ubaydullah, 21–22
ulema, see clergy, Shia

Ulum, Ayatollah Mohammed Bahr al-, 160
Umayyad dynasty, 13, 20, 21–22, 24, 144
umma (community), 34
unemployment, 84, 106, 140, 170
United Arab Emirates, 40
United Iraqi Alliance (UIA), 165, 188,
    192
United Nations (UN), 11
  High Commission for Refugees of, 12
  humanitarian coordinator from, 87, 93
  sanctions enforced against Iraq by, 23,
      83–87, 114, 121
  Special Rapporteur on human rights
      of, 51–52
United States:
  in Great Depression, 84–85
  Iran criticized by, 155, 167, 192, 202
  Iran-Iraq War and, 46, 53–54
  Iraq sanctions and, 86–87
  Iraq War objectives of, 14–15
  and Khoei's return from exile,
      121–23
  Muqtada al-Sadr viewed as enemy by,
      132, 133, 139, 141–42, 189, 195
  1991 Shia uprising and, 64–67, 69, 76
  post-Saddam governments established
      by, 134–35, 139, 153
  Saddam's downfall and, 121
  Sadrist council replaced by, 137
  SCIRI and, 132–33
  WMD and, 103
  see also Gulf War
U.S. military, 1, 2, 3, 5, 6, 10, 11, 12, 18, 67,
    139
  in battles in Najaf, 141, 144–49,
      150–62
  in Gulf War, 8
  Iraq army offensive and, 205, 207–8,
      211–12
  Iraq bombed by, 103
  Iraq invaded by, 116
  lack of planning by, 127
  "surge" by, 141, 178–79, 187–98, 199,
      203
  see also Army, U.S.; Marine Corps, U.S.

veils, 89, 93, 131, 143, 172, 173

Wadi al-Salaam cemetery, 8, 37, 42, 148,
    152, 157, 170
Wahhabi, 26
weapons of mass destruction (WMD),
    103

white martyrs' shrouds, 5, 14, 43, 80, 102, 141, 197
Witwit, Iskandar Jawad, 74

Yaqubi, Ayatollah Sheikh Mohammed Mustafa al-, 194
Yaqubi, Mohammed al-, 118
Yaqubi, Mustafa al-, 112, 145, 164
Yasseri, Maher al-, 122, 124, 126

Yassin, Mohammed, 47
Yazid, 17, 20, 21, 22
Youssif, Manale, 172, 173

Zarqawi, Abu Musab al-, 136, 143–44, 166
Zebari, Hoshyar, 116, 120, 193
Zubeidi, Mohammed Hamza al-, 77, 104
Zurufi, Adnan al-, 155

About the Author

Patrick Cockburn, Iraq correspondent for *The Independent* in London, has been visiting Iraq since 1977. He was awarded the 2004 Martha Gellhorn prize for war reporting and the James Cameron Memorial Award in 2006. He is the author of *The Occupation: War and Resistance in Iraq* (shortlisted for a National Book Critics Circle Award in 2007); *The Broken Boy,* a memoir; and with Andrew Cockburn, *Out of the Ashes: The Resurrection of Saddam Hussein.*